TORAH
THROUGH
TIME

Dedicated *l'dor v'dor* in honor of our parents,
Harvey and Judy Zalesne and Sherwin and Jackie Siff,
who taught us the richness of Torah;
and our children,
Matthew David, Adina Claire, and the one on the way,
to whom we hope to teach the same.

Kinney Zalesne and Scott Siff

TORAH
THROUGH
TIME

Understanding Bible Commentary
from the Rabbinic Period to Modern Times

Shai Cherry

The Jewish Publication Society
2007• 5768
Philadelphia

JPS is a nonprofit educational association and the oldest and foremost publisher of Judaica in English in North America. The mission of JPS is to enhance Jewish culture by promoting the dissemination of religious and secular works, in the United States and abroad, to all individuals and institutions interested in past and contemporary Jewish life.

BS
476
.C477
2007

The Jewish Publication Society
2100 Arch Street, 2nd floor
Philadelphia, PA 19103

Design and Composition by Progressive Information Technologies

Manufactured in the United States of America

07 08 09 10 11   10 9 8 7 6 5 4 3 2 1

ISBN 13: 978-0-8276-0848-1
ISBN 10: 0-8276-0848-1

Library of Congress Cataloging-in-Publication Data
Cherry, Shai.
  Torah through time : understanding Bible commentary from the rabbinic period to modern times / Shai Cherry.
     p.   cm.
  Includes bibliographical references and index.
  ISBN-13: 978-0-8276-0848-1 (alk. paper)
  1. Bible. O.T.—Hermeneutics.   2. Bible. O.T.—Criticism, interpretation, etc.
I. Title.
  BS476.C477 2007
  221.601—dc22
                                                                            2007017299

JPS books are available at discounts for bulk purchases for reading groups, special sales, and fundraising purchases. Custom editions, including personalized covers, can be created in larger quantities for special needs. For more information, please contact us at marketing@jewishpub.org or at this address: 2100 Arch Street, Philadelphia, PA 19103.

To Rivka Nomi,
my darshanit

אהבת עולם נתן בלבם
—קהלת רבה, ג׳ :ג׳

No One Drashes Her [Torah] Like Israel

—"Ein Adir Kadonai," traditional Shabbat and Shavuot song

CONTENTS

FOREWORD

To most people, the Hebrew Bible is an impenetrable book. It was written during a thousand-year period, and reflected a wide variety of internal and external political and intellectual currents. Even more difficult yet is Jewish interpretation of the Bible, which has been written for over two millennia in an even wider set of political and intellectual currents. To add to the problem, the language in which such interpretation comes down to us can be harder than biblical Hebrew, and much of this literature, such as that written in medieval times, is not yet available in translation. Consequently, most people do not have access to the rich legacy of this interpretive tradition.

The Bible is the most important of Jewish books, and much of Jewish creativity is presented as an interpretation of the Bible. This is not only true for the rich and variegated midrashic literature, and of the tradition of medieval commentators like Rashi, but of mystical tracts such as the Zohar, of many medieval Jewish philosophical works, and of modern feminist interpretation. Therefore, understanding the world of Jewish interpretation is an ideal way of gaining insight into the changes that Judaism has undergone through the ages.

Dr. Shai Cherry, an experienced and excellent educator, opens up this rich legacy in *Torah Through Time: Understanding Bible Commentary from the Rabbinic Period to Modern Times*. He does this by choosing biblical episodes that raise especially important issues. The texts he explores include: the creation of humanity in Genesis 1, which raises questions about the role of humans, God, and the earth; the enigmatic Cain and Abel story, which deals with brotherly conflict and the origins of murder; the slavery law in Exodus, which raises significant issues concerning the Bible and morality; the Korah rebellion in Numbers, which highlights the problem of authority; and the episode concerning the inheritance of the daughters of Zelophehad, which raises the topic of the status of women in Judaism. As a whole, these chapters develop themes that are of concern to contemporary readers, and emphasize a key thesis of this

book, namely that for Jewish commentators, the Bible, through proper interpretation, must speak to the crucial issues of the day.

The scope of this book is extensive. For Cherry, Jewish biblical interpretation stretches from the early post-biblical period, including writers such as
Philo of Alexandria (1ˢᵗ century C.E.) through contemporary writers who are
reflecting on the Bible today. Allegorists, rationalists, philologists, philosophers, mystics, and feminists are all represented. Moreover, rather than siding
with either the intellectual school that sees everything Jewish as reflecting
internal Jewish development, or the school that sees everything Jewish as
influenced by the outside Greek, Roman, Christian, or Moslem external
worlds, Cherry shows how ever-changing biblical interpretation is the result
of both internal and external developments. This is an important corrective
to many previous surveys.

Cherry's skill as an educator shines throughout this volume. His translations, explanations, and contextualizations of commentaries are lucid and
engaging. He offers clear charts that concisely illustrate the diversity of interpretive positions on particular texts and issues. He cites extensive suggestions
for further reading. The back matter includes useful indices and a glossary. By
making this rich tradition accessible, this book as a whole should play a significant role in the renaissance of Jewish learning that is now taking place.

Marc Z. Brettler, Dora Golding Professor of Biblical Studies,
Department of Near Eastern and Judaic Studies, Brandeis University

ACKNOWLEDGMENTS

When I began teaching a course on Jewish biblical interpretation at Vanderbilt University in 2001, I was met with a series of surprises. The first was the lack of available texts tracing Jewish commentary on biblical narrative and law from the emergence of Rabbinic Judaism, roughly two thousand years ago, until today. Even the small group of texts that did exist (in English) tended not to approach the subject in a manner appropriate for a university setting. At that point, I began to gather a wide variety of individual commentaries and compiled a reading packet for my students. My next surprise came in the form of sticker shock. Upon recovery, *Torah Through Time* was conceived.

My students at Vanderbilt consisted primarily of Protestants with a tendency toward what they considered to be biblical literalism. These students believed that the King James translation of the Hebrew Bible somehow interpreted itself in a way that the meaning was unequivocal and transparent. That was my biggest surprise. For the previous 10 years, I had shuttled back and forth between Brandeis University, outside of Boston, and Jerusalem as I pursued my doctorate in Jewish thought and theology. During that period, I bumped into relatively few Southern Baptists.

I was introduced to Jewish biblical interpretation while studying at the Pardes Institute of Jewish Studies in Jerusalem in the early 1990s. My teachers, Walter Herzberg, Judy Klitsner, and Baruch Feldstern, presented the world of Torah commentary not as the literary analysis of a static text, but as the unfolding of Jewish thought through the matrix of the Torah. They taught using an approach that contemporary literary theorists call *indeterminacy*—that is, incorporating multiple interpretations without attempting to determine the "true" meaning. Indeed, the very existence of mutually exclusive and plausible interpretations points to the impossibility of determining one true interpretation. The faculty at Pardes disabused me of the naïve notion that any translation can be "objective." All translators are constantly choosing among a field of options. Their choices, *their interpretations*, seal off large swaths of that original field—in this case, from the ancient Hebrew—while opening up new territory with previously unforeseen interpretive possibilities. Did Abraham take a knife or a hatchet to his son Isaac (Gen. 22:10)? Did Moses' mother think the infant was beautiful or good natured (Ex. 2:2)? Did Moses' siblings complain because Moses married a Cushite woman or on behalf of the Cushite woman he had married (Num. 12:1)? All translations are interpretations.

While at Brandeis, I studied with Arthur Green, whose approach to the study of Jewish texts greatly influenced my own. In many ways, I structured my course at Vanderbilt on Professor Green's course on midrash: after closely reading the biblical text, we would then delve into the history of commentary to understand how the issues of concern for the commentators changed over time. I was unprepared for my students' persistent queries. Which interpretation is right? Which interpretation do Jews believe? What does the Hebrew *really* mean?

I expected to teach a course in Jewish thought using the Torah as a familiar base text. The reality of the class was closer to literary theory. By using multiple translations and Jewish biblical commentary, the students saw that their familiar King James translation, while "authorized," was not always authoritative. Thus, the beginning of my class was dedicated to challenging my students' sense of security in their familiarity with *The Book* many considered to be the inerrant word of God.

As we delved into the commentary on selected biblical episodes, it was clear that the earliest commentators, both Jewish and Christian, were reading the Torah beyond its plain sense. That is not to say they were misreading the Torah; rather, they were generating a "deep reading" of the Torah by connecting the Bible's ancient words to the current reality of their own lives. The value of their deep readings is for the individual to judge, but intellectual honesty demands we acknowledge that many of their comments seem forced if we assume they were explaining the plain sense of Scripture as the initial authors had intended it to be understood. Only when we give these ancient commentators a sympathetic hearing can we understand that they read Scripture as religious literature. They read literarily, not literally. Since their interpretation of the Bible influenced how they wrote their commentaries, we have a responsibility to read their commentaries similarly as religious literature.

A more sophisticated approach to religious literature, one that eschews literalism, is both intellectually honest and religiously salutary. In our time, the interpretation of religious texts lies at the root of much dissension, both domestically and abroad. *Torah Through Time* presents a Jewish model of combating fundamentalism with the Bible itself. It is my hope that *Torah*

Through Time will provide a useful resource for university students, seminarians, and participants in adult education programs as we face the challenges of the future armed with the wisdom of the past.

During the writing of this book, and partially as a result of writing this book, I came to understand that a career exclusively as an academician is not my passion. From my earliest experience at an academic conference in Jewish Studies, I had the uneasy sense that many scholars were performing autopsies on what they considered textual artifacts. For me, it felt like being witness to vivisection. I sincerely hope that I have treated the comments in *Torah Through Time* with *both* academic integrity and religious sensitivity. As I complete this manuscript, I begin my official training for the rabbinate. My thanks to those Vanderbilt students who helped me to see myself more clearly.

In addition to thanking my teachers at Pardes and Brandeis, Rabbi Joel Roth merits special mention. While at the Conservative Yeshiva in Jerusalem, I studied the laws of the Hebrew slave with Rabbi Roth, who is both an excellent reader and teacher. My thanks also go to my friends and colleagues who encroached upon their own invaluable time to offer feedback and support, especially Michael Rose, Avner Ash, David Myers, Mimi Feigelson, Joan Mehlman, and the Melton Mavens of Nashville. The editors at the Jewish Publication Society kindly shepherded me through the process of writing my first book. My parents and sister remain an indefatigable, optimistic cheering squad, despite my occasionally dyspeptic disposition.

As the Rabbinic adage has it, as much as I learned from my teachers and colleagues, I learned even more from my students. My analyses of the texts in the following chapters were honed over four years at Vanderbilt and one year in Los Angeles at the Academy for Jewish Religion and at Temple Beth Am. The contributions of individual students will appear in the notes, but my gratitude goes to all who worked with me to understand the depth of wisdom these texts teach. Joanna Caravita, Rachel Dixon, and Joshua Barton deserve special note for their assistance in determining which texts would be included in this book.

This book is dedicated to my wife, Rebecca Naomi Milstein Cherry. As the thirteenth-century Jewish mystic Joseph ibn Gikitilla so presciently understood, "The *Shekhinah* in the time of Isaac, our father, is called Rebecca."

INTRODUCTION

Ben Bag Bag says:
"Turn it, turn it, for everything is in it."
—Mishnah, Avot 5:24, 3rd c. CE

BEN BAG BAG is referring to the Torah. This work is a study in how the Rabbis and their descendants turned the Torah.

Ben Bag Bag's image is particularly apt, because there are two ways to turn: spinning on the horizontal axis and overturning on the vertical axis. Spinning the Torah allows you to see different facets or faces of the Jewish crown jewel. "The Torah has 70 faces,"[1] say the later Rabbis in using the number that expresses totality, the biblically resonant seven times ten. But Ben Bag Bag's "turn it, turn it" can also be interpreted to mean turn the Torah on its vertical axis, to upend the Torah. The Gaon of Vilna, Elijah ben Solomon Zalman (1720–1797), employed a similar image when he compared the Torah to a seal whose inverted letters are only legible upon impression.[2] Turning over words of Torah, lovingly caressing them in the process, is how generations of Jews have expressed their insights about the fullness of God's word and world.

Jewish Interpretations of the Hebrew Bible

In academic circles, there is a tendency to use the term *Hebrew Bible* for what Jews have traditionally called the TANAKH[3] or simply *Torah*, and Christians have generally called the *Old Testament*. But the terms are not interchangeable. The Hebrew Bible, as academics teach it, is a composite text by multiple authors of the ancient Near East. To understand the Hebrew Bible in its original context, one must have familiarity with other ancient Near Eastern narratives and legal texts. It is a time-bound text. The Torah, however, is what the Rabbis believe to be the timeless word of God.[4] Torah is a Jewish reading of the Hebrew Bible. When the early Catholic Church read the Hebrew Bible as a Divine but superseded prequel to the New Testament, that text became the Christian Old Testament. Not only do their names indicate

1

the different assumptions of the various interpretive communities, but the content and sequence of the TANAKH and the Old Testament also differs.

Torah Through Time focuses on Jewish interpretations and specifically on Rabbinic readings of the Hebrew Bible. The Rabbis slowly emerged as the leaders of the Jewish community in the centuries following the destruction of the Jerusalem Temple by the Romans in 70 CE. A comprehensive treatment of Jewish interpretations of the Hebrew Bible would include pre-Rabbinic texts such as the Dead Sea Scrolls, the Apocrypha, Pseudepigrapha, as well as Gnostic texts. Non-Rabbinic readings might also have a voice in a comprehensive treatment of Jewish interpretations of the Hebrew Bible. For instance, early Christian writings, the philosophical treatises of Philo, the historical writings of Josephus, as well as later so-called "heretical" works from the Karaites and Sabbatians might be incorporated. I have focused on Rabbinic interpretations for two reasons. The first is the benefit of exploring the broad range of comments emerging from a single school of Judaism. The diversity of ideology amongst this religious group whose practice is quite similar (at least in the pre-modern period) is nothing short of wondrous. Second, for those interested in a comparative approach to Rabbinic and non-rabbinic interpretations of the Torah, there is the recent publication of James Kugel's *The Bible As It Was*, an annotated anthology of early comments on the Hebrew Bible by the full spectrum of ancient commentators.[5]

Hebrew in Translation

Given the nature of our investigation, the bulk of the comments in this book were originally written in Hebrew. Unless otherwise noted, I am responsible for all the translations of the commentaries. (Biblical translations, unless otherwise noted, are from the JPS TANAKH.)

The Talmud warns that one who translates literally is a liar and that one who embellishes is a blasphemer.[6] I have tried to admit my crimes so that when I paraphrase, I preface the source name with the word *from;* otherwise, I translate literally.

Roughly 90 percent of the comments in this book are available in English translations. Recently, Hebrew has become less necessary for those seeking Torah, although there is still a vast treasure house of Torah commentary yet to be translated. Nevertheless, even among those commentators who have been translated into English, many of their comments are only sensible to those who know the rudiments of Hebrew. (In *Torah Through Time,* for example, close to 20 percent of the comments rely on nuances of the Hebrew that are hidden in translation.) The most recent contribution to Jewish biblical commentary in translation, *The Commentators' Bible,* brings together the luminaries of medieval bible commentary, all of whom will be prominently featured in the following pages.

Text and/or Commentators' Context?

In our presentation of biblical commentary, some statements will seem to mirror the concerns of the commentator more than the intentions of the author or redactor of the biblical text. It has become a commonplace of literary theory to remind us that there is no objective reading of a text that is able to get outside the reader's particular frame of reference, one that is itself embedded within a larger communal framework. We all bring our experiences and worldviews to the table when reading a text.

But even when a comment might be transparently rooted in the historical moment or ideological perspective of the commentator, it would be a mistake to necessarily dismiss this reading as artificially grafted onto the biblical text. Very often, the commentator is sensitive to something in the text that generates his or her response. These textual bumps are sometimes difficult to see in translation and are dependent on the assumptions one brings to the text.

Steven D. Fraade has suggested that the early commentators of the Hebrew Bible were "double facing." Immediately before them was the Torah that they were interpreting. But they were also facing their communities who were awaiting fresh instruction.[7] Like Ezra (Neh. 8:3), whom we will introduce formally in chapter one, the commentators faced both the hermeneutical challenges of deciphering a cryptic text and the challenge shared by all preachers—to make ancient Scripture relevant to a given community at a particular time and place. Rather than see biblical commentary as a product of either hermeneutics or history, Fraade suggests that it is both.

In the words of another contemporary scholar, Daniel Boyarin, "The text of the Torah is gapped and dialogical, and into the gaps the reader slips, interpreting and completing the text in accordance with the codes of his or her culture . . . The rabbis were concerned with the burning issues of their day, but their approach to that concern was through the clarification of difficult passages of Scripture. Ideology affected their reading but their ideology was also affected by their reading."[8] Taking into account the insights of both Fraade and Boyarin, I have concluded chapters two through six with tables summarizing the textual and historical elements in each of the comments. The numbers in the tables refer to the numbers of the comments.

Starting at the Beginning

Chapter one is required reading for subsequent chapters of the book because it provides the historical background and the theoretical framework through which our commentators viewed the Torah. Terms such as *peshat* and *derash* are defined, and the history of Jewish biblical interpretation is laid out. Since this book concerns biblical interpretation and not the Bible per se, I have omitted discussion of how the Bible came into being. Nevertheless, academic assumptions of multiple authorship inform my analyses. The following chapters, two through six, do not need to be read sequentially, since they are case studies of how Jewish biblical interpretation has been carried out over the past two millennia. Each deals with a different set of substantive and interpretive issues. When reading these chapters, I recommend having a Hebrew Bible at your side, given that I frequently refer to other passages.

The subject of chapter two, the creation of humanity, is likely to be familiar to most readers. Theology, anthropology, and ecology are intertwined in this short scene. The commentators raise further issues touching on science and psychology. We will see how some Jewish thinkers have dealt with the seeming discrepancies between the Torah and later Jewish law, or *halakhah*. We will also meet the giant of medieval Jewish philosophy, Rambam. Finally, we will witness the interpretive effects of juxtaposing two different creation stories.

Chapter three treats the story of Cain and Abel, which is also familiar to most readers. In addition to the theme of fraternal conflict, this story raises the issues of God's justice and human responsibility. The post-biblical notion of heaven is introduced in this chapter, and the commentators struggle to fill in what looks like a gap in the text. Post-modern sensibilities, which resist traditional dichotomies, will help us see Cain in a more positive light. In this chapter, there are three different biblical translations which frame our inquiry and help us understand how the commentators arrived at their different interpretations.

While our previous two chapters are primarily aggadic, or non-legal, chapter four introduces the *halakhah*, the laws, of Hebrew slavery. Another distinction between this and previous chapters is that this chapter presents three sets of laws as they appear in different parts of the Torah. Much of the Rabbis' exegetical ingenuity will be devoted to reconciling the seeming discrepancies among these three codes. This chapter also presents us with a test case of how to interpret laws with which one may grow uncomfortable over time. The conclusion to this chapter highlights the distance between the plain sense of Scripture and the *halakhah*, and offers several approaches to bridge the gap.

Chapter five considers Korah and his gang of desert rebels and provides the best example of how a biblical figure can assume the identity of any commentator's foe. For some ancients, Korah represented the Dead Sea sectarians; for some moderns, Korah was a symbol of Reform Judaism. What makes Korah especially interesting is that his claim—that all the congregation is holy—is not universally rejected among the commentators. Yet, Korah himself is stigmatized as an unsavory adversary. This chapter also explores the interpretive effects of braiding several different stories into a single narrative.

Chapter six focuses on the daughters of Zelophehad and combines the halakhic with the aggadic approaches to commentary; it compares Rabbinic *halakhah* with that of the Sadducees and the Karaites. The story offers an opportunity to look at the status of women. Additionally the Hebrew text of the narrative contains several oddities that become grist for the interpreter, among them, the presence of large letters and grammatical inconsistencies. We see, as well, how independent comments can be combined later to produce radical new meanings. Finally, this episode is an important example of how a law changes within the Torah and provides an opportunity for commentators across the denominational spectrum to reflect upon that process.

The internal structure of chapters two through six is as follows: After citing a commentary, I will offer an analysis which explains (1) what prompted the comment; (2) how the commentator resolved the issue; (3) whether he used the text of the Torah in his resolution; and (4) if the historical context of the commentator or her ideology contributed to her resolution. These points are then summarized in the tables at the conclusion of each chapter. Often I will also add supporting information to provide context or parallels to the comments. On occasion, I act as a commentator myself.

The epilogue, in addition to summarizing the findings of the previous chapters, presents the latest theory of Torah. This model, adumbrated in chapter one, explains why Jews have been committed to interpreting Torah through time and why the job will never be finished. The turning of Torah continues.

NOTES

1. *Numbers Rabbah* 13:5.

2. See David Weiss Halivni, *Peshat and Derash: Plain and Applied Meaning in Rabbinic Exegesis* (New York: Oxford University Press, 1991), 30ff.

3. TANAKH is an acronym for *Torah* (Pentateuch), *Nevi'im* (Prophets), and *Kethuvim* (Writings), the three sections of the Hebrew Bible.

4. b. *Kiddushin* 49b.

5. James L. Kugel, *The Bible As It Was* (Cambridge: Harvard University Press, 1997).

6. b. *Kiddushin* 49a/b.

7. *From Tradition to Commentary: Torah and its Interpretation in the Midrash Sifre to* Deuteronomy (Albany: State University of New York Press, 1991), 13–18.

8. *Intertextuality and the Reading of Midrash*, 14 and 19. Cristina Grenholm and Daniel Patte have outlined a similar structure in their overture to *Reading Israel in Romans: Legitimacy and Plausibility of Divergent Interpretation* (Harrisburg: Trinity Press International, 2000).

Chapter 1

NO WORD
UNTURNED

THE STUDY OF Jewish biblical commentary combines literary theory, Jewish history, and Jewish thought. It is this confluence of factors, each quite complex in itself, that makes the exploration of Jewish biblical commentary so rich and exciting. This chapter sets out to explain the diversity and development of approaches used by Jews to understand Scripture during the major periods of Jewish history—Rabbinic, medieval, and modern. Since history often influences commentary, this discussion will include descriptions of the relevant historical occurrences during those periods. We begin by asking the all-important though seemingly unrelated question of: Where do Jews find God?

Theography: The Geography of God

In a beginning, though a different beginning from which the biblical redactor began, the LORD God was found walking in the Garden of Eden (Gen. 3:8). And God spoke to the humans in the Garden just as any other literary figure would communicate, through speech. God later spoke to Abraham and Moses alike (Gen. 22:1 and Exod. 3:4). In the beginning, God could be found in the familiar world of nature and human history.

With the exodus of the Israelite slaves from Egypt, God requests a change of address: "And let them make Me a sanctuary that I may dwell among them" (Exod. 25:8). During the desert sojourn, God's presence is manifested in either the Tabernacle or the Tent of Meeting, the literary and architectural precursors to King Solomon's Temple in Jerusalem.[1] At the dedication of the Temple, in the 10th century BCE, King Solomon says, "The LORD has chosen to abide in a thick cloud: I have now built for You a stately House, a place where You may dwell forever" (1 Kings 8:12ff.).

There were certainly advantages to centralizing Divine worship in the Temple: one knew where to access the Divine presence. But the major liability was that God's home was then vulnerable to attack.[2] In 586 BCE, the Babylonians exploited that vulnerability, destroyed the Temple and exiled the population of the southern kingdom of Judah. (The northern kingdom of Israel had been exiled in 721 BCE by the Assyrians.) With the destruction of God's house, our question returned with unprecedented force: Where is God? It is in the wake of the Babylonian exile that certain voices, preserved in the Hebrew Bible, began to articulate a new theography, a new venue for God's presence.

Among the classic expressions of this new theography is Psalm 119. Compare, for instance, the Book of Deuteronomy (4:4) where there is a description of Israelites who "hold fast to the LORD." In Psalm 119, verse 31, the psalmist holds fast to God's *decrees*. Throughout the Psalm, God's will as expressed in the portable Torah replaces the homeless God whose presence is now needed more than ever.[3] When Ezra brings a group of exiles back to Jerusalem in the mid-fifth century BCE, we see the blurring of boundaries between God and God's Torah. "Ezra opened the scroll [of Torah] . . . all the people stood up. . . . Then they bowed their heads and prostrated themselves *before the LORD* with their faces to the ground" (Neh. 8:5ff.). In the mind of the author, and presumably in the minds of the worshippers, the Torah has come to embody the Divine.

With the exception of mystics who seek God without an intermediary, religions generally have some structure or person in that mediating position between the seeker and God. Take Rebecca, for example, who when suffering during her pregnancy, became the first person in the Torah to "inquire of the LORD" (Gen. 25:22). Although the Book of Genesis remains silent as to where Rebecca went to pursue this inquiry, the medieval Jewish commentator, Rashbam (c.1085–c.1174), suggests that she went to an oracle, as did her ancient Near-Eastern neighbors when they wanted to inquire of their gods. The Hebrew word for "inquire" is *derash*. We might say that Rebecca was the first to *derash* (inquire of) God. According to the biblical chronology, many others followed suit.[4] With Ezra, however, we have a shift. Ezra does not *derash* the LORD, he *derashes* the LORD's Torah (Ezra 7:10). The Torah becomes the object of our inquiry, the locus in which to search for God's presence and will. The noun, *midrash*, is the product of that search through God's Torah for the Divine will.

Knowing *where* to access God is only the first step. Understanding the Divine will is the ultimate goal. Ezra was well qualified to serve in this capacity as one who interpreted God's will from the Torah. Ezra was of priestly lineage, and in the days when the Temple stood, it was the priests who mediated the Divine word to the Israelites, oftentimes through the oracle-like device of the Urim and Tumim (Exod. 28:30).[5] By the time of Ezra, the Urim and Tumim had been lost (Ezra 2:63) and were functionally replaced, as we have seen, by the Torah. Ezra is also called a *sofer*, or scribe, and is described as an expert in the Torah of Moses (Ezra 7:6). He initiates a new class of scholars, the scribes, who are able to interpret the Divine will based on their expertise in the Torah. This expertise, however, is not merely technical or confined to the necessary skills of what we might think of as a scribe.

When King Solomon dedicated the Temple in Jerusalem, he said that the LORD had "chosen to abide in a thick cloud" (1 Kings 8:12). This thick cloud has a precedent. On Mount Sinai, at the moment of God's public revelation to all the Israelites, the Divine presence was similarly cloaked in a dense cloud, behind a curtain of smoke (Exod. 19:16–18). The authors of these texts are indicating that even at moments of greatest divine transparency, God is concealed by a smoke screen. Whether in the rarified air of the desert mountains, or in the urban Temples that claim to house God, there is obscurity at the very heart of revelation.

As the theography of ancient Israelites shifts and God's Torah supplants God, God's Torah also absorbs some of the qualities previously reserved for God. In Deuteronomy, the assumption was that the Torah was not too wondrous (*niflet* in Hebrew) for any of the Israelites to follow (30:11). Our psalmist from Psalm 119 dissents. He pleads with God to open the psalmist's eyes to perceive the wonders (*niflaot*) of God's Torah (v. 18). Just as God had been shielded from our eyes, so too is the Torah cloaked in mystery. There are "textual bumps" or "surface irregularities" when reading the Torah, especially when one is looking for them. Negotiating those bumps and deciphering the meaning of those irregularities require training. And it was the scribes who assumed that role.[6] The scribes and their Torah functionally replaced the role formerly played by the priests with their Urim and Tumim. When Ezra assembled those who had returned from Babylonia, he charged his subordinates with both translating the Torah, since the refugees had forgotten Hebrew, and "giving the sense" of this mysterious message from God (Neh. 8:8).

Four Assumptions About the Bible

James Kugel, a leading contemporary scholar on the Hebrew Bible and its reception in ancient times, suggests that there were four assumptions that animated late biblical writers and early biblical interpreters. Although Kugel was not the first scholar to note these assumptions, his template will help us track the history of Jewish biblical commentary. The first assumption that Kugel lays out is that the Torah is fundamentally cryptic. We have seen how the Torah was perceived to be cryptic, which is why a special class of scribes was needed to "translate" the Torah, not only linguistically, but conceptually.

Kugel's Four Assumptions

1. The Torah is *cryptic* and cannot be understood from a superficial reading.
2. The Torah is eternally *relevant* and not merely a historical document.
3. The Torah is *perfect* without mistake, contradiction, or repetition.
4. The Torah is *Divine* in origin.[7]

The process of interpreting the Torah is influenced by how one understands the nature of Hebrew. Among the legacies of the scribes is that the Rabbis of the post-second Temple era (1st– 7th c. CE) held that Hebrew, unlike other languages, captured the essence of the thing described. In other words, Hebrew is not a language of conventions whereby we agree that the word *book* will indicate this thing you happen to be reading right now. For the Rabbis, "God spoke and the world came into being."[8] Because the world was created by the Divine language of Hebrew, language participates in the very essence of reality. The biblical word *davar* means both *word* and *thing*; this means that the word and the thing share an essence according to such an understanding of Hebrew. Many scholars of Rabbinic literature have observed that the Rabbis were inveterate punsters in large part because of the aural nature of their teachings. Although true, such a description belittles the seriousness with which the Rabbis felt Hebrew informed us about the nature of reality. For them, if two words sound alike or share certain root letters, it may well be because there is an underlying commonality that links the essences of those things.

Kugel's second assumption is that the relevance of Torah precludes it from being merely a record of genealogical and historical events. In short, the Torah is no antiquarian artifact. It was a living link, a tree of life, between God and the early Jewish community. It was the responsibility of the scribes, and later the Rabbis, to translate the seemingly irrelevant sections of the Torah into a program for contemporary living. The Torah, according to this assumption, is eternally relevant.

Kugel's third assumption that the Torah is perfect and without mistake has manifested itself in several ways. On one level, there could be no *unintended* grammatical mistakes in the Torah. Furthermore, one part of the Bible could not contradict another section. The Torah was a unified whole. Most importantly, the perfection of Scripture implies that nothing is superfluous or redundant. When the Torah repeats itself, as it does regularly, this assumption demands that the repetition is not for literary emphasis or the result of a combination of disparate documents. Only the scribe, and later the Rabbi, will be able to discern the divinely coded meanings that are not apparent to the untrained eye.

Given the assumption that nothing is superfluous in the Torah, any seeming violation of literary economy becomes an invitation for the assumption of relevance to express itself. Kugel notes that this characteristic of early biblical interpretation finds "its fullest expression in rabbinic writings."[9] He calls this aspect of Rabbinic hermeneutics "omnisignificance," whereby every word, letter, and calligraphic flourish becomes available for interpretation.

Kugel's fourth assumption is that all of Scripture is in some way Divine. Whether that means that the Hebrew Bible was the product of Divine dictation, written under Divine inspiration, or merely divinely sanctioned, varies among the commentators of antiquity and the biblical books under discussion.[10] But they all assumed the Bible to be anchored, somehow, to God. A Rabbinic text claims that when two people study Torah, the Divine presence dwells between them.[11] An even more daring text suggests that when one studies Torah, one comes to understand the mind of God.[12] Thus, engaging in Torah study was a way to interact or commune with God, filling a pressing need in the years after the Roman destruction of the second Temple in 70 CE. Studying Torah and generating novel interpretations theoretically open to all males (unlike the Priesthood with its genealogical requirements), was the vehicle through which Rabbinic Jews in the post-Temple environment maintained and fostered a relationship with God. For many, Torah study became an obsession because it was a way, the Rabbinic way, of "living in the House of the LORD, all the days of my life" (Ps. 27:4).

Letters and Spirits

There are three aspects of the Hebrew Bible that allow Kugel's four assumptions to play themselves out in myriad ways. First of all, the Hebrew Bible lacks vowels. The ancient manuscripts of the Hebrew Bible were written with consonants only. To use an English example, the consonants b and t can form many words depending on the vowels: bat, bait, bet, beet, beat, bit, boat, boot, but, and butt. If you add vowels before or after the consonants, there are additional possibilities: abate, abut, about, batty, bite, and byte. Hebrew words generally have three root letters, which only increases the opportunities for interpretation. Often, the context of a word, especially a rare word, is insufficient to determine a single meaning. Thus, every pronunciation of a biblical word is already an interpretive act of major consequence.

Another feature of the Torah is its lack of punctuation. As we will see in the next chapter, one line of Rabbinic interpretation understood what seems to be a statement, "Let us make humanity," as a question, "Should we make humanity?" More subtly, where one divides the major pauses in a scriptural verse can have profound implications for its meaning. Consider the following example:

Jacob's behavior was not always exemplary. Yet, for some Jewish commentators there was an impulse to whitewash Jacob's misdeeds. For instance, Jacob seems to lie baldly to his father in the process of acquiring the blessing meant for the first born, Jacob's older brother, Esau. Isaac asks, "Which of my sons are you?" Jacob responds to his father, "I am Esau, your first-born" (Gen. 27:18ff.). One Rabbi, ill at ease with the patriarch's lie, punctuates the verse differently: "I am [Jacob]; [but] Esau is your first-born."[13] Not only does this idiosyncratic reading exploit the lack of punctuation in the Torah, it also relies on the fact that conjugations of the verb *to be,* in the present tense, are not used in Hebrew. In an effort to exonerate Jacob, this Rabbi has given the letters of this unpunctuated verse an entirely new spirit.[14]

All texts, regardless of language, become difficult to understand over the course of time. Languages change, as do literary conventions and idioms. What might be obvious to one generation is perplexing to the next. Today, using the term *gay* to mean happy, or *queer* to mean strange, would be something of an anachronism. Or, to take a biblical example, Moses' charge to love God "with all your heart" (Deut. 6:5) needs to be explained by Mark's Jesus as including "your mind" (12:30). Apparently, what was obvious in the period of Deuteronomy had to be spelled out hundreds of years later because *heart* no longer represented the seat of both emotion and intellect as it does throughout the Hebrew Bible. Moreover, references to cultural institutions or political situations that are no longer in existence add another layer that one must penetrate in order to understand any text. Combine these factors with the peculiarities of Torah — its lack of vowels, punctuation, and conjugations of *to be* in present tense — add hundreds of years, and you have a truly cryptic document. Conversely, you have a goldmine of interpretive possibilities.

Rabbinic Approaches to Torah

Given that our focus is on the Rabbis and the textual traditions and cultures that they spawned, it is worthwhile to appreciate the extent to which they gloried in the inherent interpretability of Torah. Rabbi Yanai said, "Had the Torah been given in an unequivocal way, the world couldn't endure."[15] The very future of our existence depends on the ability of the Torah to be interpreted. The Torah, according to the Rabbis, is a tree of life (Prov. 3:18), not petrified wood. The words of Torah are compared to figs that become ripe in succession rather than simultaneously.[16] In other words, God's will is not exhaustively evident at any given time, but only in the fullness of time. The word of God is imagined as never ceasing *from Sinai*.[17]

Let her breasts satisfy you at all times

(Prov. 5:19)

Why were words of Torah compared to a breast? Just as a nursling who returns to the breast continues to find milk, so does the person who meditates on Torah continue to find new meaning therein.

(b. Eruvin 54b)

The Torah is here depicted by the Rabbis as eternally satisfying and eternally nourishing.

This commitment to continuous revelation tethers all future expressions of God's will to that of Sinai. There must be an organic connection to Sinai rather than a rupture that breaks with the past. Any claims for a new revelation or new covenant, e.g. early Christianity, are to be judged by their fidelity to the original. This Rabbinic posture toward revelation, thus, also served a polemical purpose. Nevertheless, these early Rabbinic statements point to the assumption that new interpretations will continuously be brought forth from the Torah of Sinai. The Rabbis were the midwives bringing forth new interpretations of Torah, a Torah pregnant with Divine meaning.

The Talmud also promotes dialectical argumentation as a sort of Rabbinic etude, an exercise to sharpen rhetorical skills. Every rabbi, according to the Talmud, should be able to argue that a bacon cheeseburger should be kosher.[18] Coupled with this rhetorical training is an assumption, not necessarily universal in the Rabbinic world, that verses of the Torah are amenable to multiple meanings.[19] Ben Bag Bag's somewhat cryptic claim, "Turn it [Torah], turn it, for everything is in it" reinforces the notion of pluripotence (defined below) of such late Rabbinic statements as: "The Torah has 70 faces."[20]

Kugel's notion of omnisignificance is that nothing is superfluous *within the Torah*. Everything is available for interpretation. There is a different claim, which I designate as pluripotence, that words and verses in the Torah inherently possess multiple meanings. The maximal pluripotent view of the Torah is that the letters and words of the Torah, properly interpreted, contain all the wisdom of the world. Pluripotence did not attain full expression until the mystical writings of the Middle Ages. Yet, the elements of a pluripotent view of the Torah are found already within Rabbinic culture, namely a commitment to multiple interpretations of a single biblical verse and promotion of the value of innovative readings of Torah.

In the days of King David, innocent children knew how to derash the Torah 49 ways to reach one conclusion and 49 ways to reach the opposite conclusion.

(Leviticus Rabbah 26:2)

In this Rabbinic revision of ancient history, even the unsophisticated were capable of remarkable textual dexterity.

By championing the skills of argumentation and interpretative innovation, however, there was a danger that the Rabbis might confuse virtuosity and veracity. If the Torah can mean anything, it ultimately means nothing. Given the welter of contradictory opinions, why take Torah seriously? Their answer is that all of these opinions are rooted in the Torah and God's revelation. We need to internalize the logic of each position and learn to appreciate the intrinsic worth of dispute.[21] The practical limits of Torah interpretation are communal, not methodological. The majority of sages decides the law.[22] Among those whom the Rabbis claim have no share in the coming world are they who "reveal aspects of the Torah not in accord with established norms."[23] The Rabbis here do not say that such aspects are not to be found in the Torah, only that they should not be revealed.

The Rabbinic Range

A more complete picture of the world of the Rabbis must include those who did not believe that everything in the Torah was awaiting dexterous *darshanim* (the authors of midrash) to bring forth new meanings. In one particularly pointed exchange, one of the more restrictive interpreters, Rabbi Ishmael, complained that his teacher would tell the biblical verse to remain silent while he, the teacher, interpreted it![24] The same Rabbi Ishmael is associated with the legal principle that "The Torah speaks in human language."[25] This notion precludes using every word in the Torah as an opportunity for a *midrash*. In other words, Rabbi Ishmael and those of his school were opposed to omnisignificance. Even Sigmund Freud conceded that, "Sometimes a cigar is just a cigar." In some instances, the conventions of language should not be used as a springboard for a legal ruling.

In the earliest layer of Rabbinic legal literature, the Mishnah (early 3rd c., CE), there is a statement that the laws pertaining to the release of vows "fly in the air since they have nothing [in the Torah] on which to lean."[26] If Rabbi Ishmael was not happy with the assumption of omnisignificance, which some of his colleagues employed to interpret Torah, the author of this mishnah denies Ben Bag Bag's claim that everything is in the Torah. Indeed, it seems obvious from an unadorned (or undrashed) reading of Torah that much is absent from the Torah.

Parallel to notions of omnisignificance and pluripotence, there emerged within Rabbinic Judaism the notion of the Oral Torah that was given to Moses at Mount Sinai along with the written Torah.[27] This Oral Torah contained those laws that were not included in the written Torah. The relationship between these two models, the pluripotence of the written Torah versus the giving of the Oral Torah, has been the subject of much traditional Jewish thought and contemporary scholarship.[28] The underlying question is this: Does the *halakhah* come from drashing the written Torah, or does the *halakhah* originate from the same source as the written Torah, God at Sinai, but have its existence independent of the written Torah? For our purposes, it is important to recognize that even on these fundamental issues there was no unanimity within the world of the Rabbis.

The World of the Rabbis

The most important event in Jewish history for understanding Rabbinic literature is the destruction of the second Temple by the Romans in 70 CE. Did the destruction mean that the Jews had lost God's favor? If not, what sort of God would allow the destruction of His home? If animal sacrifices could no longer be performed at the Temple, how would the individual Jew attain atonement? Where would Jews find God? The destruction of the Temple bore to the very core of Jewish self-understanding. Midrash, the weaving of an idea into a biblical verse, was the vehicle through which these urgent theological issues were addressed. The Torah was drashed by the Rabbis to help that generation of Jews understand their place in this frightening new world, much as Ezra and the scribes did after the destruction of the first Temple. One way, then, to understand *derash* is the attempt to penetrate that Divine cloud cover in each generation. Rather than asking what the Torah meant in its initial historical context, the *darshanim* ask, What does the Torah mean to us, today?

In addition to dealing with the political inferiority of the Jews in the immediate aftermath of the Temple's destruction, there were other ideological issues to contend with, as well. The competing sects of late second Temple Judaism sometimes find literary expression in the Midrash, specifically the Sadducees and the Dead Sea community. The Sadducees rejected the oral traditions of the Pharisees, while the Dead Sea sect, similarly differing from the Pharisees on many issues, also maintained a different calendrical system. (The Pharisees anticipated many of the positions later adopted by the Rabbis and are never the objects of Rabbinic dispute. For our purposes, the Pharisees can be imagined as intellectual descendants of the scribes and ancestors to the Rabbis.)

The Rabbis' two primary locales, Babylonia and the Land of Israel, were also home to dualists, people who maintained that there was both a good God and an evil God. Depending on the time and place, these people might be identified as Gnostics or Zoroastrians, and the details of their belief systems vary in important ways. But the Rabbis were not particularly interested in the nuances of opposing theologies. The notion that there were "two powers" undermined the Rabbinic perception that God was the author of all reality. These dualists, or their caricatures, also appear in Midrash.

By the second half of the Rabbinic period, the 4th through the 7th centuries, the Roman Empire had become Christian. What began as a sect of Judaism, a heretical sect from the perspective of the Rabbis, had grown into the ruling religion of the Mediterranean. Although disputes between Judaism and Christianity were performed publicly in the Middle Ages, in the Rabbinic period polemics were often written into biblical commentaries. For instance, both religious communities read *The Song of Songs* as an allegorical love poem. For the Jews, it was between God and the Community of Israel. For the Christians, however, it was between Christ and the *ecclesia*, the Christian Church. Armed with their assumptions that the Bible was cryptic, relevant, and perfect, the Rabbis parried the thrusts of Christians, dualists, Sadducees, and other sectarians in their ongoing struggle to make sense out of their post-Temple reality.

Loving God, Rabbinic Style

Before moving on to the Middle Ages, let us return to loving God (Deut. 6:5). The earliest stratum of Rabbinic literature, from the 3rd century, offers two distinct interpretations of what such an injunction entails. "Act from love" is our first comment.[29] We are to demonstrate our love for God by performing the Divine commandments from love rather than fear. Grammatically, what the Rabbis have done here is interpret love not as a verb, but as an adverb. We are to act lovingly. The problem for the Rabbis is to understand how an emotion can be commanded. In this interpretation, the charge to love God is understood behaviorally rather than emotionally.

The second comment, from the same 3rd century text, is given more flesh in its Talmudic counterpart: "'You shall love the LORD, your God' means that through you, the Name of Heaven will be beloved. When someone studies Torah and Mishnah, serves the sages, speaks to others pleasantly, conducts business honestly, what will people say about him? 'Happy is his father who taught him Torah. Happy is his teacher who taught him Torah. . . . Look at how pleasant are his ways, how refined his deeds!'"[30]

This comment continues from where the first comment stopped. Yes, loving God is about what we do; it's behavioral, not emotional. But, according to this *derash*, love is not an adverb, it's a causative verb.[31] Our actions should cause others to love God. Both comments avoid the literal understanding of the verse that we are commanded an emotion. Such non-literal readings, while characteristic of Rabbinic *derash*, begin to fall out of favor in the Middle Ages.

Peshat and *Derash* in the Middle Ages

It is, perhaps, an over-simplification to say that the concern with the unadorned, contextual meaning of biblical verses awaited the Jewish Middle Ages. But there is no evidence that during the period of the Rabbis, through the seventh century, there was any *systematic* approach to determining the Bible's meaning according to context, literary style, and philology (the study of languages). In the Middle Ages, from the 10th century, this project is known as determining the *peshat* of a verse. The *peshat*, not to be confused with the literal meaning as we will explain shortly, is what the author (or editor) intended his initial audience to understand from the words *in context*.

The term *peshat* appears in Rabbinic literature but bears a different sense.[32] For the Rabbis, the *peshat* of a verse was its generally accepted meaning. *Peshat* can mean unadorned or stripped down, but it can also mean spread out, as in something that is commonly understood. Thus in Rabbinic usage, the *peshat* was the conventional understanding of a verse for their community, regardless of whether that understanding conformed to the unadorned, contextual meaning.[33] Although we have seen Rabbi Ishmael, and there were others, express annoyance at the interpretive license of some Rabbis, none was systematically committed to interpreting all of Torah exclusively according to the methodology of *peshat*. That project was medieval, not Rabbinic.

To say that the project of *peshat* was medieval is not to say that *peshat* (in the medieval sense) was unimportant to the Rabbis.[34] It may well be that *peshat* was equally as important to the Rabbis as *derash*, but since the latter was predicated on the Torah's cryptic qualities, that's where the Rabbis invested their energy. Frequently in the throes of Talmudic disputations, the Talmud will interject: *Peshita!* That's obvious![35] The response to a *Peshita* is, "Well, yes. It's obvious, but necessary. If it weren't said you might misunderstand something else." Perhaps there is relatively little discussion of the Torah's *peshat* (which shares the same root as *peshita*) precisely because it seemed obvious.

The Emergence of *Peshat* Commentary

Systematic concern for the *peshat*, as the medievals understood the term, was precipitated by several factors. The first reason was, ironically, the pioneering work on the Arabic language done by Muslim grammarians. Their conviction that the Arabic of the Koran, their holy writ, was Divine spurred them to study the language of God. Since Arabic and Hebrew are both Semitic languages, many of the insights of the Arabic grammarians were applicable to Hebrew. With greater knowledge of Hebrew, the determination of the contextual meaning of many biblical words was advanced. This concern with grammar and philology began in the Muslim world in the 10th century, but reached its height in Northern Spain and Northern France in the 12th century.

The rise and spread of Islam also brought into wider circulation philosophical texts from Ancient Greece, now translated into Arabic. Aristotle and Plato, as well as certain Neo-Platonic philosophers, encouraged some Muslims to adopt a more philosophic posture toward Islam. The philosophical school of Islamic theology known as Kalam, which also influenced Jewish thinkers like Sa'adia Gaon (882–942), sought to bring a degree of rationalism to religion. This rationalism was applied not only to matters of theology, but also to biblical interpretation, thus promoting a more contextual appreciation of the Hebrew Bible. Also, as a result of Jewish-Muslim polemics, there was a desire to clarify the contextual meaning of the Torah.

A third factor that helps to explain the emergence of *peshat* involves a group of Jews known as the Karaites. (KRA is the Hebrew root for *read*, and Mikra is that which is read, i.e., the Scriptures; thus the Karaites are scripturalists.) Similar to the Sadducees before them, they rejected the Rabbinic Oral Torah and maintained that only the Pentateuch was authoritative for purposes of determining Jewish law. In truth, the Karaites were far from biblical literalists. They simply came to different conclusions through their exegesis than did the Rabbis. Rabbinic Judaism, for example, promoted marital relations on the Sabbath; Isaiah (58:13), after all, encourages one to be joyous on the Sabbath! The Karaites, however, prohibited sexual relations on the Sabbath based on the following verse: "You shall cease from labor [on the Sabbath] even at plowing time" (Exod. 34:21), ostensibly understanding "plowing" to be a euphemism for sex.

Although the beginnings of Karaism were in the mid-eighth century, it was not until the tenth century that we see full-scale Rabbinic attacks on this rival group. In particular, Sa'adia Gaon of Babylonia and Abraham ibn Ezra of Spain (1089–1164) are known for their fierce defense of Rabbinism against the heresy of Karaism. Both sages employ the tools of grammar and their knowledge of Arabic and Aramaic (both Semitic languages, like Hebrew) in order to champion Rabbinic Judaism's interpretation of the law. Karaism developed in the Muslim world and like Rabbinic Judaism was influenced by advances in Arabic grammar and Islamic philosophy.

Within Christian Europe, specifically in France, there were similar forces at work contributing to the emergence of the *peshat* method. Throughout the twelfth century, universities were being founded that promoted a more rational approach to the reading of Scriptures. This "renaissance," as it has been called, affected both Christian and Jewish readings of the Bible. Just as rationalism, centuries earlier, had contributed to the *peshat* approach in the Islamic world, by the 1100s, rationalism was making inroads within the Christian world.

In the Islamic sphere, the Rabbinites used the *peshat* method to argue with Karaites and the Muslims; in the Christian sphere, the Jews used the *peshat* method in their disputations with the Christians. Since much of the New Testament attempts to demonstrate that the Hebrew Bible points to the birth and life of Jesus of Nazareth, resorting to the contextual meanings of biblical verses was an obvious Jewish strategy to counter Christian readings that were frequently allegorical or typological. (An example of typology is Jesus, understood as God's son, coming from Egypt just as the Israelites had done earlier [Matt. 2:15 and Hosea 11:1]). Time and again, during this period, we read of Christian charges that the Jewish reading of Scripture is "bovine" because it deals only with the *peshat*.[36]

In both the Islamic and Christian orbits, Jews were exposed to the rationalism of members of the majority religion. Coupled with the new understandings of the Hebrew language, and a need to defend Rabbinic understandings of Scripture both from within Judaism (Karaism) and outside (Islam and Christianity), the *peshat* method of favoring contextual understandings of Scripture reached its apex by the beginning of the 13th century. With several salient exceptions, the method then lost favor until Moses Mendelssohn and the Jewish Enlightenment of late-eighteenth century Germany.

> *Reasons for the Emergence of Peshat:*
> *(1) Developments in Semitic Grammar Due to the Arabic Study of the Koran*
> *(2) Spread of Philosophy and Rationalism*
> *(3) Internal Polemics with Karaites*
> *(4) External Polemics with Christians and Muslims*

Assumptions of the *Pashtanim*

The *peshat* seekers, or *pashtanim*, were centered in Northern Spain and Northern France. Many were trained in the school of Rabbi Shlomo Yitzchaki (1040–1105) of Provence. Rashi, as he is known, wrote a running commentary on the entire Hebrew Bible, although not all of it may have survived. The importance of his commentary cannot be overstated. Although many commentators later disagreed with Rashi, none ignored him. The first machine-printed Hebrew text was not the Bible, it was Rashi's commentary on the Bible!

Rashi was concerned with *peshat*, but his methodology was not systematic. He generally recycled Rabbinic comments on the Pentateuch in order to clarify the meaning of the text. There are over one hundred and fifty commentaries on Rashi that explain his midrashic choices and the textual issues he was addressing. Rashi's students and grandsons continued his project, along with others, until the interest in *peshat* had largely run its course by the end of the 13th century.

For the *pashtanim*, Kugel's assumptions no longer held. Applying the rules of Hebrew grammar to previously obscure words allows the *pashtan* to close in on a single, contextual meaning of a given word. The Bible is only cryptic to those who do not understand how the Hebrew language functioned in the biblical period. Furthermore, not all sections are equally relevant to us today. The Bible has much information that is only of historical interest.

More importantly, the Bible is read by the *pashtanim* as religious literature in which literary style often involves repetition. There is no longer the assumption of perfection or omnisignificance among most of the *pashtanim*. Literature often contains poetic parallelism as well as figurative speech. That's the way humans talk. When Esau comes in famished from the hunt and says, "I am going to die" (Gen 25:32), he means that's he is fatigued and hungry. Although some commentators interpret his words literally, as though he would die soon because hunting is a dangerous line of work, Ovadia S'forno (1475–1550) maintains that a commitment to *peshat* means understanding how sometimes impetuous humans speak. Thus one should not confuse *peshat* with the literal meaning—humans don't speak literally. The Rabbinic *legal* principle that "the Torah speaks in human language" was greatly extended in the Middle Ages, applying its commitment to the natural use of language to the *narrative* sections of Torah.[37]

In general, the first three of Kugel's four assumptions no longer remain operative for the *pashtanim*. The Torah is not cryptic, not always relevant, and not perfect since there are repetitions for literary purposes. Only the final assumption, that the Torah is Divine, remains unscathed, although the hedge is trampled. There are hints that a hand other than Moses' was involved in the composition of the Torah. After all, as some *pashtanim* point out, Moses is recorded as dying before the final verses of Deuteronomy were completed.[38] Although what distinguishes contemporary *pashtanim* in secular universities from their medieval counterparts is the usage of historical artifacts and non-biblical texts, there is already the beginning of historical sensitivity in medieval exegesis.[39]

Torah Meets Medieval Philosophy

Just as there was a range of Rabbinic opinion, the Middle Ages similarly saw a variety of approaches to Torah. Although he has precursors, the giant of medieval Jewish philosophy is Moses Maimonides (1138–1204), known as Rambam. Born in Muslim Spain, he spent most of his life in Cairo and was thoroughly at home within the intellectual world of Islamic thought. His two greatest contributions to Judaism are his law code, *Mishneh Torah*, and his philosophical work, *The Guide for the Perplexed*, both written in the last quarter of the twelfth century.

In the Introduction to *The Guide*, Rambam informs his readers that he'll be writing in such a fashion as to hide his true views on certain controversial issues. Rambam maintains that he is only replicating the cryptic nature of the Torah itself that presents certain ideas in one way for the masses and in another way for the intellectual elite. Moses, himself, was a philosopher, as were all the prophets. Moses, using his imagination, was able to give shape to his prophecy in such a way as to lead the non-philosophers toward a more correct understanding of God than had been the case when the Israelites were in Egypt. Rambam, hoping to continue that process of intellectual refinement, spends the first section of *The Guide* arguing that the anthropomorphic language (attributing human form to God) of the Torah must be understood figuratively since God is incorporeal. To conceive of God in human terms is, according to Rambam, heretical. Since attributing human form and emotion to God, through a literal reading of the Torah, oppose philosophical reason, the Torah must be interpreted figuratively.

Rambam's philosophical system is based on that of Aristotle who maintained a strict separation between God and creation. But the Divine rewards and punishments of the Torah seem to be predicated on the behavior of the Israelites. If they obey the laws of the Torah, there will be rain, if not, drought. According to Aristotle, however, God does not know what human individuals do nor can God change nature. Rambam explains that the sections of the Torah (like Lev. 26) which outline such a system of reward for proper behavior are a lie. God does not respond to human deeds. Indeed, some medieval Jewish philosophers of an Aristotelian bent are explicit that God does not even *know* human deeds.[40] Rambam explains that at the time of the exodus from Egypt, the generally prevailing view among the Israelites was that worshipping stars guaranteed agricultural success. In order to dissuade the Israelites from engaging in idolatry, and persuade them to engage in the laws of Torah, Moses provided familiar incentives. If they worshipped God, they'd receive rain. It was a lie, but a noble lie, designed to prevent idolatry amongst the Israelites.[41]

It is apparent to me that in the Assembly at Mount Sinai, not everything that reached Moses reached all Israel. Rather it was Moses who was addressed. That is why the Decalogue is in the second person singular. He [Moses] in turn (peace upon him) went to the foot of the mountain and relayed to the people what he had heard. . . . They heard the awesome sound, but no discrete words. . . . Only Moses heard speech, and he told it to them.

(Rambam, Guide, 2:33)[42]

For my purpose is that the truths [of the Torah] be glimpsed and then again be concealed, so as not to oppose that Divine purpose which one cannot possibly oppose and which has concealed from the vulgar among the people those truths especially requisite for His apprehension. . . .

(Rambam, Guide, Introduction)[43]

Just as God's revelation was different for Moses than the rest of Israel, so does Rambam attempt to preserve the distinction between those truths appropriate for the intellectual elite and the stories and parables suited for the masses.

The *pashtanim* focus on the one plain meaning of the Torah; the Aristotelian philosophers envision at least two, the exoteric for the masses and the esoteric for the elite.[44] Actually, by the thirteenth century, a four-fold level of interpretation emerged in the mystical tradition that finds an acronym in *pardes*, the Hebrew word for orchard. The p is for *peshat*, the exoteric, plain sense of the text. The d is for *derash*, that is, the Rabbinic/legal understanding of a verse. The r stands for *remez*, allusion. This level is the philosophical or allegorical meaning of a text. Finally, the s is for *sod*, the secret, mystical meaning at the heart of the text. One commentator, Rabbeinu Bahya (1263–1340), often offers explanations on all four levels.

The Mystical Mapping of Kabbalah

In some ways, the mystical tradition is just the opposite of the philosophical tradition. If for the philosophers, God is the unmoved mover of Aristotle, for the mystics, God is the "most moved mover."[45] Jews engaged in performing the commandments with the proper intention are able to affect God in positive ways. Conversely, transgressions weaken God's powers in the world. For the Aristotelian tradition, nothing humans do can affect God. The language that begins to emerge in the 12th century (and fully blossoms with the Zohar in the 13th century) describes these changes in God's being and is called Kabbalah. The Kabbalists read the Torah as a map describing how Divine energy oscillates between God's aspects of mercy and judgment, and between God's male and female aspects, as well. These energy stations that serve as focal points for the Divine flow are generically called s'firot, though each of the ten s'firot has many names taken from passages in the Torah as well as the world of nature. The Kabbalists and the philosophers agree that God, in essence, is unknowable and totally beyond our finite minds to comprehend. For the Kabbalists, that aspect of the Divine is *Ein Sof*, endlessness.

Where the philosophers and Kabbalists disagree is whether Divine transcendence precludes God's meaningful, ongoing interaction with the world. The philosophers insist as much while the mystics consider such a claim both pernicious and untrue. The Torah, read according to the Kabbalah, unveils the mysteries of God's inner life, how human actions affect God, and how God affects our world. This concern with God's inner life reflects the mystic's concern with his own psychological states, and there is thus an emphasis on religious psychology in the writings of the Kabbalists.

Two further points about Kabbalistic exegesis are in order. The first is that unlike the philosophers who tended to see value in both layers of the Torah's meanings, one for the masses and the other for the philosophers, some mystics were quite dismissive of the *peshat*. For this group, the only part of the Torah of real worth was the mystical meaning. There is minimal spirituality to be found in the outer garb of the Torah. For the soul of the text, one had to delve into its mysteries. The method of *peshat* was not wrong, it was worthless. Only through Kabbalah can one penetrate to the Divine depths.

Alas for those fools whose minds are closed and whose eyes are shut, of whom it is said, "They have eyes but they do not see" (Ps. 115:5) the light of the Torah! They are animals, who do not see or know anything except the straw of the Torah, which is the outer husk or the chaff, of which it is said: chaff and straw are exempt from tax [since they're worthless]. The sages of the Torah, the mystics, throw away the straw and chaff, which are external, and eat the wheat of the Torah, which is internal.

(Tikkunei HaZohar, Tikkun 69, 114a, c. 1300, Spain)

Here the author of a mystical text denigrates *pashtanim*. Among some *pashtanim* there was a reciprocal feeling of disdain for those who embellished the Torah in midrashic fashion.[46]

As the depth of the Divine is endless, so are potential interpretations of the Divine text. Moshe Idel, a leading scholar in the field of Kabbalah, emphasizes that the Torah, identified in the Kabbalah with God, takes on the Divine attribute of *Ein Sof*, infinity.[47] The Torah, for Kabbalists, is maximally pluripotent; there is an infinity of interpretations ever-flowing from the Divine Torah.

The Torah contains all the deepest and most recondite mysteries, all sublime doctrines, both disclosed and undisclosed, all essences both of the higher and the lower grades, of this world and of the world to come are to be found there, but there is no one to fathom its teachings.

(Zohar I:134b–135a)

[In] Lurianic Kabbalah, every word of the Torah has 600,000 "faces," that is, layers of meaning or entrances, one for each of the children of Israel who stood at the foot of Mount Sinai. Each face is turned toward only one of them; he alone can see it and decipher it. Each man has his own unique access to revelation. Authority no longer resides in a single unmistakable "meaning" of the Divine communication, but in its infinite capacity for taking on new forms.[48]

(Gershom Scholem paraphrasing Isaac Luria,
the leading Kabbalist of the 16th century)

The Medieval Career of Rabbinic Assumptions About the Torah

We have seen that for the *pashtanim* of the Middle Ages, traditional assumptions of the Torah as cryptic, relevant, and perfect no longer hold. For many philosophers, the Torah is to be read on two different levels, the exoteric for the masses, and the esoteric for the philosophic elite. The Torah's language is designed to protect the masses from truths that are beyond their ken. The philosophers preserve the cryptic quality of the Torah for the masses while demystifying it for the elite.

As for relevance, not everything in the Torah bears contemporary significance. Rambam explicitly says that the details of which sacrificial animals are to be slaughtered are not important. "All those who occupy themselves with finding causes for something of these particulars are stricken with a prolonged madness. . . ."[49] Hence Kugel's omnisignificance does not apply for the medieval philosophers, nor is the Torah perfect in the same way as it was for the Rabbis. There are indeed parts of the Hebrew Bible that intentionally contradict each other and the philosophers will know how to decipher what is true and what is meant for the masses.[50]

In terms of the divinity of the Torah, the philosophers articulated a more sophisticated understanding of revelation than did the Rabbis. The way in which prophecy flows from God to the prophet is via the prophet's intellect and is expressed through the prophet's imagination. Hence, philosophers would be disinclined to read into the Torah anything of significance based on the spelling of a word, for instance. Language, for the philosophers, was conventional. As ibn Ezra, both a *pashtan* and a philosopher, put it, "The words are like bodies and the meanings like souls, and the body is like a vessel for the soul. Thus, there is a standard for scholars in all languages to preserve the meanings and not to worry about word changes if they have the same meanings."[51]

The medieval mystics have a very different theory of language. As for many Rabbis, words are essential in that they reflect the essence of the thing described, but in the world of Kabbalah, the Torah describes God. Indeed, for a thirteenth-century mystic, the Torah is one long name of God.[52] For the philosophers, the Torah is Divine in an attenuated sense, since it is mediated through the imagination of the prophet in comparison to the Rabbinic tradition where revelation is frequently imagined to issue directly from God.[53] But the mystics maximize the divinity of the Torah, because for them the revelation of the Torah is understood as the self-disclosure of God.[54]

As for our other assumptions, there is a similar strengthening through the exegetical activities of the medieval mystics. The Torah is certainly cryptic and needs to be read using the Kabbalistic language of the *s'firot* that describes God's inner life. The relevance of this knowledge is paramount, for it allows the medieval mystic to affect God's unity and the flow of Divine blessings into this world. The Kabbalists extend the Rabbinic understandings of the perfection of the Torah. As God is perfect and infinite, so, too, is God's Torah. The omnisignificance of the Torah is preserved by the mystics and the claim of pluripotence is maximized.

Rabbinic and Medieval Assumptions About the Torah

	Cryptic	Relevant	Perfect	Divine	Meaning
Rabbinic	Yes	Yes	Yes	Yes	Omnisignificant and pluripotent
Medieval Peshat	No	Not always	No	Yes, but a historical sense is developing	A tendency to focus exclusively on *peshat*
Medieval Philosophy	Yes	Not always	No	Yes, but through the mediation of the prophet's imagination	Exoteric for the masses, esoteric for the intellectual elite
Medieval Mysticism	Yes	Yes	Yes	Yes, since the Torah becomes identified with God	Omnisignificant and maximally pluripotent/ infinite

Moving Toward Modernity

The next major period for Jewish biblical interpretation begins by the close of the seventeenth century. Several Jews writing in Spanish were particularly exercised by the seeming opposition between the contextual meaning of a biblical verse and its Rabbinic exposition. The *pashtanim* of the Middle Ages tended to either bracket the Rabbinic interpretations of scripture as valid but not *peshat*, and therefore, not part of their exegetic enterprise, or dismiss much of Rabbinic midrash as unrelated to the text of the Torah itself. But these seventeenth-century thinkers were embarrassed and defensive about Rabbinic readings of Torah. Several of these thinkers inaugurated or anticipated developments in postmodern literary theory, attempting to bridge the gap between *peshat* and *derash* by arguing that the written word is always amenable to multiple interpretations.[55]

The effort to rehabilitate Rabbinic readings of Scripture gained momentum in the eighteenth century in response to both Christians and reform-minded Jews (beginning in 1670 with Benedict Spinoza, "the first *peshat*-Jew of modern times"[56]) pointing to the unnaturalness of midrash.[57] As the Jews of Western Europe were beginning to be allowed to participate in the civic lives of European nations, there was an increasing need to either validate the legitimacy of Rabbinic midrash or repudiate its fancifulness, often with an eye toward reforming traditional laws and practices. Two pioneers of the German Jewish Enlightenment, Naftali Herz Wesseley (1725–1805) and Moses Mendelssohn (1729–1786), each maintained that Rabbinic midrash offered a penetrating understanding of the biblical text. Wesseley emphasized that Hebrew, in particular, was polysemous, bearing within itself multiple meanings; while Mendelssohn claimed that all languages possess the capacity for multiple meanings and that the Torah, in particular, was specifically written to evoke a multiplicity of meanings.[58]

Neither of these scholars, however, advocated traditional pluripotence whereby the Torah's polysemous nature was justified by it being a Divine text. The Torah, in their modern readings, has lost its ontological uniqueness. Perhaps reflecting the increasing influence of Spinoza, the Bible was to be read like all other texts. It was still, to be sure, a divinely revealed document. But the rules of literary interpretation were not thereby changed. Other works of literature (whether world literature for Mendelssohn or Hebrew literature for Wesseley) are also polysemous and only by thorough investigation, including expertise in philology, can we appreciate the depth of meanings in great literature. Indeed, Wesseley retooled a medieval term coined by Rashbam, "deep *peshat*", to indicate that midrashim often pointed to a deeper truth about the text than was obvious from a shallow reading of the text's surface.[59] These pioneers of modern literary theory chose to promote secular literature to the ontological status of Torah rather than demote or dismiss Rabbinic midrash. In so doing, they justified their continued commitment to Jewish law within an increasingly open society.

Throughout the eighteenth and nineteenth centuries, the biblical commentaries that were generated within the Jewish community tended to be penned not by the early reformers, but by the traditionalists. Scholars have suggested that it was of little value (if not altogether counterproductive) to the liberal Jewish agenda of acculturation within Europe to expend scholarly energy on the national history of the ancient Israelites.[60] In any event, those in the traditional Jewish community extended the arc of Torah commentary. Although Jewish denominations were emerging throughout the nineteenth century, we will divide the modern commentators not by denomination but by their continued commitment to traditional assumptions about the nature of the Torah. Those we call the traditionalists often embed polemics against Reform or other critical ideologies within their Torah commentaries. They're defending the tradition.

Traditionalist Commentary

At about the same time as Mendelssohn was translating the Hebrew Bible into German (early 1780s), a religious renewal movement was sweeping through Eastern Europe under the name of Hasidism. The Hasidic masters were less concerned with justifying Rabbinic midrash than with promoting piety and describing devotion through psychologically sensitive rereadings of biblical and Rabbinic material. Hasidism popularized the Kabbalah and in so doing made it much simpler. In the process, the Kabbalistic depiction of the *s'firot* as movements within the Divine mind were turned on their head and understood as the pietist's road map to Divine communion. The Hasidic understanding of the *s'firot*, in other words, turned the Kabbalistic descriptions of God's inner being into a description of the mystic's inner being. Theosophy, the inner life of God, becomes religious psychology.[61]

The following Hasidic dialogue exemplifies Hasidism's concerns with religious psychology as well as its incorporation of mystical ideas from Kabbalah. In this exchange, the Rabbinic reticence to command an emotion has been overcome, and the issue is whether the love of one's neighbor is conditional upon his or her behavior.

A disciple once asked Rabbi Shmelke of Nikolsburg (d. 1778): "We are commanded to love our neighbor as ourself (Lev. 19:18). How can I do this if my neighbor has wronged me?" The Rabbi answered: "You must understand these words aright. Love your neighbor like something which you yourself are. For all souls are one. Each is a spark from the original soul, and this soul is wholly inherent in all souls, just as your soul is in all the members of your body. It may come to pass that your hand makes a mistake and strikes you. But would you then take a stick and chastise your hand because it lacked understanding, and so increase your pain? It is the same if your neighbor, who is one soul with you, wrongs you for lack of understanding. If you punish him, you only hurt yourself." The disciple went on asking: "But if I see a man who is wicked before God, how can I love him?" "Don't you know," said Rabbi Shmelke, "that the original soul came out of the essence of God, and that every human soul is a part of God? And will you have no mercy on Him, when you see that one of His holy sparks has been lost in a maze and is almost stifled?"[62]

Although it would be inaccurate to claim that the Hasidic masters were oblivious to critical streams of thought that so agitated the traditional Jewish leadership in Western Europe, their primary agenda was simply not dominated by those factors. Outside the Hasidic world and primarily, but not exclusively, in Western Europe, new articulations of biblical theory were emerging from Orthodox Rabbis concerned with protecting the tradition. The emancipation, beginning in France in 1790, encouraged Jews to become members of European nations while still allowing them to identify with the Jewish religion. This process of acculturation entailed education in European languages, literature, history, and the sciences.

Never before had such a potent combination of historical, intellectual, and religious factors threatened the traditional Jewish community: the emancipation of the Jews, the enlightenment, biblical criticism, evolutionary theory, Jewish Studies as an academic discipline, and Reform Judaism all erupted between 1780 and 1880. With Rabbinic tradition under siege, some rabbis responded by collapsing the *derash* into the *peshat* and claiming they were identical; others highlighted the differences between them; while still others relied on concepts of pluripotency and polysemy. Rabbi Naftali Zvi Yehuda Berlin (1816–1893) suggested that the Torah is poetry (even in its prose and legal sections) and, he therefore rejects any single interpretation at the exclusion of others.[63] All these theories were motivated by the shifting tectonic plates of modernity whereby the traditional Jewish community was displaced and marginalized as the source of values and beliefs. By the end of the nineteenth century, many Western European Jews had made the shift: their worldview was more informed by European culture than by Jewish tradition.

Contemporary Commentators

If the Hasidic masters remain largely faithful to the literary assumptions of their medieval mystical ancestors, and the traditional Orthodox commentators represent an amalgam of Rabbinic and *pashtanic* assumptions, contemporary commentators are a whole new breed. Most importantly, those whom we call contemporary reject the traditional understanding of Divine dictation to Moses at Mount Sinai. There were some important medieval precursors to this contemporary viewpoint, but the theory of multiple authorship of the Pentateuch over hundreds of years, an approach generically referred to as biblical criticism, is a modern understanding.

Asserting human authorship of the Torah does not, however, preclude Divine participation in the process. As a commentator on ibn Ezra phrased it in the mid-fourteenth century, "And since we are to have trust in the words of tradition and the prophets, what should I care whether it was Moses or another prophet who wrote it, since the words of all of them are true and inspired?"[64] But in the mid-fourteenth century, it was easier to have trust in the words of tradition and the prophets than it was by the 19th. The academic study of the Bible does not confine itself to conjecture on the authors of the text. The study of ancient Near-Eastern religions and cultures has illuminated our understanding of the biblical world and the texts produced therein.

Scholars have found parallel narratives and laws in other literatures that show how similar, and distinctive, Israelite culture was from its neighbors. The creation story, the flood, and many of the laws in the Torah have antecedents in the literature of the ancient Near East. Moreover, as scholars piece together the sources that comprise the Torah, certain theories emphasize the very political maneuverings between groups of different ideologies and those of different geographic loyalties. Given these all-too-human features of biblical literature, maintaining the unity and divinity of the text is truly a leap of faith. Nevertheless, while the academic approach to the Torah might militate against Divine authorship and unity of the entire Torah,[65] it certainly does not rule out some novel formulation of God's relationship to this human text.

Contemporary theologians and commentators are, therefore, not so much of a chronological category as a temperamental one. On the one hand, they do not completely reject the conclusions of the scientific approach to religion and the Bible; on the other hand, they remain committed to the long and rich tradition of Jewish Torah commentary, if not necessarily to the traditional understanding of the God who spoke the world and Torah into being. Abraham Joshua Heschel (1905–1972), for example, has described the Torah as a midrash on revelation which is not meant to be read literally as an account of historical revelation. He emphasizes that biblical criticism deals with transmission, not truth.[66]

Contemporary commentators do not rely on the Torah for science or history. Much of the Torah is best understood as the Israelite reaction to myths and laws earlier articulated by Israel's neighbors. There's also an understanding that the text of the Torah itself may have changed over centuries of scribal replication. Furthermore, there's no compulsion to reconcile biblical texts that are in seeming contradiction. Some may see it as two simultaneous voices set in opposition by a redactor; others might see a natural development in which both the earlier and later understandings have been preserved. Taken together, these new assumptions about the nature and transmission of the Torah undermine Rabbinic assumptions of the Torah's relevance and perfection.

Each letter, word, or verse of the Torah is no longer perceived to be overflowing with Divine meaning. It might just be a scribal error. Kugel's assertion of omnisignificance does not hold for contemporary commentators. But contemporary literary theory, often called *postmodern*, has corroborated the Rabbinic assumption that the Torah is cryptic. For contemporary commentators, though, the Torah's obscurity is not predicated on Divine provenance, but is an inherent feature of all literature.

According to Wesseley, Mendelssohn, and those postmodern theorists who follow in their path, words and sentences bear within them multiple meanings. Literature is polysemous. Another characteristic of some contemporary literary theories functions similarly to polysemy although it is based on different assumptions. Some literary theorists claim not that multiple meanings inhere within any given text, but that determining the single authoritative sense of a text is impossible. All texts are indeterminate in nature. Thus, some interpretations might be better than others, depending on the criteria, but no interpretation can ever attain final truth. The effect of such a theory is to invite multiple interpretations, since there is no conclusive way to validate any given reading.[67]

Modern Assumptions About the Torah

	Cryptic	Relevant	Perfect	Divine	Meaning
Hasidic	Yes	Yes	Yes	Yes	Omnisignificant and maximally pluripotent/ infinite
Traditional Orthodox	Strategy varies	Strategy varies	Strategy varies	Yes	Strategy varies
Contemporary	Yes	Not always	No	Not exhaustively	Not omnisignificant but polysemous or indeterminate or botanical

The Botanical Model

In addition to literary theories stressing polysemy or indeterminacy, there is yet another approach which has yet to be dignified with a name. Let us call it the botanical model. Like polysemy and indeterminacy, the botanical model is well rooted in Rabbinic sources. "Just as one finds new figs on a fig tree each time one searches, so too does one find new meanings in the Torah each time one searches."[68] Or, in the words of a contemporary Jewish Bible scholar, ". . . the meaning and significance of a passage (an event, an utterance) may not be realized until activated by later circumstances or contemplation."[69]

The botanical model credits the authors of all texts with the potential of having embedded in their art the capacity for meanings to emerge over time. Figs don't ripen on a tree all at once. For the Rabbis, since God is the author of both nature and Torah, they share a certain feature. In this case it is the emergence of novelty. Many contemporary readers who do not assign any unique, Divine status to the Torah nevertheless agree that literary texts have the potential to reveal latent messages to later readers. Polysemy points to multiple meanings that inhere in a text at a given moment. The botanical theory emphasizes the potency of texts to have dormant meanings awakened over time. The following Rabbinic *aggadah* captures that moment of activation:

> *Rav Yehudah said in the name of Rav: When Moses went up on high, he found the Holy One, blessed be He, sitting and adorning the letters [of the Torah] with crowns. He said, "Master of the universe, who slows you down [by making you affix these crowns to the Torah's letters]?"*

*He responded to him, "There will be a man in the future, at the end of
many generations, Akiva son of Joseph is his name, and on every little tittle,
he will derash heaps and heaps of halakhah."*
"Master of the universe, show him to me."
He said, "Turn around."
*Moses went and sat down at the back of eight rows [of students.] He didn't
know what they were talking about. He became weak.*
*When Akiva reached a certain point, one of his students asked, "Rabbi,
from where do you know this?"*
He said, "It is a halakhah of Moses from Sinai."
Moses' mind was settled.[70]

One might think that if Moses received the Torah from Sinai, he would
recognize the content. Part of the force of this *aggadah* is that the author is
admitting that the Judaism of Akiva, Rabbinic Judaism, would be initially
unrecognizable to Moses! Upon hearing Akiva's teaching, Moses becomes
weak, disoriented. Where is the revelation that he had transmitted to the
Israelites? It is only when Akiva links his teaching to that of Moses' that
Moses recovers. The question, then, is why does Moses regain his strength?

Of course, it might be that Moses is just happy to have the connection
made to him. According to the theory of indeterminacy, we can't rule that
interpretation out. What an interpreter should do, though, is point out that
Moses is described, by God (the literary character) no less, as the most
humble man on earth (Num. 12:3). Now it seems strange for a rabbi who
knew God's description of Moses to create an *aggadah* that presents Moses as
so self-centered.

Alternatively, and to my mind more plausibly, Moses served as a vehicle
for revelation without fully understanding the content. In the Rabbinic mind,
Moses may have been something akin to their own contemporaries who were
responsible for transmitting traditions even though they, themselves, were not
sages.[71] They were blessed with excellent memories and served as ancient tape
recorders. Perhaps when Moses heard Akiva's rendition, he understood God's
revelation for the very first time. In this reading, Akiva may not only be more
intelligent than Moses, but Akiva may be even a better teacher than God!

Finally, and for my present purposes, the most illuminating interpretation
is one consonant with the botanical model that we have seen elsewhere in
the Talmud. According to this model, Moses understood quite well what he
received from God at Sinai, but *only* what he received from God at Sinai.
Akiva, living a thousand years after Moses, understands not only Moses'

Torah, but some of its implications, as well. Akiva has the advantage of time, of seeing how the words of Torah, like ever-ripening figs, have revealed their latent meanings in the intervening centuries between Sinai and Akiva's Israel. Akiva, like a good therapist, draws out the implications of his patient's words and combines them to derive a fresh insight. Moses recovers from his sense of disorientation once he hears that Akiva is drawing his teachings from him. Only then does Moses awaken to the dormant implications of his Sinai experience.[72]

Every generation has followed Akiva's example and generated fresh insights from Moses' message. There has been no word unturned. "The unbelievably rich hermeneutical literature subsumed generically under the rubric of *parshanut ha-Miqra,*' the exposition of the Scriptures, supplies all the essential ingredients of Jewish intellectual and spiritual history."[73] Turn the commentary, turn the commentary, for all is in it. For those desirous of adding to the storehouse of Jewish thought, expressing oneself through the medium of Torah commentary, regardless of one's literary theory, is unexceptionally traditional. And for many Jews, still today, God's presence is found not in nature, or history, or even the synagogue, but in the Torah and its commentaries.

A modern interpreter of Judaism described the activity of the earliest commentators as follows: "It is not just a continuation or development [of the Bible] but a new act of weaving undertaken by master weavers of rare power."[74] Weaving is a wonderful metaphor for our *darshanim.* (*Text* is etymologically related to *textile,* both coming from the Latin word meaning *weave.*) Our *darshanim* are weaving the text of the Torah into the fabric, the contexts, of their lives. Their comments are themselves literature, which means that they possess the same qualities and opportunities for interpretation as the Torah itself. Some comments are clearly products of their time, reflecting the concerns and milieu of the authors; other comments are timeless, reflecting the universal human condition; and, finally, there are comments that are ahead of their time, reaching toward a moment when "nation shall not take up sword against nation" (Isa. 2:4) and "everyone will dwell in safety, everyone under his own vine and under her own fig tree" (1 Kings 5:5).

NOTES

Much of the material that would supplement chapter 1 is out of print, in Hebrew, or in relatively inaccessible or inconvenient scholarly tomes. What follows is a user-friendly guide of further resources for students of Jewish biblical interpretation. There are two essays that cover much of the same material, with different perspectives, as we have here: Michael A. Signer,

"How the Bible Has Been Interpreted in Jewish Tradition" and from a more comparative perspective with Christianity, Stefan C. Reif, "Aspects of the Jewish Contribution to Biblical Interpretation." Michael Fishbane has published several similar surveys; the most accessible is found in his essay, "Hermeneutics," in *Contemporary Jewish Religious Thought*. In addition, Gershom Scholem has an important essay in his *The Messianic Idea* in which he treats the relationship between "Revelation and Tradition."

For those looking for additional information on specific periods or schools of biblical interpretation, the essays in *Back to the Sources* (ed. Barry Holtz) and *The Jewish Study Bible* (ed. Marc Z. Brettler and Adele Berlin) are both good places to begin in addition to the sources in the notes for this chapter. Michael Fishbane has several wonderful chapters in the first two sections of his *The Garments of Torah* that deal with interpretive issues in the Bible and early Rabbinic literature. Nahum Sarna has several essays that focus on *pashtanim* in his *Studies in Biblical Interpretation*. For a treatment of the reading strategies of both medieval mystics and philosophers, see Frank Talmage, "Apples of Gold: The Inner Meaning of Sacred Texts in Medieval Judaism." Arthur Green has recently published a very readable *Guide to the Zohar* that treats historical and hermeneutical issues.

Rivka Horwitz summarized several contemporary views in "Revelation and the Bible According to Twentieth-Century Jewish Philosophy"; Edward Greenstein applies contemporary literary theory to the Torah in "Deconstruction and Biblical Narrative"; and Susan A. Handelman has also written extensively on Jewish hermeneutics and modern literary theory in *The Slayers of Moses*. A thoughtful rejoinder to Handelman, combined with a lucid explanation of the emergence of Torah-centered, Rabbinic Judaism, can be found in William Scott Green, "Romancing the Tome: Rabbinic Hermeneutics and the Theory of Literature."

For those specifically interested in the Hebrew Bible and its sources, two books bear reading. The first is Richard Elliott Friedman's *Who Wrote the Bible?* And the second is Brettler's *How to Read the Bible*. Finally, for those seeking an overview of Judaism, my "Introduction to Judaism" through The Teaching Company (www.teach12.com) is humbly recommended.

1.   For an analysis of the distinctions between the two venues of the Divine presence in the desert, see chapter 5 of Israel Knohl's *The Divine Symphony: The Bible's Many Voices* (Philadelphia: The Jewish Publication Society, 2003).

2.   The Ark of the Covenant, as a unique, physical object, was also vulnerable. The Bible records that Philistines stole the Ark during a military campaign (1 Sam. 4).

3.   For further examples within this Psalm, see the commentary by Adele Berlin and Marc Zvi Brettler in *The Jewish Study Bible,* ed. Adele Berlin, Marc Zvi Brettler, and Michael Fishbane (New York: Oxford University Press, 2004), 1415–1424.

4.   See Exod. 18:15, 1 Sam. 9:9, Ezek. 20:1 and Jer. 21:2.

5.   But see also Deut. 17:8ff.

6.   James L. Kugel provides a fuller explanation of this transition in *The Bible As It Was* (Cambridge: Harvard University Press, 1997), 1–49.

7.   Ibid., 20–21.

8.   *Genesis Rabbah* 4:4 and many others.

9.   Kugel, 21.

10. Abraham Joshua Heschel discusses different conceptions of revelation in Rabbinic Judaism in his *Heavenly Torah: As Refracted Through the Generations*, trans. and ed. Gordon Tucker with Leonard Levin (New York: Continuum, 2005).

11. m. *Avot* 3:2.

12. *Avot d'Rabbi Natan* 3:2.

13. Simplified from *Genesis Rabbah* 65:18.

14. Amos Frisch penned an illuminating article on this subject, "R. Jacob Zvi Mecklenburg's Method in the Issue of the Patriarchs' Sins," *Journal of Jewish Studies* 8:1 (Spring, 2002): 107–119.

15. y. *Sanhedrin* 21a.

16. b. *Eruvin* 54a/b.

17. Onkelos on Deut. 5:18.

18. b. *Sanhedrin* 17a, *mutatis mutandis*.

19. b. *Sanhedrin* 34a.

20. *Numbers Rabbah* 13:15. Seventy (7×10) is the Rabbinic number signifying totality.

21. t. *Sotah* 7:7.

22. b. *Baba Metzia* 59 a/b. Using the term of literary theorist Stanley Fish, the sages comprise the interpretive community that establishes parameters for legitimate interpretations of Torah. The Rabbis also established, in theory, rules of halakhic interpretation that they then inserted into the morning liturgy. For more on these rules and the more expansive rules ostensibly governing aggadic interpretation, see Saul Lieberman, "Rabbinic Interpretation of Scripture," in *Essential Papers on the Talmud*, ed. Michael Chernick (New York: New York University Press, 1994), 429–460.

A brilliant and disturbing example of interpretive license, or excess, is Vladimir Nabokov's *Pale Fire* (New York: Putnam, 1962). Not coincidentally, the protagonist is isolated from the salutary safeguards of an interpretive community.

23. b. *Sanhedrin* 99a.

24. *Sifra, Tazria* 13:2.

25. b. *Kiddushin* 17b.

26. m. *Hagigah* 1:8.

27. m. *Avot* 1:1, b. *Shabbat* 31a and *Sifra, Bechukotai* 8:3.

28. See Jay M. Harris, *How Do We Know This? Midrash and the Fragmentation of Modern Judaism* (Albany: State University of New York Press, 1995) and Moshe Halbertal, *People of the Book: Canon, Meaning, and Authority*, trans. Naomi Goldblum (Cambridge: Harvard University Press, 1992).

29. *Sifre*, 32.

30. b. *Yoma* 86a. Norman Lamm has brought together a wonderful variety of interpretations on this verse and those surrounding it in *The Shema: Spirituality and Law in Judaism* (Philadelphia: The Jewish Publication Society, 2000).

31. Hebrew, unlike English, has a specific grammatical form for causative verbs, *hiphil.*

32. See b. *Hullin* 6a.

33. For more on this distinction between the Rabbinic and medieval uses of *peshat*, see Jose Faur, "Basic Concepts in Rabbinic Hermeneutics," *Shofar* 16, no. 1 (Fall, 1997): 1–12. See also Raphael Loewe, "The 'Plain' Meaning of Scripture in Early Jewish Exegesis," in *Papers of the Institute of Jewish Studies London*, vol. 1, ed. J. G. Weiss (London: Institute of Jewish Studies, 1964), 140–85.

34. Loewe makes the point that the Rabbis employed other terms besides *peshat* that indicate "a semi-articulate feeling towards a distinction between literal and non-literal exegesis," 175.

35. E.g., b. *Brachot* 20b.

36. Avraham Grossman, "The School of Literal Jewish Exegesis in Northern France," in *Hebrew Bible/Old Testament*, vol. 1, pt. 2, ed. Magne Saebo (Gottingen: Vandenhoeck & Ruprecht, 2000), 330.

37. On the development of this principle, see Isadore Twersky, "Joseph ibn Kaspi: Portrait of a Medieval Intellectual," in *Studies in Medieval Jewish History and Literature*, ed. Isadore Twersky (Cambridge: Harvard University Press, 1979), 231–57, esp. 239ff.

38. See Rashi, citing from b. *Baba Batra* 14b/15a, and ibn Ezra on Deut. 34:5. See also ibn Ezra on Gen. 12:6.

39. Shaye J. D. Cohen explores "historical exegesis" in anti-Christian polemics by three medieval *pashtanim* in "Does Rashi's Torah Commentary Respond to Christianity? A Comparison of Rashi with Rashbam and Bekhor Shor," in *The Idea of Biblical Interpretation*, eds. Hindy Najman and Judith H. Newman (Leiden: Brill, 2004), 449–472.

40. See Gersonides, *Wars of the Lord*, 3:4.

41. *The Guide of the Perplexed*, 2 vols., trans. Shlomo Pines (Chicago: University of Chicago Press, 1963), 3:30. All translations from *The Guide* are by Pines unless otherwise noted. *Leviticus Rabbah* 22:8 presents a similar notion.

42. L. E. Goodman, *Rambam: Readings in the Philosophy of Moses Maimonides* (New York: Viking Press, 1976), 381, translation slightly altered.

43. *Guide*, 6ff.

44. Not all philosophers were Aristotelian, nor were all Aristotelians committed to esoteric language. See *The Cambridge Companion to Medieval Jewish Philosophy*, ed. Daniel H. Frank and Oliver Leaman (New York: Cambridge University Press, 2003) and Robert Eisen, *Gersonides on Providence, Covenant, and the Chosen People: A Study in Medieval Jewish Philosophy and Biblical Commentary* (Albany: State University of New York Press, 1995).

45. This language is that of Abraham Joshua Heschel in *The Prophets: An Introduction*, 2 vols. (New York: Harper Torchbooks, 1962).

46. See Eric Lawee, "The 'Ways of Midrash' in the Biblical Commentaries of Isaac Abarbanel," *Hebrew Union College Annual* 67 (1996): 107–42.

47. Zohar 2:60a/b. See also Moshe Idel, *chap. 3, Absorbing Perfections: Kabbalah and Interpretation* (New Haven: Yale University Press, 2002) and Elliot R. Wolfson, "The Hermeneutics of Visionary Experience: Revelation and Interpretation in the Zohar," *Religion* 18 (1988): 311–45.

48.   *On the Kabbalah and its Symbolism* (New York: Schocken Books, 1960), 13. The first two chapters of Scholem's text are quite important for our study.

49.   *Guide*, 3:26, p. 509.

50.   See, for example, ibn Tibbon's exegesis of Job in Robert Eisen, *The Book of Job in Medieval Jewish Philosophy*, 79–110.

51.   Ibn Ezra, long commentary to Ex. 20:1.

52.   Ezra ben Solomon, *Commentary on Talmudic Aggadot*. Cited in Scholem, "The Meaning of the Torah in Jewish Mysticism," in *On the Kabbalah and its Symbolism*, 39.

53.   For example, Pirkei d'Rabbi Eliezer, 40.

54.   Josef Stern has a helpful essay distinguishing between these two understandings of language in his essay, "Language," in *Contemporary Jewish Religious Thought: Original Essays on Critical Concepts, Movements, and Beliefs*, ed. Arthur A. Cohen and Paul Mendes-Flohr (New York: The Free Press, 1982), 543–51.

55.   See comments on Joseph Lopez and Izhak Orobio de Castro in Shalom Rosenberg, "Emunat Hakhamim," in *Jewish Thought in the Seventeenth Century*, ed. Isadore Twersky and Bernard Septimus (Cambridge: Harvard University Press, 1987), 285–341.

56.   Simon Rawidowicz, "On Interpretation," in *Studies in Jewish Thought*, ed. Nahum N. Glatzer (Philadelphia: The Jewish Publication Society, 1974), 83–126, 109. Spinoza was dedicated to reading the Torah as it was, without projecting later ideas onto the text. For a synopsis of Spinoza and his approach to Torah, see Harris, 121–31. For a critique of Spinoza, see Rawidowicz, 106–26.

57.   Edward Breuer notes the changing perception of Rabbinic midrash. "Whereas in the medieval period Jews were depicted as obstinate literalists, the early modern period saw a growing tendency to identify Jewish scholarship with non-literal, and therefore inferior, exegesis." *The Limits of Enlightenment: Jews, Germans, and the Eighteenth-Century Study of Scripture* (Cambridge: Harvard University Press, 1996), 85.

58.   For more on these two figures and their contributions to Jewish Biblical interpretation, see Jay M. Harris, chap. 6, *How Do We Know This?* and Breuer, chap. 6, *The Limits of Enlightenment*.

59.   See Edward Breuer, "Naphtali Herz Wesseley and the Cultural Dislocations of an Eighteenth-Century Maskil," in *New Perspectives on the Haskalah*, ed. Shmuel Finer and David Sorkin (London: Littman Library of Jewish Civilization, 2001), 27–47.

60.   For a review of these ideas, see S. David Sperling, *Students of the Covenant: A History of Jewish Biblical Scholarship in North America* (Atlanta: Scholars Press, 1992), 23–29.

61.   See Arthur Green's introduction to *Menahem Nahum of Chernobyl: Upright Practices, The Light of the Eyes* (New York: Paulist Press, 1982), 1–27.

62.   With slight modifications from Martin Buber, *Tales of the Hasidim* (New York: Schocken Books, 1991), 1:190.

63.   See Harris, chap. 8, *How Do We Know This?*.

64. Joseph Bonfils, *Tsaphenat Pa'aneach* on ibn Ezra's comment on Gen. 12:6. Cited in Jon D. Levenson, *The Hebrew Bible, the Old Testament, and Historical Criticism* (Louisville: Westminster/John Know Press, 1993), 67.

65. The unity of the Bible only comes into effect once the editor has brought together the individual traditions that comprise the whole.

66. Abraham Joshua Heschel, *God in Search of Man: A Philosophy of Judaism* (New York: Farrar, Straus and Cudahy, 1955), 185–220, *passim*.

67. See David Stern's essay, "Midrash and Hermeneutics: Polysemy vs. Indeterminacy," in his *Midrash and Theory: Ancient Jewish Exegesis and Contemporary Literary Studies* (Evanston: Northwestern University Press, 1996), 15–38. What Stern calls polysemy, I have called pluripotent. For an example of indeterminacy in biblical studies, see Susan E. Gillingham, *The Image, the Depths and the Surface: Multivalent Approaches to Biblical Study* (London: Sheffield Academic Press, 2000).

68. b. *Eruvin* 54 a/b.

69. Moshe Greenberg, "To Whom and For What Should a Bible Commentator Be Responsible?" in *Studies in the Bible and Jewish Thought* (Philadelphia, The Jewish Publication Society, 1995), 239. Greenberg cites James D. Smart. This model bears functional resemblance to the reader-response theory associated with Stanley Fish. In the botanical model, though, the text contains the dormant interpretations; for Fish, new readers bring new interpretations to bear on the text.

70. b. *Menachot* 29a.

71. See Jose Faur, *Golden Doves with Silver Dots: Semiotics and Textuality in Rabbinic Tradition* (Bloomington: Indiana University Press, 1986), 95.

72. Keen readers will have noticed that my first interpretation uses the context of the Hebrew Bible itself to evaluate the *aggadah*. My second suggestion incorporates the context of the authors of the *aggadah*. My third interpretation had to do with my own purposes in citing the text in the context of the present work. Such attention to the frame and context of our comments will be characteristic of the chapters to follow.

73. Nahum Sarna, "The Authority and Interpretation of Scripture in Jewish Tradition," in his *Studies in Biblical Interpretation* (Philadelphia: The Jewish Publication Society, 2000), 68.

74. Rawidowicz, "On Interpretation," in *Studies in Jewish Thought*, 91.

Chapter 2

THE CREATION
OF HUMANITY

GENESIS 1:26–31

(A.)²⁶ And God said, "Let us make man in our image, after our likeness. They shall rule the fish of the sea, the birds of the sky, the cattle, the whole earth, and all the creeping things that creep on earth."²⁷ And God created man in His image, in the image of God He created him; male and female he created them.²⁸ God blessed them and God said to them, "Be fertile and increase, fill the earth and master it; and rule the fish of the sea, the birds of the sky, and all the living things that creep on earth."²⁹ God said, "See, I give you every seed-bearing plant that is upon all the earth, and every tree that has seed-bearing fruit; they shall be yours for food.³⁰ And to all the animals on land, to all the birds of the sky, and to everything that creeps on earth, in which there is the breath of life, [I give] all the green plants for food.³¹ And God saw all that He had made, and found it very good. And there was evening and there was morning, the sixth day.

(JPS TANAKH)

(B.)²⁶ God said: Let us make humankind, in our image, according to our likeness! Let them have dominion over the fish of the sea, the fowl of the heavens, animals, all the earth, and all the crawling things that crawl about upon the earth!²⁷ God created humankind in his image, in the image of God did he create it, male and female did he create them.

(Everett Fox, *The Five Books of Moses*)

Creating Pluralism

Although there are two creation stories in the Book of Genesis, we begin with the narrative that has pride of place, chapter 1. In these six verses, which focus on the latter part of the sixth day of creation, the Torah treats issues of theology, anthropology, and ecology. Our commentators begin their exploration of these issues by seizing upon the most salient difference between this act of creation and those that preceded it. God's creation begins as a solo act. Although the word God in this chapter has a plural suffix (the *im* ending of *Elohim*), its predicates are all in the singular. This grammatical curiosity might be a literary hint that all those gods in the ancient Near-Eastern pantheons have now been consolidated under the generic and grammatically singular term *Elohim*. If so, then the introduction of plurality in verse 26, "Let *us* make adam," is all the more bizarre.

> 1. *Rabbi Joshua said in the name of Rabbi Levi: God consulted with the work of the heavens and the earth.*
>
> > (*Genesis Rabbah*, Rabbinic compilation edited by 5th century, Land of Israel)

Rabbi Levi's comment has the advantage of remaining within the confines of our story to supply an answer for the mystery of the plural. God consulted all that He had created up until that moment. Not only does Rabbi Levi's intuition resonate with contemporary scientific accounts and environmentalist sensibilities, but it is also sensitive to the rhetoric of our chapter.

The God of creation, at least in the opening chapter of the Torah, is not a commanding God. God's first utterance, grammatically, is less a command than an enthusiastic invitation: "Let there be light," as opposed to "Shine!" or "Illuminate!" (Grammarians refer to this tense of persuasion as the jussive, or in our verse, since it is first person rather than third person, the cohortative.) Everett Fox punctuates our verse with an exclamation point. The NJPS translation, more in keeping with the Hebrew, uses a softer point. The grammar of creation suggests the willing acceptance of a Divine invitation.[1]

It can be argued, of course, that God's invitation is far more commanding than any human imperative. But the same might be true for any C.E.O. The medieval commentator Rashi does not cite this Rabbinic comment, but he does tell us we should learn humility from this verse since even God consults with His subordinates. For Rabbi Levi, human humility isn't only a reflection of God's humility, but derives from our essential commonalities with the rest of creation. After all, humans and other land animals share the sixth day as a birthday.

2. Everything formed on a given day was incorporated into the things formed on the next day. When God created the human, He included all the elements that were present already from the creation of the animals which preceded humans. . . . Let us make adam (v. 26) is in the plural since the earth brought forth the body, just like the earth brought forth the bodies of the rest of the animals, while God imbued humanity with the intellectual soul. . . . God created (v. 27) indicates the emergence of the human soul that God created out of nothing and was unlike anything that had previously been created.

(Malbim, 1809–1879, Central Europe; cf. Ramban)

Malbim is one of the very first Jewish thinkers to seriously deal with the theological implications of biological evolution. In traditional Jewish fashion, he discusses contemporary ideas of science within his biblical commentaries. Although this statement, culled from his comments on verses 25–27 of our chapter, contains only a brief reference to the incorporation of earlier life forms in later ones, Malbim was an early evolutionist. In 1996, Pope John Paul II acknowledged that "if the human body takes its origin from pre-existing living matter, the spiritual soul is immediately created by God."[2] Malbim anticipates this papal distinction between humans and the rest of the animal kingdom and insists the biblical text tells us as much.

Malbim points out that the predicate in verse 26 is *make*, while in verse 27 it's *create*. Making is something anybody can do; but creating is an exclusively Divine activity. The *making* of humanity is derivative of the animal world. Verses 11, 21, and 24 supply precedents for the elements of the earth contributing to further creation. Just like the earth brought forth every living creature, every living creature contributed to bringing forth, or *making*, the physical qualities of humanity. The *creating* of humanity in the Divine image, however, is the infusion of the intellectual soul that God alone created for us. Rabbi Levi's comment spoke of God consulting with the works of creation; Malbim's comment, based on the medieval commentary of Ramban, has God collaborating with creation. Malbim is not afraid of God partnering with creation to produce further creation; rather, he is afraid of scientists and philosophers explaining creation in an exclusively naturalistic way that leaves no room for Divine input.[3]

3. Since Genesis 1 states clearly that the human being is in God's image and the human being is male and female, it follows that God's image—and God—must be both male and female. . . . Both male and female qualities are contained in this God. As the human being encompasses both

*masculine and feminine, so too does the Divine Being. . . . I suggest that
we hear God's internal dialogue, the female and male aspects of Divinity in
conversation with each other, checking to be sure both sides are represented in the creation of humanity.*

(Elyse Goldstein, contemporary, United States)[4]

Rabbi Goldstein adds a contemporary feminist perspective. Men shouldn't
make decisions themselves that affect their female counterparts. Maybe father
knew best in the 1950s, but no more. The male and female aspects of God
conferred with one another before making the momentous decision to
create something in their image. Rashi thought that God consulted with the
angels to teach us humility. Goldstein thinks that God is modeling good relationship skills.

*4. Rabbi Simon said: At the time that God came to create the first human,
the ministering angels formed opposing parties, some in favor of creation,
some against. . . .*

*5. Rav Huna the Great of Tzippori said: The ministering angels were argu-
ing back and forth about whether God should create adam until the Holy
One, blessed be He, said to them, "Why are you debating?! The human is
already made."*

(from *Genesis Rabbah*; cf. *Targum* Pseudo-Jonathan)

According to Rabbi Simon, the anomalous plural of our verse indicates
that God is consulting the heavenly host. The *darshan* reads our verse as a
question from God to the angels, "Should we make adam?" (Since the
Torah contains no punctuation, such a reading is plausible.) The *darshan*
then lets us eavesdrop. But, one might reasonably ask, where did the angels
come from? Genesis one does not tell us about God creating the angels. In
fact, nowhere in the Hebrew Bible is there a mention of the creation of
angels.

Angels might not be mentioned in our chapter because they are not the
concern here. We do know from elsewhere in the TANAKH, however, that
God does consult with the heavenly host, at least according to the vision of
the prophet Micaiah as recorded in 1 Kings 22:19–22. (Rashbam points out
this parallel in his commentary.) Although this explanation goes outside our
chapter, it does remain within the framework of the TANAKH. By contrast, the
Council of Sirmium in 351 CE dogmatized the Christian reading of our verse
that the Father was addressing the Son.[5] Another anachronistic reading,

found in Jewish sources, is that God was using the "royal we."[6] Such usage, however, is not found elsewhere either in the Tanakh or in the other literatures of the ancient Near East.

The angels of these midrashim, like our commentators themselves, are disputatious. The best part of Rabbi Simon's midrash, which I truncated here but will return to in the Epilogue, envisions God throwing one of the angels out of heaven in order to reach a majority in favor of creating adam! We have here an explanation for human contentiousness—if we are created in their image, no wonder we can't get along. James Madison wrote, "If men were angels, no government would be necessary." Madison clearly did not have the angels of *Genesis Rabbah* in mind!

In Rav Huna's comment, when God tells the angels that the human has already been created, the *darshan* is quoting God in Genesis 1:26. With a slight change of vowels, which are also absent from the Torah, the first person plural can be read as the passive. Rather than, "Let us make (*na'aseh*) adam," the *darshan* changes the vowels to read, "Adam has been made (*na'asah*)." The angels are too absorbed in their own deliberations about whether or not humans should be created that they miss the glory of God's creation. The letter *nun* of *na'aseh*, signifying the plural subject, has been neutralized, leaving only God as the creative agent. Rav Huna may have been responding to Gnostic interpretations of our verse that imagine evil angels creating the physical material of humanity. The Gnostics believed that all of creation was the product of evil forces in the world.[7] With Rav Huna's reading, God's unique ability to create is protected, and the subsequent plurals in our verse, *our image* and *our likeness*, remain as reminders that whatever God creates, whether angels or human, entails division and divisiveness.

Why, one might ask, would the Rabbis have the angels arguing against the creation of humanity? Did they fear for their own position in the Divine economy? Or, did they know something about us, something sinister? The intellectual ancestors of the Rabbis, too, had misgivings about our creation. The Talmud contains a legend that the House of Shammai and the House of Hillel debated for two-and-a-half years about whether it was better for humans to have been created or not. After taking a vote, the majority decided that it would have been better *for humans* had we not been created. But, since we have, let us examine our past deeds and scrutinize our future ones.[8] The onus of living up to our potential as bearers of the Divine image and likeness, the depressing reality that so few do, and the vulnerabilities attendant to inhabiting a physical body weighed down the Rabbis and their angels.[9]

Imagining the Image

For those who take it for granted that God is incorporeal, the notion that we humans are created in the Divine image *must* refer to something other than our physical body. Yet there are biblical verses which can plausibly be read as suggesting that God *does* have physical form (Exod. 33:20 and Isa. 6:5). Perhaps the presence of these verses explains why the assumption of Divine incorporeality does not inform Rabbinic comments. "In all of rabbinic literature there is not a single statement that categorically denies that God has body or form. . . . Instead of asking, 'Does God have a body?' we should inquire, 'What kind of body does God have?.'"[10]

> 6. *Resh Lakish said in the name of Rabbi Shimon ben Menasya: The knob of Adam's heel outshines the sun, how much more so his countenance.*
> (*Leviticus Rabbah* 20:2, Rabbinic compilation edited by 5th century, Land of Israel; cf. Baba Batra 58a)

According to this tradition, Adam had a body of light. Working backwards, God's image must similarly be luminous. Indeed, in one of the oft-repeated passages from the Torah, we have the all-too-familiar phrase translated literally by Everett Fox: "May YHWH shine his face upon you and favor you!" (Num. 6:25.) God is associated throughout the Torah with light and fire imagery. God reveals himself to Moses through the burning bush (Exod. 3:1–4), later speaks to all of Israel from "the midst of the fire" (Deut. 5:4), and appears to Ezekiel as "what looked like fire" (Ezek. 1:26–28).

With this understanding, God has a body or form but it is not quite corporeal. The first humans, made in the Divine image, somehow lost their luster. Opinions vary as to the reason.[11] But one human, according to the Torah, does regain the aura. When Moses descends from Mt. Sinai with the second set of tablets, he is unaware that his face is radiating light (Exod. 34:29). The disappointing epilogue to the story is that Moses was forced to veil his face in public after descending from the mountain of God. The Israelites were not ready to recognize the illuminating image of God in their leader (Exod. 34:33). Perhaps that is why the culmination and climax of Judaism's central prayer, a map which traces the necessary blessings for a world at peace, reads: "God will bless us all, as one, through the light of the Divine countenance." In the Rabbinic imagination, the moment we regain the image and recognize the image in all humanity, we will have entered the Messianic era.

7. *But* tselem *[image] designates natural form, i.e., the principle which substantiates a thing and makes it what it is, its reality as that thing. In man's case this is the source of human awareness and it is on account of such intellectual awareness that it is said of man that "He created him in the form of God."*

(Rambam, 1138–1204, Egypt)[12]

Rambam was one of the leading Aristotelian philosophers of the Middle Ages. He maintained that it was nothing short of heresy to understand God in corporeal terms. Indeed, he devoted the first section of his philosophical work, *The Guide for the Perplexed*, to explain away the anthropomorphisms and anthropopathisms of the Torah (attributing human form and emotions to God).

In our comment, Rambam understands *image* not as bodily, but as Aristotelian form, that underlying principle which *informs* the object in question. For us humans, according to the Aristotelian philosopher, our form is the intellect. We think, therefore we are human. Our intellectual awareness and capacity are what distinguish us from the rest of God's creation. For Rambam, our intellect is the human soul.[13]

Rambam is not only reflecting Aristotle in this comment, but Hellenistic philosophy in general.[14] The Hebrew Bible has a monistic anthropology—our body and soul are a unified whole. The dualism of body and soul, or more extreme, body versus soul, is foreign to the TANAKH. Anthropological dualism is a product of Hellenism, generations before Aristotle, which distinguished between the immortal soul and the mortal body. Pauline Christianity incorporates this Hellenistic anthropology (see, e.g., II Corinthians 5:1–4) in a way that Rabbinic Judaism resisted. According to one contemporary scholar, "Rabbinic Judaism, in contrast, defined the human being as an animated body and not as a soul trapped or even housed or clothed in a body."[15]

Maimonides' interpretation of the image of God as incorporeal also countered certain trends that emerged in the early Rabbinic period associated with ancient Jewish mysticism. The depiction of God in grossly anthropomorphic terms, with gigantic dimensions, was central to the *Shiur Komah*, a text from the early centuries of the Common Era. A talmudic legend imagines the first human to be humongous, having ostensibly been created in the image of God.[16] *Shiur Komah* gives the cosmic dimensions of the God after which that human was modeled. Medieval Jewish mysticism, beginning with the late-twelfth century text, *Bahir*, rehabilitates the image of the Divine body and provides a foundation for the distinctive vocabulary of the Kabbalah.

8. [The plural language in our verse] can be compared to a king who is sovereign over all. He wants to demonstrate that everything is included in him and he is everything. Therefore he speaks about himself in the plural. So, too, the Holy One, blessed be He, when He wanted to show that the entire universe is His, that everything is included in His hand, He spoke in the plural to show that He is everything.
(Zohar Hadash, Midrash Hane'elam, 16, 13th c., Spain)

Although much of the Zohar, as well as later Kabbalah, often depicts the Divine in the shape of a human, this comment suggests that humans don't just correspond to the image of God, but are actually *in* the image of God, i.e., inside the Divine. All of creation, not just humans, is included in and encompassed by God. This theological stance, sometimes called panentheism, indicates that all of creation is within God, but that God also transcends the limitations of what we perceive as creation. The Zohar calls that which is beyond all human ability to comprehend, the *Ein Sof*, or endlessness.

In the Rabbinic period, God's image was often understood as physical, somehow corresponding to our own physical being but on a much larger scale.[17] Alternatively, God was depicted as a light being, having an image but not a body. In the Middle Ages, the philosophical tradition rejected any kind of bodily form for God, instead emphasizing our intellectual form as that which links us to the Divine. The Kabbalistic tradition insists that we can know something about the inner life of God by better understanding ourselves. In some symbolic way, the image of the Divine incorporates the intellectual aspects so important for the philosophical tradition, but within a framework that includes the emotional and sexual aspects of embodiment, as well. Finally, we saw an example of how the Kabbalists suggested that all of creation is comprehended by God, *in* God's image. In this interpretation, *image* is not a representation of God's being, it *is* God's being.[18]

Modern Images of Likeness

In addition, and perhaps in response, to Rambam's emphasis on the intellect, the mystical tradition emphasized the power of imagination. The Hebrew for imagination is *dimyon*, which echoes both the name *adam* (human) and our likeness (*d'mut*) to the Divine. (We are called *adam* in Genesis one because we are created in the Divine likeness.[19] The second creation story (2:7) links our name to the substance from which we were created, *adamah*, the earth.) The union of intellect *and* imagination corresponds to humans being made in the image *and* likeness of God.

9. *"Adam" is from the same root as dimyon (imagination), and the aleph is extra. The advantage of humanity over all other creatures is our power of imagination.*

(Rabbi Bunim of Przysucha, 1765–1827, Poland)[20]

10. *There is no doubt that the term "image of God" in the first account refers to man's inner charismatic endowment as a creative being. Man's likeness to God expresses itself in man's striving and ability to become a creator.*

(Rav Joseph B. Soloveitchik, 1903–1993, Lithuania and United States)[21]

Rabbi Bunim represents that stream of thought which resists the glorification of the intellect at the expense of the rest of the human being. Realistically, not everyone can be a scientist. So, is it fair to use intellect as the exclusive, or even primary measure of one's humanity? Rabbi Bunim isn't only interested in expanding our pool of who can be considered fully human, his anthropology underscores that we are more than just disembodied intellects. Our imaginative faculty brings out what is distinctive about us humans. We can imagine a different world. No other animal has that capacity.

Rav Soloveitchik brings Rambam together with Rabbi Bunim. Marrying our intellect and imagination, we can work toward a better world. But it is not just the capacity with which we're endowed, it is the need, the yearning to express ourselves creatively that is the marker of the Divine likeness. God imagines a world and creates it. We can, too.

11. *We humans are the only creation able to do what we consider to be good, according to our will. And in this, we are likened to our Creator. "The superiority of humans over beasts is naught" (Eccles. 3:19). Only the "naught," the power to oppose and say, "No!" This is according to His likeness.*

(Aharon Lewin, 1879–1941, Poland)[22]

Rabbi Lewin creatively rereads that biblical existentialist, Kohelet, who asserts that there is no difference between humans and beasts. For the Rabbi, the difference is our ability to say "no." We are like God because we have free will. Indeed, as one modern commentator points out, we don't look all that different from monkeys, so our verse *must* mean something other than physical resemblance.[23] Unlike monkeys, we can engage in long-range planning. Or, as we tell college students (and graduate students), you are deferring benefit. It's true that we're often impulsive, but we do not have to be. It's that measure of self-restraint that makes us fully human. And when we resist the temptation to cash in early, to cut corners or indulge in immediate gratification, that is when we are most like God, slowly and patiently working toward the fulfillment of the vision. That is why we read about the *six days* of creation. Eventually, Genesis promises us, the seventh day will arrive.

Alternatively, or additionally, Rabbi Lewin's comment might be about saying "no" to others, rather than to ourselves. To be godly, we must oppose the behavior of the beasts, in human garb, who follow their animal instincts. They have their designs for domination, but we are warned against following the multitude or the mighty to do evil (*Exod.* 23:2). We have the power to oppose and say, "No!" Relinquishing that prerogative, abdicating that responsibility, puts us on the same plane as the beasts. According to the *halakhah,* "just following orders" is no excuse for criminal behavior.[24] A chilling postscript for our commentator: Rabbi Lewin, a communal leader in Poland, was murdered by the Nazis in July of 1941.

All of the commentators in this section focus on our *likeness* to God. Although one could chalk up the repetition ("in our image, after our likeness") to poetic style, a traditional assumption about the Torah is that all repetition is meaningful. Being created in the image must then mean something different than being created after the likeness. Similarly, the different prepositions, *in* and *after,* must bear significance. The medieval commentator S'forno makes the point that, unlike God, not all of our choices, by which we exercise our likeness to God, are for the best. That's why our deeds are only "after" God's likeness rather than "in" God's likeness.

Framing Creation

Verse 27 introduces the feminine into Torah. But it introduces the masculine, too. Throughout this chapter, I have awkwardly translated the *adam* (with a lower case *a*) of our previous verse as humanity or humankind, as does Fox. In our present verse, we are informed that humankind, as a species, comes in two genders and both are created at the same time. That is exactly how several medieval commentators, who focus on the immediate context, understand *adam,* as humanity.[25] That is how Everett Fox translates it. So why do we have this idea that Eve, a single woman, was created after Adam, a single man? Because she was, at least according to the second story of creation that begins with the second half of Genesis 2:4.[26]

There are two differing accounts of creation in the Hebrew Bible. (The Christian Bible doubles that! There are four different gospels retelling the birth, ministry, death, and resurrection of Jesus.) Before feminist sensibilities raised our awareness about language, *man* could refer to men or to men and women. Hebrew works the same way. If we take the first creation story in isolation, it's clear that the term *adam* refers to the species known as humans. All the animals in Genesis one were created as entire species. It's equally clear that the *adam* of Genesis two is a single individual, not yet masculine, perhaps, but singular. It is only when we read Genesis one anticipating the second creation story in Genesis two that we conflate these two discrete narratives. One popular method to resolve the real contradictions between these two accounts of human creation is to understand the *adam* of 1:26 as singular and 1:27, which introduces the feminine, as a preview of the future creation in Genesis 2.[27] The Torah is telling us, according to this line of thinking, that there *will be* a woman created later on the sixth day, but we'll have to await the next chapter to get the full story.

Given the juxtaposition of these two creation narratives, attempts at interpreting the *adam* of Genesis one as a single male are understandable. Rabbinic assumptions about the perfection of the Torah preclude the possibility that there should be contradictions. As we saw, a few of the medieval *pashtanim* (*peshat* seekers) anticipated modern Bible scholars by acknowledging that we have two different stories of creation, though without suggesting that the human authors of these different areas lived hundreds of years apart and in different parts of the Land of Israel. As a result of reading these stories together as a single description of the creation of Adam and Eve, interpretative possibilities emerge from the biblical landscape.

12. *Rabbi Jeremiah, son of Elazar said: "At the time that the Holy One, blessed be He, created the first human, He created it as a hermaphrodite, as is written, 'male and female He created them . . . and called their name Adam on the day He created them.'"* (Gen. 5:2).

Rav Samuel, son of Nachman said: "At the time that the Holy One, blessed be He, created the first human, He created it with two faces and then cut it and made backs for each."

They challenged him: "And He took one of his ribs." (Gen. 2:21).

He responded to them: "'One of his sides.' Like it says, 'the side of the Tabernacle' (Exod. 26:20)."

(Genesis Rabbah)

The first human being, in the singular, was a hermaphrodite. That explains why verse 27 includes both male and female. The name of that entity, according to Gen. 5:2, was *Adam*. The male and female were distinct personalities sharing the same body. Rav Samuel then goes further into the anatomy of Adam. It had two faces, one on each side, with corresponding genitalia. What God then did was to split this primordial androgyne in two and sewed up each of their back sides.

So far, this midrash has explained how *Adam*, understood to be a single person, could be both male and female. The midrash then voices opposition. "Wait a second! You're ignoring the verse that says God took man's rib and made woman." But Rav Samuel has a ready retort: "I'm not ignoring anything. You're misunderstanding the verse. Just like *tsela* means *side* in the description of the Tabernacle, so, too, it means side here. God took one of the sides of the hermaphrodite and split it down the middle." Now, our midrash has the additional benefit of reconciling the two creation narratives. That's efficiency!

This Rabbinic midrash has had far-reaching influence on subsequent Jewish understandings of the creation of humans. Many midrashim suggest that to be fully human, man and woman require one another in order to reflect the first Divinely-created human.[28] A similar image of a hermaphrodite being split apart occurs in Plato's *Symposium*. When the halves of these former wholes find each other, lifelong partnerships result.[29] For Rav Samuel, it seems any human couple can house the Divine Presence, as did the sides of the Tabernacle.

This midrash of the hermaphrodite could not have been the original intention of the author of either creation story. But I can't say that such a conception was *necessarily* foreign to the biblical editor or redactor who juxtaposed our stories in purposeful sequence. There is a possibility that the redactor sought to conflate these two stories, rather than to present two opposing stories side by side. If conflating or merging was the redactor's intention, something like a hermaphroditic human may have been how the redactor intended his audience to read Genesis one. Said differently, our redactor may have believed that these two stories express different aspects of creation that are complementary, not contradictory. The word *tzela* usually means side, so why not in the second creation story, too? Genesis one, in isolation, doesn't mention Eve (or Adam). But reading Genesis one, after knowing the story of Genesis two, frames the creation of humanity in such a way that the reader is now receptive to either a single hermaphrodite, or a single couple, the Adam and Eve of Genesis two.

Engendering the Image

13. Image *is male and* likeness *is female.*

(Zohar 3:35b, Tzav)

Each Hebrew noun is either masculine or feminine; Hebrew has no neutered *it.* The Zohar's grammar is correct: *image* is male and *likeness* is female.[30] The grammar of theology and anthropology is, therefore, gender inclusive. But the Zohar is doing more than teaching grammar.

According to Kabbalah, each human appendage corresponds to the Divine image which is also understood as a map of the energy flows *within* God. The name for these energy stations is the *s'firot.* In the world of the *s'firot,* the upper nine *s'firot* reflect the male image. The tenth *sefirah,* sometimes called the *shekhinah,* or Divine presence, is depicted as female. Altogether, the male and female *s'firot* comprise the totality of the Divine image and likeness. For the Zohar, only when the masculine and feminine aspects of God are in union will the Divine blessings flow. The mystic's charge is to unite the male and female *s'firot* through ritual acts and also through proper sexual union. The male mystic coming together with his wife stimulates the corresponding elements in the world of the *s'firot* to join. When male and female, image and likeness, achieve union, the bounty of Divine munificence overflows from the *s'firotic* world and brings blessings into our own.[31] Stripping the myth and metaphysics from this mystical interpretation, sex is good for a marriage.

14. Jung taught that in each of us there are personality traits more commonly associated with the opposite gender. The goal of a healthy individual is to integrate the anima/animus within each psyche. In the language of Genesis, "masculine" and "feminine" together make up the Divine image—not "male" and "female" that distinguishes the sexes in other animals (Gen. 7:2). Each human has masculine and feminine within him or herself, and our goal is to integrate those elements in our dedication to following in God's ways (Deut. 28:9). A couple, regardless of gender, should also enjoy a holy balance of traditionally masculine and feminine energies.

(Meshi, contemporary, United States)

When God created the human *zakhar u'nekevah,* our other commentators read the Hebrew as *male and female.* Meshi reads it as *masculine and feminine.* Meshi is more concerned with psychology than anatomy. His comment strikes the contemporary chord of getting in touch with your inner, opposite gender. While the mystical tradition focuses on the interplay *between* male and female, it is, nevertheless, true that both male and female aspects are operating *within* the Divine world as represented by the *s'firot*. The unity of God is a cardinal principle of Judaism. Meshi is suggesting that the unification of our own traditionally masculine and feminine attributes is essential for us as we strive to imitate God.

The Other Woman

15. Lilith and Adam were created as equals. When Lilith desired to lie on top during intercourse, Adam refused, saying that he was superior. Lilith flew away by pronouncing the ineffable name of God. Angelic attempts to persuade Lilith to return to Adam failed.
>   (from *The Alphabet of Ben Sira* [c. 9th c.]; cf. *Genesis Rabbah* 18:4)

Lilith appears once in the TANAKH (Is. 34:14) as a night demon, having no connection to the creation stories. Rabbinic creation legends include the story of a woman, created prior to the Eve of the Garden of Eden, whom Adam rejected. These story lines merge in the early Middle Ages as another approach to resolve the tension between our two creation stories. The *adam* that was created male and female in Genesis one was a couple. The woman, Lilith, claimed equality with her male counterpart—the plain sense of Genesis one—and Adam couldn't tolerate it.[32] So Lilith gets replaced by Eve, who is made from Adam; this somehow makes him superior.[33]

Not only does the Lilith legend resolve the seeming contradiction between our two creation stories, it also provides an explanation for what remains a medical mystery: crib death. In medieval tradition, Lilith becomes the embodiment of the femme fatale, avenging herself by killing infants and by seducing men in their sleep to cause nocturnal emissions. The mystical tradition further develops the legend of Lilith so that she becomes the queen of demons. *The Alphabet of Ben Sira* may have been written as a farce, but the Lilith legend took on a life of its own.[34] The latest twist in this legend comes as Jewish (and gentile) women have re-appropriated Lilith and claimed her as the archetypal feminist. Indeed, according to *The Alphabet of Ben Sira*, Lilith *was* more powerful than Adam: she knew how to use the power of the Divine name.[35]

Legislating a Blessing

Since the Rabbinic period, there has been an understanding that there are 613 commandments (*mitzvot*) in the Torah. According to Rabbi Simlai, 365 prohibitions correspond to the days in the solar year, and 248 imperatives correspond to the parts of the human body.[36] My reading of Rabbi Simlai's statement is that we should always strive to embody God's will. In his language, we should be walking Torahs at every moment.

During the Middle Ages, there was a concerted effort to identify those 613 *mitzvot*. Although there are many differences in the listings, the mitzvah to "be fruitful and multiply" is on every list. But, please notice, that the language of command is absent from verse 28. Procreation is a blessing, not an object of legislation for the author of Genesis one.

16. Concerning human beings, the blessing, which is the granting of the power and ability, is separated from the fulfillment, that is from using the power and ability for the purposes which God intended them. The fulfillment is directed to the human beings who are to carry it out as a duty, from their own free will.

(Samson Raphael Hirsch, 1808–1888, Germany)

Hirsch, the father of Modern Orthodoxy, slips the idea of commandment into this blessing. He contrasts our verse with verse 22 in which God similarly blesses the creatures of the fifth day. The wording there, though, is slightly different. In our verse, *God blessed them* and then immediately *God said to them*. So what is the import of the extra phrase, "and God said to them"? Hirsch suggests that all creatures have the urge to procreate (Hirsch knew something about biological evolution, too), but only humans have the capacity to channel that urge in the service of God. And therein lies the mitzvah. Hirsch turned a seeming redundancy in our verse into an occasion to preach the merits of self-discipline.[37]

Hirsch was part of a larger movement in the late nineteenth and early twentieth centuries to demonstrate that Rabbinic interpretations of Torah were somehow reasonable. If the Torah deems procreation a blessing, why does Jewish tradition treat it as a mitzvah? Hirsch's response is that by paying close attention to the wording of the Torah, we see that procreation is both a blessing common to all creatures and a special responsibility of humanity. In Freudian terms, God's *blessing* speaks to the id, and God's *saying* speaks to the superego.

17. The man is obligated to be fruitful and multiply, but not the woman.
Rabbi Yohanan ben Baroka disagrees. They're both obligated. The verse
says, "God said to them, "Be fruitful and multiply." "

(Mishnah, Yevamot 6:6, 3rd c., Land of Israel)

What's the biblical basis for exempting women from this commandment?
Rabbi Il'a said in the name of Rabbi Elazar, son of Rabbi Shimon: The con-
tinuation of the verse says, "fill the earth and conquer it." It's a man's way to
conquer, not a woman's.

(Gemara, Yevamot 65b, 6th c., Babylonia)

The Mishnah is the first literary product of Rabbinic Judaism. Although almost entirely composed of laws, it's not a legal code. Our mishnah (small m for the individual unit of legal discussion) is a good example of why the *Mishnah* (capital M for the entire collection) is not a code. Codes don't preserve dissenting opinions or legal deliberations.

Our mishnah follows in the wake of yet another dispute: how many children fulfill the mitzvah of being fruitful and multiplying? The House of Hillel, according to whom the *halakhah* usually follows, says one male and one female, based on our creation story. Just as God created one of each gender, so should we. But, the next mishnah asks, who is the "we"?

Our mishnah exempts women from this obligation, even in the face of a rather strong challenge from Rabbi Yohanan. Since the Mishnah rarely justifies its laws by associating them with a biblical verse, the *Gemara* (the later and larger part of the *Talmud*) frequently begins by asking about the biblical basis for the laws presented in the *Mishnah*. Our gemara (the individual unit, as opposed to the entire corpus) is no exception. Focusing on the meaning of the verse rather than the grammar, Rabbi Il'a reads the verse backwards. Since conquering applies to men, he reasons, so does the first part of God's charge concerning procreation. Although this midrash deals exegetically with women's exemption, there are likely to be additional factors.

Today, celibacy is an idea associated with conservative politics in its response to pre-marital sex. But in late antiquity, celibacy was a way of dedicating oneself exclusively to God. St. Paul endorsed celibacy in *I Corinthians* 7, and celibacy became a virtue in the Christian community.[38] Some Rabbis, too, were mightily attracted to a life exclusively dedicated to knowing God's will through Torah study, but the *halakhah* rejected that option. Perhaps male access to Torah study provided them with an opportunity to pursue communion with God in a way that was generally closed to women, and thus men had to be commanded to procreate and women did not. Perhaps the bio-logical urge for children is stronger in women than in men. I suspect that for a combination of these sociological and physiological reasons, the Rabbis felt that men had to be commanded to procreate, while women would do so even without the explicit mitzvah. Of course, all knew that women are necessary participants in the process of procreation, but legal systems sometimes bracket biology in pursuit of social policy.

> 18. It's not far from the truth to say that the Torah exempted women from the commandment to be fruitful and multiply and obligated only men because Divine decrees and His ways are "ways of pleasantness and all her paths peaceful" (Prov. 3:17). The Torah did not impose on the Jew what her body could not bear. . . . Both members of the first couple were blessed with the obligation to procreate. But after the sin, since the woman will experience pain and danger in childbirth, she is exempt.
>
> (from Meir Simcha HaKohen of Dvinsk, 1843–1926, Russia)[39]

Another efficient comment. Rabbi Meir Simcha concedes that the simple meaning of our text is that both male and female are included in the blessing/mitzvah. But that changes after the punishments are doled out in the Garden of Eden. Since women will experience pain in childbirth (Gen. 3:16), and many women die in the process (there is actually a special blessing for having successfully withstood the dangers of childbirth), the Torah will not command a woman to do what is life threatening. This Orthodox Rabbi acknowledges the plain sense of our verse, shows how the following creation story changed the law, *since the Torah's ways are pleasantness*, and thereby justi-fied Rabbinic law as it appears in the Mishnah. Rabbi Meir Simcha defended this *halakhah* as well as Orthodoxy, in general, at a time when traditional Judaism was under siege from the forces of assimilation and Reform Judaism.[40]

Filling and Fulfilling

One might expect that the *halakhah* would require more than two children from each Jewish couple, especially in light of the tragedies that have punctu-ated Jewish history. Or, from a purely textual perspective, the blessing/mitzvah to procreate is immediately followed by the clause, "fill the world." So why stop with two? Indeed, based on a different verse (Isa. 45:18), Jewish leaders throughout the ages have encouraged large families.[41] In the 19th century, at a time of record Jewish population, one Orthodox Rabbi offered a very different understanding of our verse.

> 19. The word "fill" refers to filling a void. In Ecclesiastes (6:7) the verb is used in the sense of fulfillment. God's blessing in our verse, then, is that we'll have the intellectual and creative capacities to develop all the tools required for our efficient utilization of material resources. But since this blessing involves the desire to accumulate material wealth, we're also given a warning: Conquer it! We're commanded to conquer the urge toward acquisitiveness, toward materialism. We must not become enslaved to materialism. God's first statement to humanity bears not only on the physical, but also on the moral, which is the true goal for which humanity was created.
>
> (Jacob Zvi Mecklenburg, 1785–1865, Germany)

Rabbi Mecklenburg offers the innovative reading that rather than filling the earth, we are blessed with the intellectual and imaginative abilities to fulfill our desires *from* the earth, from the material resources that the earth provides us. But the blessing is mixed. Ability and ambition slide imperceptibly toward avarice. The last clause of this sequence, "conquer it," does not refer to the antecedent, "the earth," but to an aspect of the blessing itself.

The seeming prescience of this comment, originally written in the wake of the Industrial Revolution, is striking to a twenty-first-century reader. Not only does Mecklenburg's comment point to the rampant materialism of our own culture, but it also precludes the mindless exploitation of our natural resources.[42] It's not the earth that we're to conquer, but our own rapaciousness. Only by conquering our passions, rather than becoming their slaves, will we fulfill the blessing of this verse.

Rabbi Mecklenburg's comment offers the additional benefit of emphasizing that the Torah is spiritually edifying, not *just* a book of laws. This concern with *Bildung*, edification, pervades the world of mid-nineteenth-century German Orthodoxy. In part, traditional German Judaism, or what comes to be known as Orthodoxy, is reacting to the charges of the leading German philosopher, Immanuel Kant. He asserted that Judaism is an externally imposed legal system of spiritually and morally empty ritual acts. Notice that Samson Raphael Hirsch, above (extract 16), concludes his comment with an emphasis that we accept the obligation of the commandments from our own free will. Traditional Judaism was also on the defensive from Reform Judaism that sought to substitute traditional *halakhah* with characteristically Protestant expressions of piety. For Rabbi Mecklenburg, the purpose of all the laws is not only a stable body politic, but a pious one.

The Humane Associations

The *halakhah* prescribes that Jews are not to cause unnecessary pain to any animal. This mitzvah, *tza'ar ba'alei chayim*, comes under scrutiny to determine what constitutes "unnecessary." Our verses provide a springboard for reflection on our relationship with other creatures. The terminology of our verses is puzzling. On the one hand, we are charged to "rule" the animal world; in the very next verse, though, we are instructed to be vegetarians. Indeed, the plain sense of verse 29 also prohibits human consumption of all animal products! What sort of "rule" is that? Or, as Philo, the first Jew to understand the Torah to incorporate systematically both commandment and allegory, will ask: what kind of animal is that?

> 20. *As for the deeper meaning, it is to be interpreted as follows: He [God] desires that the souls of intelligent men . . . should strike terror and fear into beasts, which is the exercise of the will against evil, for evil is untamed and savage. And [he wishes that they should rule] over the birds, [that is] those who are lightly lifted up in thought. . . . Moreover, [he wishes that they should rule over] the reptiles, which are a symbol of poisonous passions. . . .*
> (Philo, 20 BCE–50 CE, Egypt)[43]

Philo's allegorical interpretation would warm the hearts of contemporary environmentalists. We are not charged to rule animals, but people who behave like animals. We need to tame those wild beasts. Those flighty individuals, too, need to be grounded by those of us in control of our passions. In another text, Philo promotes vegetarianism for the reason that indulging in flesh is to "change oneself into the savagery of wild beasts."[44] Although Philo's writings were lost to the Jewish community for hundreds of years, his philosophical and allegorical reading of the Torah was employed by many medieval Jewish philosophers. On a practical level, though, there is still the question as to the limits of sovereignty. Humans can't eat animals, at least not until after Noah and his family disembark (Gen. 9:2), but are we licensed as benevolent despots or tyrants?

21. Rabbi Hanina said: "If one is meritorious, you will rule (urdu); if not, they will descend (yerdu)."

(Genesis Rabbah)

Although Rabbi Hanina doesn't specifically answer our question, he does insist that we have to earn the privilege of ruling the animals through good behavior. If we're meritorious, ostensibly including how we behave toward the animals, then we'll rule. If we're not, if we abuse our position, we'll descend to an even lower status than the animals, at least that's how Rashi understands our midrash. The Hebrew root for *rule* (resh, dalet, hey) is nearly identical to the root for *descend* (yod, resh, dalet). Rabbinic eyes see the similarity and read out the warning. The subsequent midrash in *Genesis Rabbah* makes it clear that only when we fulfill our potential to act in the Divine image will we rule. An alternative, and more ominous, reading of Rabbi Hanina's midrash is that if we are not worthy, the animals will descend on us.

22. Although the Torah allows us postdiluvians to consume flesh, there's clearly a pervasive bias against the killing of another one of God's creatures for human enjoyment. It wasn't the initial plan, according to Genesis, and even the most bloodthirsty of carnivores will change their ways in the messianic days (Isa. 11). In between, where we are, the Torah tells us that eating a carcass renders us tamei, ritually impure, and requires us to wash our garments (Lev. 11:39–40)! In the days before washing machines, that's a serious disincentive. These days, for those of us in the industrialized world, we can eat quite healthfully without animal protein. So, why continue to support the slaughtering of God's creatures? The Book of Psalms reaches its religious crescendo with the command: "Everything with the breath of life, sing praises to God!" (Ps. 150:6) An animal's dying gasp for air is not part of the Psalmist's Divine symphony.

(Meshi, contemporary, United States)

Philo espoused vegetarianism because of what eating meat does to us; Meshi agrees and also expresses concern about what it does to the animals. Meshi strings together biblical verses and combines them with a contemporary sensitivity to animal rights in order to argue for vegetarianism. Given Judaism's prohibition of causing unnecessary pain to animals, coupled with all of the non-animal protein available to contemporary consumers, Meshi challenges us to justify the continuation of animal slaughter. He is pushing us toward the Messianic days that the prophet Hosea envisions will involve a rapprochement of animals and humans (2:20). Then our fellow creatures, in whose image we were partially created according to *Genesis Rabbah*, will lose the fear and dread of us that has characterized our postdiluvian world (Gen. 9:2).[45]

Good, No Good, and Very Good

The first chapter of Genesis is quite rhythmic. God speaks, acts, sees, and judges creation to be good. Usually. On the sixth day, our day, God begins by creating land animals. They're good, according to God in verse 25. Then God creates humans. But the daily refrain falls silent.

> 23. *When describing the formation of the animals, the Torah says, "And God saw that this was good." That means that their very existence is the only thing that God expects of them. But with the formation of humanity, the Torah surprisingly omits "this was good." Unlike the animals, we have to strive to actualize our potential.*
>
> (Joseph Albo, 1380–1435, Spain)[46]

We're unique, according to this medieval Spanish philosopher, because we're essentially incomplete. Humans are created with free will, with the potential for perfection, and with the capacity for evil, as Albo witnessed in his own lifetime. (Spanish massacres against Jews erupted in 1391, about a century before the expulsion of Jews from Spain in 1492.) There's nothing necessarily good about us; we have to work for it. Other animals follow their nature and are complete. We are a work in progress, constantly striving to improve ourselves, intellectually and ethically. Albo predicates his philosophical distinction on the disconcerting silence of the text, reminding us to pay attention to both what is written and what is not.

In the late Middle Ages, Jews living in Christian Spain were under strong pressure to convert. Eventually, those that refused were exiled from Spain in 1492. For hundreds of years prior to the expulsion, there were public disputations between Rabbis and Priests orchestrated by the Church and the government to promote Jewish conversion to Christianity. Joseph Albo represented the Jewish community in one such disputation in Tortosa in 1413. Albo's comment here about the perfection of humanity, or lack thereof, might be a polemic against the Christian notion of The Fall. Since humanity had not been created as perfect beings in Genesis one, there's no reason to see the subsequent disobedience in the Garden of Eden as the origin of human imperfection.[47]

24. In previous verses, the word "ki" preceded tov *(good) to indicate potential. But in our verse (v. 31), we find "v'hinei tov" which expresses actuality. Had human beings not been created, all previous creation would have been in vain. Thus, the Torah characterized pre-human creation as potentially good,* ki tov. *Only when humans were created can we retrospectively perceive the goodness and beauty of all creation.*

(Shlomo Ephraim of Lunschitz, 1550–1619, Poland)

Rabbi Shlomo Ephraim, also known by the name of his commentary *Kli Yakar*, anticipates the twentieth-century paleontologist Stephen Jay Gould: natural history could have been different.[48] The story that the Torah tells is the story of our creation, but up until the moment we were created, a different story may have unfolded. "Radical contingency" is how scientists describe the precarious, unscripted unfurling of life's pageant. The universe had the potential for self-conscious life from its inception, true. But only with the unlikely emergence of humanity can we look backwards and marvel at the journey of life that has culminated, for the moment, with a creature intelligent enough to appreciate the course of natural history. Perhaps the *Kli Yakar* is also hinting at the idea that if God's projects can go awry, how much more can human projects. In the nuclear age, it might also be added that even a completed project poses unanticipated perils.[49]

25. In Rabbi Meir's Torah, they found written "and found it very (me'od) good," "and found death (mavet) good."

(Genesis Rabbah)

For Rabbi Meir, death is very good. It's not clear if this was a note he wrote in his copy of the Torah, or if his Torah actually concludes the account of creation with such an evaluation. It's equally unclear what he means. Rabbi Meir was a student of Rabbi Akiva who was flayed alive by the Romans during the Bar Kochva Revolt (132–135 CE). Many Jews were murdered during this period, and Rabbi Meir's comment might be a midrashic method of promoting the status of martyrdom, without quite encouraging the act. A similar midrashic flourish turned a verse in Psalms (116:15) from "The death of His faithful ones is *costly* in the LORD's sight" into "The death of His faithful ones is *precious* in the LORD's sight."[50]

One of the pitfalls of analyzing biblical interpretation is the tendency to shoehorn comments to fit the historical setting or religious agenda of the commentator. That's what I did in the above paragraph (and do throughout the book). But, sometimes, that approach is misguided. The problem is knowing when. In all cases, though, it's limiting. In our particular midrash from Rabbi Meir, the Rambam understands him to be suggesting that death is what allows new life to enter the world.[51] Rabbi Mecklenburg extends that idea and suggests that the dynamic progress of natural history is only possible through death. The Malbim, commenting from a more mystical perspective, suggests that death is good since we return to our Creator. These understandings of Rabbi Meir don't invoke the historical circumstances of Rabbi Meir to exalt martyrdom, they give us an appreciation for the finitude of life.

> 26. Everything in existence, looked at in connection with everything else, is
> very good. That which is relatively bad only appears as bad when looked at
> alone, in isolation, compartmentalized in time and space.
> (Samson Raphael Hirsch, 1808–1888, Germany)

God's answer to Job from out of the whirlwind (ch. 38) is echoed by the father of Modern Orthodoxy: if we could see the big picture, we'd understand. There does *seem* to be evil in creation, but if so, how can God declare it all very good? Hirsch notes that God's evaluation is not on the products of the sixth day alone but on *all* of creation. Only as a whole are things very good.

The End

Why is this day different from all others? On all other days, the Torah doesn't include the definite article. On the sixth day, it does.

> 27. A hey (the definite article) was added to "sixth day" at the conclusion
> of the account of creation to impose on Israel the condition that they will
> accept upon themselves the five books of Torah. Another interpretation of
> the sixth day: all of existence hangs in the balance until the sixth day, the
> sixth of Sivan which is designated as the time of the giving of the Torah.
> (Rashi, 1040–1105, France)

Two comments, one idea. Creation is incomplete without revelation. Rashi gets there by focusing on the anomalous definite article. His first comment utilizes *gematria*, the correspondence between letters and numbers. *Hey* is the fifth letter of the Hebrew alphabet and signifies the number five. Thus, *the* sixth day points to the *five* books of Moses, which if the Israelites do not accept, according to the lengthier rabbinic midrash from which Rashi cites, the world will be returned to primeval wild and waste. No law, no order.

Creation and revelation were perceived by many Rabbis to be dual aspects of God's work, one in nature and one in human history. They expressed this sentiment through such statements that just as there were ten utterances at Sinai (the Decalogue), so did God create the world through ten speech acts ("And God said . . .").[52] Rashi's comments point to the power of humanity, though he was speaking only of the Jews. We control the fate of the world. Like God, we can create. Equally like God, we can destroy that which we've created. God did so through the Flood. According to Torah, humans do so when we ignore (or misunderstand, as we'll see in the next chapter) the Divine voice.

Rashi's second comment emphasizes the *sixth,* as in the sixth day of the Hebrew month *Sivan,* when Jews celebrate Shavuot (Pentecost), commemorating the giving of the Torah at Mount Sinai. God created the laws of nature *and* gave the Israelites laws to live by. But we have to live up to the laws. As the Rabbis said, through our administration of justice we are partners with God in the creation of the world.[53] The end of God's workweek provides the Rabbis and Rashi an opportunity to remind us that our work has just begun. God's creation hangs in the balance.

Summary of Comments

Comment	Problem	Resolution	Textual Mechanism	Historical Circumstance
1.	To whom is God speaking?	Creation	Context and use of cohortative	None
2.	Why are different verbs and numbers used between vv. 26 and 27?	Prior creation makes the body of *adam,* but only God creates the soul	Only God creates in TANAKH	Evolutionary theory and materialist philosophies in late-19th century that deny a role for God in the world
3.	To whom is God speaking?	The male and female aspects of God are discussing creation	No one else is mentioned for God to be speaking to	Contemporary feminism
4.	To whom is God speaking?	Angels	Reading the verse as a question	None

continued

Comment	Problem	Resolution	Textual Mechanism	Historical Circumstance
5.	Who creates humanity?	Only God	God is telling the angels that the human has already been made (the passive of "Let us make")	Gnostic myths which involve evil angels creating human matter
6.	What does *image* mean?	Light	God is described with light and fire imagery elsewhere in the Torah	None
7.	Is *image* physical?	*Image* is the Aristotelian form, which for humans is the intellect	None	Confrontation with Aristotelian philosophy in the Middle Ages
8.	To whom is God speaking? What does *image* mean?	God uses the "royal we" to show that all of creation is *inside* His own image	*In*, like in English, can also mean inside	Panentheistic tendencies of Jewish mysticism
9.	What does *Adam* mean?	Comes from *dimyon*, imagination	Similarity of root letters	Promotion of non-intellectual virtues in the mystical and Hasidic traditions
10.	What does *likeness* mean?	Striving to become a creator	Context. God creates in *Genesis* and we're in His image	Modern, existentialist values to take responsibility for our own world
11.	What does *likeness* mean?	The ability to plan, reflect, exhibit self-restraint, and oppose others perpetrating evil	Context. Creation is well planned and unfolds over time	Post W.W. I reflections?
12.	a. How can *adam* be both male and female? b. Two different accounts of creation	a. Adam was a hermaphrodite b. God took the female side from the male side of the hermaphrodite	a. Ambiguity of *adam* as singular or generic b. *tzela* usually means side	None

continued

Comment	Problem	Resolution	Textual Mechanism	Historical Circumstance
13.	a. What is the difference between image and likeness? b. How can *adam* be both male and female?	a. Image is male, likeness is female, b. To be fully human, male needs female, and vice-versa	Gendered grammar of *image* and *likeness*	Mystical concerns with gender and sexuality
14.	How can *adam* be both male and female?	*Adam* has both traditionally masculine and feminine traits	No necessary distinction between male/masculine and female/ feminine in Hebrew	Contemporary psychology and mystical insight
15.	What happened to the first woman?	She insisted on equality, was denied, and avenges herself	*Adam* was understood as a pair which included male and female	Patriarchy, misogyny, farce taken seriously?
16.	What's the difference between *blessing* and *saying*? Why is procreation a mitzvah?	*Blessing* is said to our libido. *Saying* to our superego, and, hence, a mitzvah	Differences between vv. 22 and 28	Modern Orthodox desire to justify the Oral Torah; post-Darwinian discussions of differences between humans and other animals
17.	Are women obligated to procreate?	No	Conquering, from later in the verse, is a male activity. So, too, must be the obligation to procreate	Religious attraction to celibacy as a way of exclusively focusing on one's relationship with God
18.	Were women initially obligated to procreate?	Yes	After the punishments in the Garden, child bearing is dangerous and therefore women have been exempt from this mitzvah since then	Orthodox desire to show consonance between traditional *halakhah* and Torah

continued

Comment	Problem	Resolution	Textual Mechanism	Historical Circumstance
19.	a. Is "filling" meant physically? b. Are we commanded to conquer the earth	a. No. It's meant in the sense of filling a void. b. No. We're to conquer our desire to be fulfilled by material possessions	a. "Fill," like in English, can also mean fulfill. b. Don't read "fill the earth," but "fulfill [yourselves] *from* the earth." c. Conquer *it* refers to the blessing, not the earth	a. Jews have not filled the earth b. The materialism following the Industrial Revolution and a prescient environmental consciousness c. German Orthodox defensiveness that Judaism is legalistic and not edifying
20.	How do we rule the animals if we can't eat them?	Animals here are understood as symbolic of different kinds of humans	Understanding the animals allegorically	Hellenistic tendency to allegorize
21.	What are the limits of our ruling the animals?	We must be virtuous	Similarity between *rule* and *descend* in Hebrew	None
22.	Since we were initially to be vegetarians, should we eat animals now that we can?	No.	Entire context of TANAKH	Contemporary concern for animal rights and the deadening effects of the slaughter industry on humans
23.	Why is the refrain "and it was good" missing in reference to humans?	Because we are created as an unfinished product	Poetic rhythm and refrain of Genesis one	Jewish-Christian disputations in Spain in late Middle Ages
24.	Why *v'hinei* tov?	Previous creation was only potentially good, whereas with humans, all of creation has been retroactively redeemed	Distinction between *ki* and *hinei*	None

continued

Comment	Problem	Resolution	Textual Mechanism	Historical Circumstance
25.	Why is creation deemed *very* good?	*Very* points toward death	"very" (*me'od*) and "death" (*mavet*) sound somewhat similar	Increase in martyrs during the Bar Kochva Revolt?
26.	Why is *all* of creation deemed *very* good?	Only as a whole can creation be seen to be very good	Unlike other days, the evaluation of day 6 includes all previous days and is judged to be very good, not just good	None
27.	Why *the* sixth day	It points toward the 5 books of Torah (using gematria) or the sixth of Sivan, the revelation of God's will	This is the only day to receive the definite article	Rabbinic tendency to link creation and revelation/ legislation

NOTES

1. William P. Brown compares the creation accounts in Genesis 1 and Plato's *Timaeus* with an eye toward the participation of primordial matter in creation. "Divine Act and the Art of Persuasion in Genesis 1," in *History and Interpretation: Essays in Honour of John H. Hayes*, ed. M. Patrick Graham et. al. (Sheffield: JSOT Press, 1993), 19–32.

2. For this and other religious responses to evolution, see *Darwin: A Norton Critical Edition, Third Edition*, ed. Philip Appleman (New York: W. W. Norton & Co., 2001), 527–33.

3. I am particularly interested in issues of Judaism and evolution. See my "Three Twentieth-Century Jewish Responses to Evolutionary Theory," *Aleph: Historical Studies in Science and Judaism* 3 (2003): 247–90 and "Crisis Management via biblical Interpretation: Fundamentalism, Modern Orthodoxy, and Genesis," in *Jewish Tradition and the Challenge of Darwinism*, ed. Geoffrey Cantor and Marc Swetlitz (Chicago: University of Chicago Press, 2006), 166–87.

4. *ReVisions: Seeing Torah through a Feminist Lens* (Toronto: Key Porter Books, 1998), 47ff.

5. For early Christian interpretations of our verse, see H. H. Somers, "The Riddle of a Plural (Gen 1:21 [sic]): Its History in Tradition," in *Folia. Studies in the Christian Perpetuation of the Classics* 9 (New York: Catholic Classical Association of Greater New York, 1955), 63–101. For medieval Jewish responses to this interpretation, see also David Berger's *The Jewish-Christian Debate in the High Middle Ages* (Philadelphia: The Jewish Publication Society, 1979).

6. See Ibn Ezra who cites Sa'adia Gaon and then refutes him.

7.   Jacob Neusner offers an insightful analysis of *Genesis Rabbah* as a polemic against Gnosticism in his "*Genesis Rabbah* as Polemic," *Hebrew Annual Review* 9 (1985): 253–265. For Gnostic views on our verse, see Jarl Fossum, "Gen 1,26 and 2,7 in Judaism, Samaritanism, and Gnosticism," *Journal for the Study of Judaism* 16:2 (1985): 202–239. See also Alexander Altmann, "The Gnostic Background of the Rabbinic Adam Legends," in *Studies in Religious Philosophy and Mysticism* (Ithaca: Cornell University Press, 1969).

8.   b. *Eruvin* 13b.

9.   This midrash has enjoyed a successful career. For a Hasidic treatment, see Abraham Joshua Heschel's *A Passion for Truth* (New York: Farrar, Straus and Giroux, 1973). For a more contemporary analysis, see Simi Peter's "'Na'aseh Adam': Should We Make Adam? A Midrashic Reading of Genesis 1:26," in *Torah of the Mothers: Contemporary Jewish Women Read Classical Jewish Texts*, ed. Ora Wiskind and Susan Handelman (New York: Urim Publications, 2000), 291–306.

10.   Alon Goshen Gottstein, "The Body as Image of God in Rabbinic Literature," *Harvard Theological Review* 87, no. 2 (1994): 172.

11.   Ibid., 178–86.

12.   Translated from the Arabic in *The Guide for the Perplexed* 1:1 by Goodman, *Rambam*, 56.

13.   Marvin Fox wrote a very helpful essay on Maimonides' understanding of humanity in his *Interpreting Maimonides: Studies in Methodology, Metaphysics, and Moral Philosophy* (Chicago: University of Chicago Press, 1990).

14.   The earliest Jewish Hellenistic philosopher has a similar reading. See Philo, *On the Creation*, 134.

15.   Daniel Boyarin, *Carnal Israel: Reading Sex in Talmudic Culture* (Berkeley: University of California Press, 1993), 33.

16.   b. *Hagiga* 12a.

17.   E.g., *Leviticus Rabbah* 34:3.

18.   Joseph Dan writes extensively on early Jewish mysticism. See his *The Ancient Jewish Mysticism* (Tel Aviv: MOD Books, 1993). See also Gershom Scholem, *On the Mystical Shape of the Godhead*, trans. Joachim Neugroschel (New York: Schocken Books, 1991), chaps. 1 and 6, for a discussion of anthropomorphism and the *s'firot*. Arthur Green, my teacher, translates some of these concepts into a contemporary idiom in his *Ehyeh: A Kabbalah for Tomorrow* (Woodstock: Jewish Lights Publishing, 2003).

19.   Naphtali Zvi Yehuda Berlin, *Ha'amek Davar*.

20.   Aharon Yakov Greenberg, ed. *Torah Gems*, trans. Shmuel Himelstein (New York: Chemed Books & Co, 1998).

21.   *The Lonely Man of Faith* (New York: Doubleday, 1965), 12.

22.   *Torah Gems*. Cf. *Meshekh Chochmah* on Deut. 6:5.

23.   Benno Jacob, *The First Book of the Bible: Genesis*, trans. and ed. Ernest I. Jacob and Walter Jacob (New York: Ktav Publishing House, 1974), 10.

24.   b. *Baba Kamma* 51a. For an interesting article exploring the halakhic principle of individual responsibility for crimes committed during modern wars, see Samuel Hugo Bergman's essay, "Can Transgression Have an Agent?" in his *The Quality of Faith: Essays on Judaism and Morality*, trans. Yehuda Hanegbi (Jerusalem: World Zionist Organization, 1970).

25.   See Chizkuni and S'forno.

26.   The NJPS translation formats these stories so that the reader sees the break in the verse and the separation between the two narratives.

   The most readable account of how the disparate elements of the TANAKH came together as a single book is Friedman's *Who Wrote the Bible?* For an academic account of the possible relationships between the two creation narratives, see James Barr, "Adam: Single Man, or All Humanity?" in *Hesed ve-Emet: Studies in Honor of Ernest Frerichs*, ed. Jodi Magness and Seymour Gitin (Atlanta: Scholars Press, 1998), 3–12.

27.   See Rashbam.

28.   *Genesis Rabbah* 17:2.

29.   Plato, *The Symposium*, 192e.

30.   Mark Goodman graciously reminded me of the gendered grammar.

31.   Elliot Wolfson is the most prolific author on issues regarding gender and Jewish mysticism. For a brief overview, see his "On Becoming Female: Crossing the Gender Boundaries in Kabbalistic Ritual and Myth," in *Gender and Judaism: The Transformation of Tradition*, ed. Tamar R. Rudavsky (New York: New York University Press, 1995).

32.   The comment of Rashi on v. 28, taken from the Talmud, similarly imposes patriarchy on this immaculately egalitarian description of creation.

33.   For a fuller biography of Lilith, see Judith Baskin's "Constructing Eve" in her *Midrashic Women: Formations of the Feminine in Rabbinic Literature* (Hanover, NH.: Brandeis University Press, 2002). *Which Lilith? Feminist Writers Recreate the World's First Woman*, ed. Enid Dame et. al. (Northvale, N.J.: Jason Aronson, 1998) is a collection of contemporary feminist writings on Lilith.

34.   For a literary analysis of *The Alphabet of Ben Sira*, see David Stern, "The *Alphabet of Ben Sira* and the Early History of Parody in Jewish Literature," in *The Idea of biblical Interpretation: Essays in Honor of James L. Kugel*, ed. Hindy Najman and Judith H. Newman (Leiden: Brill, 2004), 423–48.

35.   I owe this insight to my student, Meredith Hammons. Indeed, many artistic depictions of Lilith show her winged.

36.   b. *Makkot* 23b/24a.

37.   David Shapiro provides many sources concerning procreation in "Be Fruitful and Multiply," *Tradition* 13:4 (1973): 42–67. Robert Gordis explains the historical development of the commandment, "'Be Fruitful and Multiply'—Biography of a Mitzvah," *Midstream* 28:7 (1982): 21–29.

38.   For a treatment of Gnostic attitudes toward sexuality that influenced early Christianity, see Elaine Pagels, "Exegesis and Exposition of the Genesis Creation Accounts in Selected Texts from Nag Hammadi," ed. Charles W. Hedrick and Robert Hodgson, Jr. (Peabody, MA: Hendrickson Publishers, 1986), 257–85.

39. *Meshekh Chochmah* on Gen 9:7.

40. For other examples of Rabbi Meir Simcha's use of biblical history to resolve tensions within the Torah, see Yaakov Elman, "The Rebirth of Omnisignificant biblical Exegesis in the Nineteenth and Twentieth Centuries," *Jewish Studies, an Internet Journal* 2 (2003): 199–249.

41. Emil Fackenheim, a late-20th century Jewish philosopher and survivor of the Shoah (Holocaust), encouraged Jews to accept as a 614th commandment that each couple should have one more child than they would otherwise. He urged this self-imposed obligation in order to prevent Hitler from enjoying a posthumous victory.

42. The *halakhah* developed a category, *bal tashchit*, "do not destroy." This precept is the halachic safeguard against conspicuous consumption. See Eilon Schwartz, "Judaism and Nature: Theological and Moral Issues to Consider while Renegotiating a Jewish Relationship to the Natural World" in *Judaism and Environmental Ethics: A Reader*, ed. Martin D. Yaffee (New York: Lanham Books, 2001), 297–308.

43. *Questions and Solutions in Genesis.* Translated in Jeremy Cohen, *"Be Fertile and Increase, Fill the Earth and Master It" : The Ancient and Medieval Career of a Biblical Text* (Ithaca: Cornell University Press, 1989), 75.

44. Cited in Roger T. Beckwith, "The Vegetarianism of the Theraputae, and the Motives for Vegetarianism in Early Jewish and Christian Circles," *Revue de Qumran* 13, nos. 1–4 (1988): 407–410.

45. In addition to the essays on the treatment of animals in *Judaism and Environmental Ethics*, ed. Martin D. Yaffe, see the books of a husband-wife team from Massachusetts, Roberta Kalechofsky and Richard H. Schwartz, who operate Micah Publications. Specifically, see her *Judaism and Animal Rights: Classical and Contemporary Responses* (Marblehead, MA: Micah Publications, 1992) and his *Judaism and Vegetarianism* (New York: Lantern Books, 2001).

46. *Book of Principles*, 3:2.

47. My student Anthony Elman reminded me of the polemical context of Albo's comment.

Ramban participated in a disputation in Barcelona in 1263. His record of that event has been translated into English in *The Disputation at Barcelona*, ed. and trans. Charles B. Chavel (New York: Shilo Publishing House, 1983). The BBC also produced a film based on Ramban's account. *Disputation and Dialogue: Readings in the Jewish-Christian Encounter*, ed. Frank E. Talmage (New York: Ktav Publishing House, 1975) also contains relevant primary sources.

48. *A Wonderful Life: Burgess Shale and the Nature of History* (New York: W.W. Norton & CO., 1989).

49. Hans Jonas has done an admirable job of linking the facts of natural history with a religious sensibility and Jewish commitment to ethical behavior. See his collection of essays in *Mortality and Morality: The Search for the Good after Auschwitz*, ed. by Lawrence Vogel (Evanston: Northwestern University Press, 1996).

50. *Tanhuma*, Pekude 7.

51. *The Guide for the Perplexed*, 3:10.

52. Psikta Rabbati 21. The Rabbinic notion that creation is incomplete without revelation is an updating of the biblical understanding that creation is incomplete without God's presence in the Tabernacle. The literary connections between Genesis one and the end of Exodus, when the Tabernacle is completed, are drawn out by Peter Kearney in "Creation and Liturgy: The P Redaction of Ex 25–40" *Zeitschrift für die Alttestamentlische* Wissenschaft 89:3 (1977): 375–387.

53. b. *Shabbat* 10a.

Chapter 3

THE SONS OF ADAM AND EVE

GENESIS 4:3–8, 13

T HE TORAH'S VERDICT on life outside the Garden is mixed. On the one hand, there's the fratricide. On the other hand, it didn't have to be that way. And that possibility, resounding with Divine authority, holds out the hope for a better future. Let's look in on Cain and Abel through the windows of three translations and two millennia of Jewish interpretation.

Translations/Interpretations of Cain and Abel

King James Version	JPS TANAKH	Everett Fox, *The Five Books of Moses*
And Adam knew Eve his wife; and she conceived and bore Cain, and said, I have gotten a man from the LORD.	Now the man knew his wife Eve, and she conceived and bore Cain, saying, "I have gained a male child with the help of the LORD."	The human knew Havva his wife, She became pregnant and bore Kayin. She said: Kaniti/I-have-gotten A man, as has YHWH!

continued

King James Version	JPS TANAKH	Everett Fox, *The Five Books of Moses*
2 And she again bore his brother Abel. And Abel was a keeper of sheep, but Cain was a tiller of the ground.	2 She then bore his brother Abel. Abel became a keeper of sheep, and Cain became a tiller of the soil.	2 She continued bearing—his brother, Hevel. Now Hevel became a shepherd of flocks, and Kayin became a worker of the soil.
3 And in process of time it came to pass, that Cain brought of the fruit of the ground an offering unto the LORD.	3 In the course of time, Cain brought an offering to the LORD from the fruit of the soil;	3 It was after the passing of days that Kayin brought, from the fruit of the soil, a gift to YHWH,
4 And Abel, he also brought of the firstlings of his flock and of the fat thereof. And the LORD had respect unto Abel and to his offering:	4 and Abel, for his part, brought the choicest of the firstlings of his flock. The LORD paid heed to Abel and his offering,	4 and as for Hevel, he too brought—from the firstborn of his flock, from their fat-parts. YHWH had regard for Hevel and his gift,
5 But unto Cain and to his offering he had not respect. And Cain was very wroth, and his countenance fell.	5 but to Cain and his offering He paid no heed. Cain was much distressed and his face fell.	5 for Kayin and his gift he had no regard. Kayin became exceedingly upset and his face fell.
6 And the LORD said unto Cain, Why art thou wroth? And why is thy countenance fallen?	6 And the LORD said to Cain, "Why are you so distressed, And why is your face fallen?	6 YHWH said to Kayin: Why are you so upset? Why has your face fallen?

continued

King James Version	JPS TANAKH	Everett Fox, *The Five Books of Moses*
[7] If thou doest well, shalt thou not be accepted? And if thou doest not well, sin lieth at the door. And unto thee shall be his desire, and thou shalt rule over him.	[7] Surely, if you do right, There is uplift. But if you do not do right Sin couches at the door; Its urge is toward you, Yet you can be its master."	[7] Is it not thus: If you intend good, bear-it-aloft, But if you do not intend good, At the entrance is sin, a crouching-demon, Toward you his lust—But you can rule over him.
[8] And Cain talked with Abel his brother: and it came to pass, when they were in the field, that Cain rose up against Abel his brother, and slew him.	[8] Cain said to his brother Abel . . . and when they were in the field, Cain set upon his brother Abel and killed him.	[8] Kayin said to his brother Hevel . . . But then it was, when they were out in the field That Kayin rose up against Hevel his brother And he killed him.
[9] And the LORD said unto Cain, Where is Abel thy brother? And he said, I know not: Am I my brother's keeper?	[9] The LORD said to Cain, "Where is your brother Abel?" And he said, "I do not know. Am I my brother's keeper?"	[9] YHWH said to Kayin: Where is Hevel your brother? He said: I do not know. Am I the watcher of my brother?
[10] And he said, What hast thou done? The voice of thy brother's blood crieth to me from the ground.	[10] Then He said, "What have you done? Hark, your brother's blood cries out to Me from the ground!	[10] Now he said: What have you done! A sound—your brother's blood cries out to me from the soil.
[11] And now art thou cursed from the earth, which hath opened her mouth to receive thy brother's blood from thy hand;	[11] Therefore, you shall be more cursed than the ground, which opened its mouth to receive your brother's blood from your hand.	[11] And now, damned be you from the soil which opened its mouth to receive your brother's blood from your hand.

continued

King James Version	JPS Tanakh	Everett Fox, *The Five Books of Moses*
[12] When thou tillest the ground, it shall not henceforth yield to thee its strength; a fugitive and a vagabond shalt thou be in the earth.	[12] If you till the soil, it shall no longer yield its strength to you. You shall become a ceaseless wanderer on earth."	[12] When you wish to work the soil it will not henceforth give its strength to you; wavering and wandering must you be on earth!
[13] And Cain said unto the LORD, My punishment is greater than I can bear.	[13] Cain said to the LORD, "My punishment is too great to bear!"	[13] Kayin said to YHWH: My iniquity is too great to be borne!

One *peshat* reading of this story emphasizes human freedom, responsibility, and the power to overcome our inclinations (v. 7). It's true that sin is at the door, whatever that may mean, but we don't have to be its victim. We have the capacity, so God tells us as He tells Cain, to rule over it. No determinism or predestination in this text. Indeed, the rejection of determinism and the embrace of free will are central to the Torah's assumption that we can "choose life" (Deut. 30:19) by following the dictates found within the Torah.

While responsibility is the central message of this story, along the way there are some perplexing details. Why does God play favorites by accepting Abel's offering but not Cain's? What is the nature of the sin at the door? Why is God seemingly insensitive to Cain's suffering? What did Cain say to his brother? And, finally, does Cain show any character development? Does he regret killing his brother? As if those problems weren't enough, the commentators will manufacture a few more where there are none in the verses themselves, just to have a peg upon which to hang their own thoughts. We begin with such an example.

Why Bring an Offering?

Cain and Abel understood the great mystery of sacrifices and offerings, as did Noah. Our Rabbis said that the first man also sacrificed a bull (b. Avodah Zarah 8a). This should shut the mouths of those whose explanations of the sacrifices generate anxiety and dismay.

(Ramban, 1194–1270, Spain)

In Leviticus, sacrifices are part of a divinely mandated service. But, here in Genesis, there is no command to offer a sacrifice. What moved our actors to sacrifice? (Or, to update the question: What motivates us to pray? *Avodah*, which in biblical Hebrew generally refers to sacrificial service, in post-biblical Hebrew usually refers to prayer.) Was it a spontaneous expression of gratitude for a bountiful flock or harvest? Was it a desperate plea for a better future in the wake of drought or plague? Was it a way for these early men to reach out and connect with their Creator? Or something else, something even more?

Ramban (Rabbi Moshe ben Nachman, or Moses Nachmanides) reveals that Cain and Abel understood the magnitude of their actions. He recycles the Talmudic concept of *tzorech gavoah*, supernal need, and asserts that God has needs which we have the power to fulfill.[1] We add strength, as it were, to the godly forces in the universe. Pagans offered gifts to their gods in order to curry favor with them. They were bribes. The Jewish mystical tradition, here represented by Ramban, subtly inverts that relationship. Sacrifices are not primarily for us but for God. God lacks something and we freely gift God what He lacks. Nevertheless, according to Ramban's kabbalistic scheme, a byproduct of fulfilling the supernal need is that God's overflowing goodness can reach us. A felicitous byproduct, to be sure, but a byproduct, nevertheless. Fundamentally, this relationship is a covenant, a *b'rit*. Each party to the *b'rit* has something to offer the other.

This notion of a God in need is a central motif of medieval Jewish mysticism. Attendant to that claim is the related idea that human actions affect God. He is not, to use theological language, impassible. God cares passionately about what we do and is changed by our behavior. God is not an island. The TANAKH, especially the prophets, describes the needs of God, and the Rabbis later develop the theme. But it is the medieval mystics, Ramban among them, who articulate and systematize this theme in the face of opposition from the medieval Aristotelian philosophers who emphasize Divine transcendence and impassability.

So now we know whose "interpretations of the sacrifices generate anxiety and dismay." Ramban has in mind Rambam (Rabbi Moshe ben Maimon, or Moses Maimonides), the giant of the Jewish Aristotelians. In his *The Guide for the Perplexed* (1:59 and 3:32), Rambam implies that perfect worship is through silent meditation alone. Sacrifices, he avers, were instituted after the sin of the Golden Calf when it became clear that the Israelites needed something concrete through which to express their devotion to God. Like the other pagan nations, Israel needed to engage in sacrificial service, the only difference being the correct address of Israel's sacrifices. They were directed to the one, true God, rather than to the idols of the other nations.

Behind Rambam's reading is the Aristotelian conviction that God is impassible and self-sufficient. God has no needs. God certainly cannot be bribed or affected by human offerings. Rambam's God, like Aristotle's, is perfect and transcendent. For Rambam, sacrifices are a noble lie or a gracious ruse. Ramban seeks to counter the claim, which to him seems so pernicious, that the underlying reason for the commandments is human need rather than Divine need. Ramban, like the mystical tradition in general, resisted the philosophical reading of Judaism propounded by the Aristotelians. In his comment above, Ramban points out that far from being a Divine concession to the Israelites in the desert, sacrifice is one of the very first human activities.

This medieval debate on the meaning of long-discontinued animal sacrifices may have served as a proxy for the very live issue, in that period as well as our own, of the function and value of prayer. And that may explain why Ramban is so sharp tongued, even toward someone whom he otherwise held in great respect. Rambam understood that the prayer service satisfies our need for concrete religious expression. This is a way for us to talk to ourselves about God. Extrapolating from Ramban's comments on sacrifice, prayer is far more than a psychological concession; it is a living dialogue and an expression of the *b'rit* linking God and the Jewish people.[2]

Rambam may be right about sacrifices and prayer as psychological concessions, but Ramban has a better reading of the biblical and rabbinic traditions. The idea of *b'rit* is fundamental to the Hebrew Bible and all subsequent Jewish thought. Often it is the mystical tradition, unembarrassed by "primitive notions," that preserves the *peshat* of the Hebrew Bible more authentically than do philosophical reconstructions. Of course, determining the *peshat* of the Torah and determining the truth about God are two different enterprises.

"For the Lord your God . . . shows no favor" (Deut. 10:17). Really?

Cain's offering was from the fruit of the soil, from the refuse.
(Genesis Rabbah, Rabbinic compilation edited
by 5th century, Land of Israel)

The Rabbis were determined to find a justification for God's actions. They assumed that the verses themselves, read properly, would unlock the mystery of Divine motivation. In addition to the assumptions that the Rabbis had about the Torah, they had a few about God, too. And one of them was that

God shows no favor. As father Abraham rhetorically asked, "Shall not the Judge of all the earth deal justly?" (Gen. 18:25). The Rabbis, too, were committed to preserving the Divine characteristic of justice, and this comment does just that. It explains why God rejected Cain's offering. Cain had brought second-rate produce.

Our comment focuses on the verse's wording that Cain offered *fruit of the soil*. Perhaps the Rabbis are emphasizing that the offering lacks a positive modifier, and thus the juxtaposition with Abel's first-rate offering is unflattering. This explanation would emphasize what is absent from the text.

Another way to interpret our comment emphasizes what is present. *Genesis Rabbah* may be reading our verse with the accent on *soil/ground*. Cain's offering was not fruit that grew *from the soil*, which is the *peshat* reading, but was fruit that had fallen *to the ground*. (Notice that the King James translation of verse 3 allows for this midrashic reading slightly better than do the modern translations. Fruit doesn't fall to the soil, it falls to the ground.) Prepositions are prime midrashic material because of their intrinsic plasticity. In this case, the text has no preposition whatsoever because it employs a grammatical form called a construct (*s'michut* in Hebrew) that places two nouns together to indicate a possessive relationship. *Genesis Rabbah* offers a very different understanding of *how* the fruit belongs to the ground than we originally thought when reading our narrative.

With either explanation, our comment throws into relief what is explicit in the text, namely that Abel brought from the fatted firstborns while Cain's produce is not described. There is clearly a lack of symmetry in the descriptions of their offerings. *Genesis Rabbah* tweaks the asymmetry so that it is no longer, as in the Torah, silent about Cain *and* positive about Abel; rather, now it is negative about Cain *but* positive about Abel. Not only are prepositions plastic, so are conjunctions. The Hebrew prefix, *vav*, can signify both *and* and *but*. Although each of our translations of verse 4 has the initial *vav* as *and*, the Rabbis read it as a conjunction of opposition to distinguish Cain's gift from that of Abel. Look back at the translations of verse 2 and notice the same phenomenon. KJV has Abel's occupation in opposition to Cain's, while the NJPS and Fox translations maintain relative neutrality.

There is a tendency within Rabbinic thinking to simplify the complexity of the Torah's characters. They prefer polarization. The Esau of Genesis, for instance, might not be a paragon of virtue, but neither is he what the Rabbis describe—a personification of vice who commits the three cardinal transgressions of Rabbinic Judaism: idolatry, adultery, and murder![3] Some Rabbis, like many political leaders, prefer black and white.

3. Cain's offering was brought with impudence; Abel's with humility.
(Zohar, Midrash HaNe'elam, late 13th century, Spain)

Here's another way to explain God's preference. It didn't have to do with the quality of the sacrifice, but with the spirit in which it was offered. Our *darshan* is addressing the issue that the text raises by mentioning God's response to both the gift *and* the giver (v. 4 and 5). One might expect that God would only respond to the sacrifice being offered. But, since the text explicitly mentions God's response to the giver, many commentators understand that the problem was really with the person rather than the offering.

For the mystical tradition, there is unprecedented emphasis on inwardness. This theme, of course, is present and pervasive in the TANAKH and Rabbinic literature. The Mishnah, for example, says: "It doesn't matter how much you sacrifice as long as you focus your attention on God."[4] But it was the Kabbalists and the later Hasidic masters who made inwardness or awareness (*kavanah*) central to their religious renewal movements.

In a similar vein, we have a comment from the Hasidic tradition on the seemingly superfluous words in verse 4 "for his part." Rabbi Bunam said, "Abel brought himself. He sacrificed himself."[5] Don't take this comment literally. Abel did not commit suicide. Rather, he dedicated himself, entirely, to God's service, and that's why God had regard for Abel and his gift. There was nothing half-hearted in Abel's approach. He understood, suggests Rabbi Bunam, that Divine service is an all-consuming affair that is not to be compartmentalized into synagogue attendance and everything else.[6]

4. The serpent came into her and she became pregnant with Cain, as it says, "And the human knew his wife Eve." What did he know? That she was already pregnant.
(Pirkei d'Rabbi Eliezer 21, 8th century, Land of Israel;
cf. *Targum* Pseudo-Jonathan on Gen. 4:1)

In this reading, Adam didn't know Eve in the biblical sense. He knew something *about* her.

The idea that Cain was evil from the very beginning is dominant throughout the mystical tradition and reflects a certain sympathy for the type of theological dualism that characterizes Gnosticism and Zoroastrianism. The serpent, in this reading, represents demonic forces in the world that are seeking to proliferate in order to wreak havoc in human affairs. But here we need to be careful. Normative Rabbinic tradition and medieval Jewish mysticism do not depict two *independent* forces in the universe. That's heresy. There is still only one force. But, borrowing from the contemporary film-maker George Lucas' theology, the force has a dark side. In Kabbalah, the mystics call it the *sitra achra*, the other side. The other side of a single force. According to the Kabbalistic myth, the *sitra achra* feeds off violations of the *mitzvot* (commandments). It's parasitic on our transgressions. The model, though stunningly anthropocentric (the deeds of human beings, rather than God, animate the Divine system), is consistent. Just as our deeds affect the Divine reality for the good, so do they for the bad.

Of the explanations we have seen so far for God's favoritism, this one seems particularly troubling. If we understand the story to be about our ability to overcome the temptation of sin, then biology should not dictate our destiny. This comment seemingly links God's rejection of Cain, and Cain's subsequent murder of Abel, to his being the offspring of the serpent. If so, is this a case of visiting the sin of the parents upon the children (Exod. 20:5)? There is such a theology in the Hebrew Bible and its unmerciful logic is carried forward through the Christian dogma of Original Sin.[7]

Some contemporary Bible scholars understand our story to be underlining that connection between biology and destiny. According to them, our story might have originally served the function of explaining the enmity between the Israelites and the neighboring Kenites, the descendants of Cain.[8] In this case, the etiology would indeed rely on the logic of *Pirkei d'Rabbi Eliezer* that the Kenites were bloodthirsty because they descended from a murderer. As a leading contemporary Bible scholar puts it: "[I]n biblical genetics it is axiomatic that the founder's chromosomes are passed on with unvarying accuracy from generation to generation."[9]

But already in the TANAKH there is opposition to this type of biological determinism. "A child shall not share the burden of a parent's guilt" (Ezek. 18:20). Our comment, after all, does *not* connect Cain's origins and his actions.[10] Our comment may have just the opposite message: Even if you were born to evil parents in a totally dysfunctional family, the ever-present inclination to continue the downward spiral into a cycle of moral poverty can be overcome, as God seems to say in verse 7. Also for the etiological purposes of our tale, Cain's deeds might still explain why the Kenites are the enemies of the Israelites, but only because they have consistently refused to control their tempers. Verse 7, even on the heels of comments like those of *Pirkei d'Rabbi Eliezer*, precludes fatalism.

The rejection of the biology-is-destiny outlook, moreover, is absolutely central to the TANAKH. Consider the Messiah. The authors and redactor of the

TANAKH go out of their way to highlight his tainted pedigree. First there is the act of incest between Lot and his daughter that establishes the Moabites (the etymology of *Moav* is *from father*, see Gen. 19:36f). Then we have Tamar's deceptive act of harlotry with Judah which bears Peretz (Gen. 38). And, finally, we have Peretz's descendant, Boaz, violating a biblical prohibition by marrying Ruth the Moabite (Deut. 23:4 and Ruth 4:13). Their great-grandson was King David and the Messiah will be his descendant (Isa. 11:1).

And what's so amazing about David? When he is confronted with his own misdeeds, rather than rationalize, he says starkly, "I stand guilty before the LORD!" (II Sam. 12:13.) (Contrast King David to the whining Cain: "My punishment is too great to bear!") Confession is the first station on the road of *teshuvah* (repentance.) And the TANAKH's glorification of King David as the ancestor of the Messiah is testimony that one's past iniquities do not necessarily doom one's future.

5. Cain may have brought the sacrifice after Abel had.
(from Radak, c.1160–c.1235, France)

Part of what's so galling about our story is that Cain is not acknowledged by God for having been the first to think of the idea of offering a sacrifice. Radak (Rabbi David Kimchi) focuses on the grammatical structure of verse 4 which suggests that Abel had first offered his high-quality sacrifice, and it was Cain who then imitated Abel with an inferior offering.

In a comment on an earlier biblical passage, Rashi points out that the grammatical sequence of subject then predicate, rather than the more common biblical sequence of predicate then subject, means that a clause might be understood in the past perfect.[11] Although Rashi does not apply that grammatical insight to our verse, Radak does. Through the grammatical rules that he had learned in Muslim Spain, where they were emphasizing such things, he mitigates a seemingly unfair biblical passage. Radak suggests the following translation: And Abel *had* brought, also, from the firstlings of his flock [before Cain].[12] This reading takes some of the sting out of God's preferential treatment.

What none of the traditional commentators wants to allow for is the possibility that God was acting arbitrarily or unjustly. The Rabbinic psyche skirts the idea, from a safe distance, by putting such a disorienting thought into the mouth of Cain (see comment 17 below).[13] Not until we emerge from the Shoah, the Holocaust, do we find a thinker willing to articulate in his own voice a somewhat similar notion.

6. Or did God wish to make the point—even then—that injustice is inherent in the human condition?

(Elie Wiesel, contemporary, United States)[14]

But even Wiesel, witness to unimaginable injustice, dulls the point by posing it as a question and juxtaposing it with others, not privileging one viewpoint above any other. Moreover, the issue for Wiesel is not Divine justice but human injustice. God was simply trying to teach Cain the lesson that the two are easily confused in a world graced by free will. People don't always get what they deserve. If you read only the ending of our story, you might conclude that Abel's death was a sign of Divine disfavor.[15] We should remember, however, that God's regard for Abel did not even protect him from his own brother. The converse is also true. It is seductive to imagine that our success is a sign of Divine favor. Do not identify the victor with the virtuous, or the vanquished with the wicked. Such simplistic reductionism is a vulgar perversion of God's role in history.

The Doors and Perception

In the revelation at Mt. Sinai, God "appears" in a dense cloud (Exod. 19:9). God's communiqué to Cain in verse seven seems to be equally opaque. (Notice our three different translations. Fox preserves the difficulties.) But biblical opacity generates midrashic creativity.[16]

7. The Holy One, blessed be He, said to Israel: My son, I created in you a yetzer ha-ra. I also created within you Torah as an antidote. As long as you engage in Torah, the yetzer ha-ra will have no control over you, as our verse says, "If you do well, you will rise above." But if you don't engage in Torah, then you'll be delivered into its hands, as our verse continues, "But if you don't do well, sin crouches at the door." And not only that, but there will be internal vacillations, as the next verse says, "its desire will be for you." But if you want, you can rule over it, as the conclusion says, "You will rule over it."

(Sifre Deuteronomy, *Ekev 45*, Rabbinic collection compiled in 3rd century, Land of Israel; cf. Midrash on Psalms, *119:64*)

Both Torah and the *yetzer ha-ra* (the inclination to do evil) are part and parcel of who we are. Torah is not in the heavens, it is "in your mouth and in your heart" (Deut. 30:14). God may have created us with the toxic *yetzer ha-ra*, but we enjoy the antidote of Torah to right our ways. In this classically

Rabbinic comment, the praises of Talmud Torah are sung. (Talmud Torah is often translated as *learning Torah*. But since *Torah* is best translated as *teaching*, *Talmud Torah* becomes *learning teaching!*)

Sin, according to this midrash, springs into action when you exit the door of the *beit midrash*, the study house. When you stop studying Torah, that's when you expose yourself to temptation. The Rabbis advise that when you feel yourself tempted, get thee to a *beit midrash!* There, you will engage in holy vacillations, the give and take of Talmud Torah. On the outside, the vacillations will not be between you and your *havruta*, your study partner, but between your own strengths and weaknesses, your super-ego and your id.

8. *The yetzer ha-ra is produced in the human individual at his birth: "Sin coucheth at the door."*
(Rambam, *The Guide for the Perplexed* (1190), III:22, p. 489; see also b. Sanhedrin 91b)

9. *At the door of your house your sin crouches to cause you to stumble in all your paths.*
(Ramban, 1194–1260, Spain)

10. *But if you do not improve your deeds you will find the sin crouching at the door of your grave. That is to say that as soon as you leave this world, you'll be punished in the world of the souls.*
(Rabbeinu Bahya, 1263–1340, Spain; cf. Onkelos and Rashi)

These verses are like a medieval Rorschach test. Behind door number one we have Rambam, the medieval Aristotelian philosopher, who internalizes sin by identifying it with the Torah's psychological observation that humans have the tendency to do wrong (Gen. 6:5). Note that the Christian concept of Original Sin is about who we are in our very essence. To use the philosophical term, Original Sin is an ontological condition. For normative Jewish tradition, the *yetzer ha-ra* is a psychological tendency, *not* an ontological condition. The Rabbinic innovation in the field of human psychology is to complement the biblical *yetzer ha-ra* with the *yetzer ha-tov*, the inclination to do good and practice random acts of kindness. The downward pressure exerted on the biblical earthling to do evil awaits the Rabbinic period to meet its equal and opposite force. But, perhaps the Rabbis were not quite as innovative as I've suggested. After all, as we saw in the previous chapter, the Torah's Adam is both like (*domeh*) God *and* from the earth (*adamah*).

Rambam understands the *sin* from our verse not as an external force luring us into temptation, but as an internal tendency leading us astray from what we know intellectually and from religious tradition to be the proper path. *The door* is the door to this world and from the moment we enter, our *yetzer ha-ra* is there, like the Freudian id, to sate its passions.

Behind door number two is Ramban who conceives of "sin" as a personal tempter. Every time we make a decision, walk through the door, our demon is there to lead us astray. On a ritual level that may be why we remind ourselves of God's presence and expectations as we cross every threshold by affixing a *mezuzah* to our doorposts (Deut. 6:9). It's dangerous out there. Sin is lurking, waiting for an opportunity to pounce. Sin is not some internalized tendency or predisposition as it is for the philosopher. Ramban is a mystic and believes there are ungodly forces at work in the universe lying in wait to entrap those who are not vigilant.

Look back at the translations to verse 7. Couching and crouching may be rhymes, but they are also opposites. Couching and lying (NJPS and KJV) are passive states. In these translations, "sin" is an obstacle to be negotiated lest you trip over it. Rambam's reading is closer to these translations. For Fox and Ramban, sin is crouching, scanning the horizon for the right moment to spring forth toward its prey.

Door number three takes us out of this world, *olam ha-zeh*, and into the next, *olam ha-ba*. Rabbeinu Bahya maintains that upon arrival to that coming world, we will not be greeted by harps and an angelic choir, but by an exhaustive catalogue of our iniquities. This is a sobering thought. Here, *sin* represents neither the internal *yetzer ha-ra* nor demonic forces but a collective noun, waiting patiently to remind us in too many cases of long-forgotten transgressions.

Rabbeinu Bahya's comment retrojects into the TANAKH the concept of the World to Come. The TANAKH emphasizes life in this world. Systematic notions of heaven and hell are simply not in evidence. They are an important part of both the Jewish and Christian traditions, but they begin their literary career in earnest in post-biblical thought.

The World to Come is important because it enables the fulfillment of God's justice. If we wish to keep our assumption that God is just, and if we wish to trust our senses—exposing us to the harsh reality that neither are the good always rewarded nor the wicked always made to suffer—we need a new dimension in which God's justice can be fulfilled. As Rabbeinu Bahya projects into God's warning, murder will out, though not necessarily in this world. Rabbeinu Bahya is telling us that we should not be deceived by the injustices of this world. Cain gets away with murder, but it's only a temporary reprieve.

11. Cain did not understand what God had told him. . . . Cain thought that the body and its powers were all there was to a human being. Thus, he did not know whom God meant when He spoke of sin that couches at the door within, desiring to lure him into transgression, but whom he can overcome. He did not know who this sin was, and since only he and Abel were around then, Cain thought that God meant Abel. That is, that God was telling him that Abel intended to lure him into the pit, but that Cain had the strength to overcome him.

(Malbim, 1809–1879, Central Europe)

This comment is breathtaking, modern, and very scary. Malbim suggests that the murder of Abel was all just a misunderstanding. Cain was not intellectually mature enough to handle the abstract language that God used about sin couching at the door. What sin? What door? Cain was a simple farmer, a man of the soil. There is an implicit, if unintended, criticism of God in Malbim's comment. Teachers and parents need to speak *to* their students and children, not over their heads. God should have known better than to use abstract language with someone whose developmental level was inadequate to the task.

Cain looked around and saw Abel. He put what he heard together with whom he saw and reasoned that God must be referring to Abel when God spoke about "sin couching at the door." And then God went on to say that he is to overcome *him*. (Remember, Hebrew is a gendered language and has no way to say *it*. Look back at Fox's translation.) So, Cain overcame Abel instead of his own *yetzer ha-ra*. In Malbim's reading, the murder was not a crime of passion; from Cain's perspective it was executed with a Divine mandate. The message is that when we misunderstand God, we end up killing each other.

Malbim is the first commentator we've seen to present multiple perspectives simultaneously. (Cubism is a parallel movement in the world of art.) Malbim explains his reading of what God meant and what Cain understood. Malbim (like Rambam) interprets the sin in God's speech to Cain as internal temptation; while Cain understands it to be an external and concrete threat.

Malbim was a bitter foe of the newly emerging Reform movement. In his 1860 introduction to his commentary on Leviticus, he railed against the reformers, calling them "Karaites and deniers." He insisted that the Rabbinic interpretation was the *peshat* of the Torah and that contrary to the conclusions of academic scholarship, both the written and Oral Torahs were given at Sinai. Was Malbim hinting that Reform Jews, like the medieval Karaites, don't understand God's method of communication because they read Jewish texts literally? Was Malbim claiming that the Orthodox community, however, correctly understands God's abstract language by reading the Torah and subsequent Jewish tradition midrashically? The stakes in the dispute over understanding God's word are high: brothers kill each other.[17]

"It's Not What You Said . . ."

12. Rabbi Yitzchak Meir of Ger was asked: What is the meaning of God asking Cain why his face has fallen? How could his face not fall since God had not accepted his gift?
The Rabbi replied: God asked Cain, "Why has your face fallen? Because I did not accept your sacrifice or because I accepted your brother's?"
(1799–1866, Poland; cf. Sforno)[18]

13. God did not ask Cain about his sins that had prevented his sacrifice from being accepted. Rather, he asked why Cain was drowning in grief. Excessive grieving over a transgression is worse than the transgression itself since it drags one into even more transgressions.
(Rav Y. Y. Trunk of Kutno, 1820–1893, Poland)[19]

Both comments are motivated by God's seemingly insensitive remark that follows on the heels of God's rejection of Cain and his sacrifice. If one reads God's words (v. 6) as though delivered in a taunting tone, we have to ask why God would be rubbing Cain's rejection in his downfallen face? The Hasidic Rabbi Yitzchak Meir suggests that God was emphasizing the *Why* of the question. "*Why* has your face fallen?" How difficult it is to be happy for one's brother when one is not enjoying similar success! A Hasidic addition to the Decalogue might be: Thou shalt not begrudge your neighbor.

The Hasidic master is very sensitive to the wording of the verses. Cain first responds to God's rejection with distress or anger (v. 5), and only after with embarrassment or a sense of humiliation. Rabbi Yitzchak Meir assumes that God's second question in verse 6 is not redundant. First Cain is angry at being rejected. He then feels humiliated when Abel's offering is accepted.

In his comment, Rav Trunk highlights the focus on joy and ecstasy that one finds in much, though by no means all, of Hasidic literature. There is a tendency among religious personalities to abuse themselves over their imperfections. Rav Trunk suggests here that self-flagellation is self-defeating. Rav Trunk's reading of verse 6 emphasizes the word *so*. "Why are you *so* distressed?" It is entirely appropriate to be upset if the emotion facilitates self-improvement. The problem here is that Cain is *so* upset that his emotions are themselves an obstacle to moral progress.

What I translated as "drags" (*goreret*) suggests two mutually reinforcing trends. First, if we're feeling like wastrels, we're more inclined to commit additional sins in the future. Secondly, we're more likely to dredge up, or drag up, those past indiscretions that have dogged us for years, therefore making us feel even more like inveterate sinners and inclining us to commit even more transgressions. On Yom Kippur, in addition to forgiving those who have wronged us (including God), Hasidic wisdom suggests we need to forgive ourselves, too. The beauty of Rav Trunk's comment is that it not only gets God off the hook for being insensitive, it makes God both insightful and caring.

Silence and Speculation

Through the use of ellipsis dots, the NJPS and Fox translations call attention to the problem with the Hebrew of verse 8. Whenever you have a verse that begins with *"Ploni says to Almoni"* (the Hebrew equivalent of "Tom says to Harry"), you expect to then hear what Ploni said to Almoni. Here, however, we seem to have missing dialogue that may have illuminated the motive for the murder. Silence rather than speech. This is another tailor-made moment for the commentators to fill in the gap. Of course, there are ways to smooth over the problem, as the KJV translation does.[20] But, the Rabbis found it more illuminating to fill the space. The Rabbis of *Genesis Rabbah* bring three midrashim back to back—dueling midrash, as it were.

> 14. They said: "Come let us divide up the world. One will take the real estate, the other the movables." One said: "The land you're standing on belongs to me!" The other said: "Well, what you're wearing belongs to me! Strip!" "Buzz off!"
> 15. This one said: "In my half of the world the Temple will be built." And the other said the same.
> 16. The quarrel was about the first woman. An additional baby, a twin, had been born with Abel. Cain said: "I'll take her because I am the first born." Abel said: "I'll take her because she was born with me."
> (Genesis Rabbah, Rabbinic compilation edited
> by 5th century, Land of Israel)

The first thing to appreciate in these midrashim is the Rabbis' total lack of discomfort with presenting multiple interpretations. These three dialogue boxes appear one after the other in our Rabbinic text. The Rabbis (or, at least, the editors of Genesis Rabbah and Rashi who cites all three midrashim) were true believers that the Torah has 70 faces.

As for content, these ancient comments strike an amazingly contemporary chord. Speculating on the roots of human violence, the first darshan suggests that aggression is rooted in acquisitiveness, our rapacious greed. Part of what's interesting in this series of explanations for fratricide is the claim that this impulse is universal. The darshan doesn't blame Cain alone. Abel's avarice warrants equal condemnation. Some commentators have linked the name Cain to the word koneh, meaning owner or one who has acquired. But this comment in Genesis Rabbah claims that both brothers covet their neighbor's possessions.[21] As Ramban later states explicitly, perhaps what the darshan is indicating is that all acquisitions are ultimately hevel (Abel's Hebrew name): evanescent.[22]

While for our first darshan the love of money is the root of all evil, for our second, it is religion. (Since the killing of Abel was preceded by religious offerings, this explanation comes closest to a deep peshat reading.) Ostensibly, the real estate has been divided equitably, but there is a desire for a monopoly on Divine access. Such a monopoly was enjoyed by the priests when the Temple stood in Jerusalem. But once the Second Temple was destroyed, Rabbinic Judaism underwent a democratization of sacred space in which God's presence was imagined to be accessible in synagogues and houses of study throughout the Land of Israel and the Diaspora.[23]

In the ancient world, tribal deities were assumed to be attached by a metaphorical umbilical cord to a particular piece of sacred space, usually on a mountaintop. Moreover, the power of these gods was often geographically circumscribed. Second Temple Judaism tried to maintain both a House of the Lord (the Temple in Jerusalem), as well as the theological conviction that the Lord fills the heaven and earth.[24] The Talmud calls the Temple the "navel of the world," implicitly relegating the other lands and those peopling them to the periphery.[25] Could our comment be a daring critique of temple-centered religion, the jealousies they provoke, and the wars waged in their name?

Helen of Troy may have launched a thousand ships, but according to our third darshan, Cain and Abel's sister was her prototype. And from where exactly did this alleged sister come? There is no mention of her in the biblical text. Perhaps the biblical author saw nothing wrong with assuming the presence of other people not specifically mentioned in the text, such as Cain's wife. Alternatively, the biblical editor or redactor may have lifted our story from another source that referred to such a person. However, neither proposed solution would conform to the Rabbis' assumptions about the Torah. For them the Torah, when properly read, contains everything. So the Rabbis maintained that each additional appearance of the small word *et* in verses 1 and 2 are pregnant with the births of sisters who do not come explicitly into play until later in our drama. They are therefore birthed in midrashic space and textual silence.

Because biblical Hebrew is such a fluid language, it needs "markers" to prevent confusion because of ambiguous word order. One such marker is *et*, indicating the direct object. Never translated, it nevertheless makes translation possible. Remember the first sentence of Genesis? If we didn't have an *et* before the Hebrew words for *heaven* and *earth*, we might think that they themselves were the gods responsible for creating the fullness of the world. But since we do have an *et* before each of those nouns, we know that they were the created objects, not the creating gods.

Although Cain and Abel's sister is not part of the biblical story we have in front of us, she nevertheless fulfills an important exegetical and legal function. We know that Cain takes a woman and has a child (v. 17). But the only other woman explicitly mentioned in this part of the Torah is Eve. Sex with your mother—that was a problem for the Rabbis. So, the Rabbinic solution was to marry Cain off to his sister. Sex with one's mother is both incest and adultery, assuming Dad is still around, as he is in our story. Sex with your sister is *merely* incest. So, *et* solves the exegetical problem of whom Cain took as a wife, while minimizing his transgressions.[26]

Is this midrash yet another example of "blame it on the woman"? I doubt it. The point of the midrash, demonstrated time and time again in human and non-human communities, is about reproductive rights. On a personal level, who gets to have sex? On an evolutionary scale, whose genes get to make it into the next round?

Money, religion, and sex are a concise, if not exhaustive, inventory of the sources for conflict according to our Rabbinic sages. And, to emphasize the point that these are universal human urges, there is no single aggressor or victim. Both Cain and Abel are equally complicit in what seems to be a natural inclination toward cupidity, religious exclusivism, and concupiscence.[27]

17. Cain said, "God isn't fair! Why was my offering not received favorably and yours was?" Abel replied, "My sacrifice was accepted because my good deeds exceeded yours." Cain answered, "There is no justice and no judge, there is no world to come and no reward or punishment for the righteous and wicked." About this the brothers quarrelled.

(from Targum Neophyti, Aramaic rendition of Torah, 2 c.[?], Land of Israel)

The textual bump, as previously mentioned, is that the verses say that God responded to both the gifts *and* to the givers. Why mention the givers? Because, according to the *Targum*, God's acceptance of the offerings was *entirely dependent* on the deeds of those who offered them, and completely independent of the gifts themselves. By this interpretation, Cain's offering may even have been better than Abel's. Moreover, it is not that Cain was evil and full of bad deeds; he just wasn't good *enough*. Specifically, he wasn't as good as Abel. The *Targum* is setting a high bar!

This comment comes from the period after the Romans had destroyed the Second Temple in Jerusalem. The post-Temple Rabbis would not want their flock to conclude that God's favor was dependent on sacrifices. For once the Temple was gone, so was the sacrificial system. The Rabbis needed to find new ways to fulfill the function previously served by the sacrifices. (The early Jewish-Christian community faced the same problem and resolved it through the vicarious sacrifice of Christ for the sins of humanity.[28]) Rabbinic Judaism replaced sacrifices with *teshuvah* (repentance), *Talmud Torah*, *avodah* (now understood as prayer rather than sacrifice) and deeds of loving-kindness as methods of atonement and communion with God.[29]

Although it's a sweeping generalization, there's much truth to the claim that Judaism is more concerned with deed than creed. Even though the *Targum* emphasizes deeds, creed does creep in. The *Targum* implies that Cain has been keeping bad company with Greek philosophers and Sadducees.[30] Like the Sadducees who opposed the Pharisees' more expansive exegetical tendencies, the *Targum's* Cain denies the World to Come. The Hellenistic Epicureans, of course, would deny it, too. For the *Targum*, Cain espouses those ideas that are outside of normative Rabbinic Judaism. Although there's an emphasis on deeds, a few beliefs that serve as the logical underpinnings of the religion enjoy the status of Rabbinic doctrine if not quite Rabbinic dogma.[31] In this reading, the first murderer was a heretic. No God, no moral brakes. The *Targum* anticipates Immanuel Kant's postulates of practical reason[32] and Fyodor Dostoevsky's moral and theological speculations in *The Brothers Karamozov*. Paraphrasing both the *Targum's* Cain and Kant, Ivan Karamozov mused, "If there is no God, all things are lawful."[33]

Although our comment obviously emerged from the Rabbinic confrontation with Hellenistic thought, its message is timeless. For the *Targum*, Cain is an Apikorus (Epicurean) waging a war of ideas with Abel. But intellectual wars can degenerate into bloodshed between brothers, perhaps mirroring the civil strife between the less Hellenizing Jews (like the Pharisees) and the more Hellenizing Jews (like the Sadducees and priests) from the second century,

BCE, until the destruction of the Temple.[34] The *Targum* brings home two timely messages: the power of ideas and the need for a morality grounded either in religion or philosophy.

> *18. Cain said to himself that God had meant Abel, his brother. Therefore, Cain rose up against him and killed him, in fulfillment of what the Lord had told him: "you can overcome him."*
>
> (Malbim, 1809–1879, Central Europe)

The Malbim's strategy is similar to the KJV in that he rejects the notion that there is missing dialogue. For Malbim, what is missing is better understood as interior monologue. Look back at his comment. *Cain said to his brother Abel* is reread as *Cain said [to himself that God had been speaking] about his brother, Abel*. Malbim provides us with an understanding of what was going on inside Cain's confused mind. For Malbim, the omniscient narrator has shifted perspectives from providing external dialogue to interior monologue. As noted above, the murder is thereby transformed into a misguided act of Divine obedience. On the midrashic level, both the Rabbis and Malbim add something to the verse, either dialogue or interior monologue, in order to fill in the gap. On the technical level, Malbim replaces *to* ('l [*aleph lamed*]) with *about* ('l [*ayin lamed*]) in order to finesse his comment. Exchanging one silent letter for another (*ayin* for *aleph*) voices an entirely different reading.

> *19. Cain tried to speak to Abel, but the words wouldn't come.*
>
> (Sandy Eisenberg Sasso, contemporary, United States)[35]

> *20. Cain spoke to his brother, Abel. What did he say? We don't know. Perhaps he simply repeated to him the words he had just heard. It hardly seems to matter. Cain, grief-stricken, wanted to, had to unburden himself. All he wanted was someone to talk to, to commune with. To feel a presence. And break his solitude. To have a brother, an ally when confronting God.*
>
> *And Abel? Abel remained aloof. He did nothing to console his brother, to cheer him up or appease him. He who was responsible for Cain's sorrow did nothing to help him. He regretted nothing, said nothing.*
>
> (Wiesel)[36]

Sasso and Wiesel's comments don't fill in the gap; they *explain* the gap. For Sasso, Cain's inner turmoil prevented him from articulating to his brother what was bothering him. Like Moshe striking the rock out of anger rather than reasoning with the stiff-necked people of Israel (Num. 20:11), Cain's anger and consternation clouded his judgment and led him to strike his brother. Before Cain became blinded by emotion, he was muted by it.

Wiesel turns the tables and places Abel in the dock. The break in the text does not reflect Cain's inability to speak, as it does for Sasso, but Abel's refusal to engage in dialogue with his pained brother. (Notice that Wiesel, like the King James, gets around the textual caesura by translating the predicate of the verse as "spoke" or "talked" rather than "said.") Deuteronomy 22:3 demands that we do not remain indifferent, and Abel was guilty of doing just that according to Wiesel's reading. It is no coincidence that one who survived the fiery furnace of the Shoah preaches sensitivity to the suffering of others.

21. The text is showing us that there was a breakdown in communication between the brothers. This breakdown led directly to Abel's death.

(Meshi, contemporary, United States)

For the pre-moderns, the text has a lacuna. For Meshi, another contemporary Jewish thinker, the text presents the image of a fissure. Onkelos, the second-century convert to Judaism, also converted the Torah into the common language of his day, Aramaic. He translates/interprets Gen. 2:7 as Adam becoming a speaking spirit rather than as the NJPS translation has it, a living being. Once Cain and Abel renounced their commitment to dialogue, to speaking with one another, they abdicated from what distinguished them from other beasts—their ability to communicate—and, thus, fell under the law of the jungle.

22. Alternatively, perhaps the author does not want us to know what was said between the two brothers because of how we might misinterpret or abuse the information.

(Meshi)

Sometimes authors use a technique called intentional ambiguity, leaving the reader uncertain about authorial intent. Meshi, here, suggests intentional concealment. If we were privy to Cain and Abel's conversation, we might delude ourselves into thinking that the content of what they said was so antagonistic that it somehow justified their coming to blows. But we know that there are no words that can ever justify killing your brother. So rather than allowing for the possibility that future readers might make such a mistake, the conversation between the brothers was preemptively edited out.

The traditional commentators fill the silence with their own speculation on the missing conversation and the motive for the murder. We moderns, however, speculate on the meaning of the silence. To us, traditional theologians often seem like ventriloquists, forcing their images of God to mouth their own notions. Chastened and more wary, we moderns often choose to content ourselves with speculating on the meaning of Divine silence.

The Fallout

23. In the beginning, each variety of vine and tree brought forth 926 different kinds of fruit. After Cain killed Abel, the vines and trees went into mourning and they only brought forth a single kind of fruit. In the coming world, the vines and trees will once again blossom with a full bounty.

(from Tanhuma, Introduction, 158)

This midrash answers the question about the nature of God's curse on the ground in verses 11 and 12. The *Tanhuma* imagines God's garden as a colorful cornucopia that becomes washed out from grief in the wake of the fratricide. But there's a message here beyond the horticultural.

Initially, in some idealized past, it was obvious to all that different-looking fruits shared the same roots. As the creation story teaches, the brotherhood of humanity is the consequence of the fatherhood of God. We are all, equally, created in the Divine image. But very early in our mythical past, something went wrong. Our common root was denied and one brother killed another. Now it is much more difficult to see that all people and all religions share the same root. It looks like each tree produces its own unique fruit that shares little with the fruit of other trees. But it was not always that way, says *Tanhuma*. Nor will it be that way forever. In the words of the prophet Zechariah, "In that day, the LORD shall be one with one name" (14:9). We will relearn that we all have one Father (Mal. 2:10). Like many different fruits which blossom from a single tree, there are manifold people and religious expressions connected to the same Divine root.

Such a reading sounds suspiciously contemporary. Could *Tanhuma* have been that progressive? It is an unavoidable danger when reading any text for the interpreter to overlay his or her ideology onto the text. Indeed, this has occurred in many of the comments analyzed in this book. But there are two safeguards against such "unintentional midrash." The first is for authors to be self-conscious whenever interpretation and personal ideology overlap. The second safeguard is for the author to match an interpretation with ideas or themes in the broader context of the work. In our case, biblical verses, like those in Zechariah and Malachi, allow us to reconstruct a vision of the future in which all people recognize that they are all children of the same God. Furthermore, Deuteronomy 4:19 suggests that God has ordained different avenues of Divine service for different nations. One characteristic of the World to Come is that we will have learned to appreciate the 925 other ways of relating to God, while still finding our own way most fruitful for us. In the first chapter, I suggested that there are some ancient comments that seem ahead of their time. This comment from *Tanhuma* may be one.

The Immortality of Self-Love

24. For nowhere in the Torah has Cain's death been explicitly mentioned. This shows allegorically that folly is a deathless evil, never experiencing the end that consists in having died, but subject to all eternity to that which consists in ever dying.

(Philo, The Worse Attacks the Better[37])

Philo is an important figure in examining Jewish interpretations of Torah. Although his allegorical readings were not known in the Jewish world until the nineteenth century, Philo represents an early Jewish attempt at reading the Torah as religious *literature*. That's not to say that he dismissed the plain sense of Scripture and read Torah only as allegory, as some of the early Christians did (who were themselves influenced by Philo). Rather this Hellenistic Jew struggled to preserve the political and sociological elements within the Torah while adding a philosophical dimension through his allegorical interpretations.

In Philo's extended allegory of Cain and Abel, Cain represents self-love while Abel symbolizes love of God. Although many commentators claim that Lemech killed Cain (Gen. 4:23), the Torah is not explicit on this point. Philo exploits this lacuna to make an important psychological observation. Self-love, symbolized by Cain, is a constant threat to the religious (and philosophical) life. Placing our needs and desires above the love of God is idolatry. The lure of idolatry lingers. And idolatry, like Cain, is ultimately fatal.

The Power of Teshuvah

25. How do we know that Cain repented? And Cain said to the LORD, "My sin is too great [for You] to bear, i.e., forgive."

(P'sikta d'Rav Kahana, Shuva 11, Rabbinic collection, c. 5th century, Land of Israel; cf. Targum Onkelos)

This chapter began with the suggestion that the story of Cain and Abel was about free will and human responsibility. But is that all? Look back at the

NJPS and Fox translations of verse 13. Is Cain complaining, as the NJPS would have it? Or is he confessing, as the Fox translation might suggest? The Hebrew *'avon* can mean both iniquity and its consequence, namely, punishment. To complicate matters further, the verb *bear* (in Hebrew, *min'so*) is floating without a pronoun to anchor it to a specific actor. So whom does Cain mean to bear the sin? Himself or God? Ambiguity is a mother of midrash.

In this reading from *P'sikta d'Rav Kahana*, our story is also about the power of *teshuvah*, frequently translated as repentance, but literally *returning* or *responding*. According to this interpretation, Cain admitted his sin and understood the gravity of his offense.[38] He demonstrated character development. He grew. He returned to God's words from verse 7 and responded that he could have, and should have, overcome the temptation to harm his brother.

In addition to exploiting the opportunity to manufacture a precedent for *teshuvah*, which was particularly important after the destruction of the Temple and the cessation of animal sacrifices to effect atonement, *P'sikta d'Rav Kahana* also solves a textual perplexity. If we read the text solely in its plain (*peshat*) sense, Cain gets away with murder! Although he is punished by being condemned to be a "ceaseless wanderer" (v. 12) he then settles down in the Land of Nod (v. 16). Cain even receives Divine protection from being murdered himself (v. 15).[39] For the Rabbis, only *teshuvah* could explain such a Divine about-face. Although the Torah emphasizes free will and human responsibility, the ultimate message of this story, according to this traditional reading, is the power of *teshuvah* to change our future.[40]

Summary of Comments

Comment	Problem	Resolution	Textual Mechanism	Historical Circumstance
1.	Why sacrifice?	Supernal need	None	Kabbalistic assumption
2.	Why reject Cain's gift? Why an asymmetry in the descriptions of the gifts?	Inferior gift	Ambiguity of prepositions, conjunctions and the relationship between nouns in construct state	None
3.	Why reject? Why mention both gift and giver?	Impudence of giver	Emphasize giver	Mystical emphasis on kavanah

continued

Comment	Problem	Resolution	Textual Mechanism	Historical Circumstance
4.	Why reject? Gift and giver? Why "know" from v. 1?	Cain was the offspring of the serpent and therefore prone to evil	Emphasize giver/Unusual use of "know" in verse 1	Dualistic influences
5.	Shouldn't Cain get credit for initiating offerings?	Abel may have offered before Cain	Grammar of subject-predicate sequence indicating past perfect	Medieval attention to grammar under Arabic influence
6.	Why reject?/Why aren't God's favored protected?	To teach a lesson about the inherent injustice of being human	The righteous are not rewarded	Post-Shoah reflections
7.	Opaque pronouncement	Doing right = Talmud Torah Sin = *yetzer ha-ra* Door = Beit Midrash	None	Rabbinic value of Talmud Torah
8.	Opaque pronouncement	Sin = *yetzer ha-ra* Door = Entrance to this world	None	Aristotelian philosophy
9.	Opaque pronouncement	Sin = Demon Door = House	None	None
10.	Opaque pronouncement/Cain gets away with murder	Sin = Your sins Door = Entrance to the next world	None	Post-biblical concern with the next world
11.	Opaque pronouncement	Cain misunderstood God	Lack of un-gendered nouns in Hebrew	Modern tendency to shift perspectives/ Polemic with Reform Judaism?
12.	Redundancy in God's question/God's insensitivity	God's questioning Cain's *reason* for being angry in addition to embarrassed	2 different questions/ Emphasis on *Why?*	Hasidic emphasis on religious psychology
13.	God's insensitivity	God's insight and concern	Emphasis on *so*	Hasidic emphasis on religious psychology
14.	Missing dialogue/motive	Material wealth	Cain's name meaning acquisitive?	None
15.	Missing dialogue/motive	Religion	The sacrifices preceding the murder? (biblical context)	None
16.	Missing dialogue/motive	Woman	Whom does Cain later marry? (biblical context)	None

continued

Comment	Problem	Resolution	Textual Mechanism	Historical Circumstance
17.	Missing dialogue/motive	Abel: Emphasis on deeds Cain: Talks like an Apikorus/Sadducee	Emphasize givers from vv. 4–5	Hellenistic environment of post-Temple Judaism/Polemic with Sadducees
18.	Missing dialogue/motive	Interior monologue	Exchanging *ayin* for *aleph* to get the preposition *about*	Modern tendency to shift perspectives/ Polemic with Reform Judaism?
19.	Missing dialogue/motive	Cain's inability to speak	Missing dialogue	None
20.	Missing dialogue/motive	Abel's indifference	Abel's silence throughout text	Post-Shoah reflections
21.	Missing dialogue/motive	Lacuna represents communication breakdown	Visualization of text	Universal
22.	Missing dialogue/motive	Pre-emptive editing	Missing Dialogue	Universal
23.	What is the curse of v. 12?	Trees now only offer one kind of fruit	None	Messianic yearnings
24.	Why is Cain's death not mentioned?	Cain = Self-love which never dies	None	Hellenistic allegory
25.	Why wasn't Cain a ceaseless wanderer? Why was Cain protected?	*Teshuvah*	Ambiguity of 'avon and lack of pronoun	*Teshuvah* rather than sacrifice as atonement in post-Temple Judaism

NOTES

For those interested in how this story has been reworked in modern literature, Ricardo J. Quinones offers a partial survey and analysis in his *The Changes of Cain: Violence and the Lost Brother in Cain and Abel Literature*. Honor Matthews has brought together dramatic renditions of this story in his *The Primal Curse: The Myth of Cain and Abel in the Theatre*. There is also musical midrash on the story. The libretto of Scarlatti's "Il Primo Omicidio" offers several interesting midrashim, and the music itself is a powerful vehicle to convey the pathos of the tale.

1.   b. *Moed Katan* 9a and Ramban on Gen. 2:8, Exod. 29:46, and Lev. 1:9. See also Daniel Matt, "The Mystic and The Mizwot," in *Jewish Spirituality*, vol. 1, ed. Arthur Green (New York: Crossroad Publishing House, 1994), 367–404.

2.   For a comparison of these two thinkers, see Josef Stern, *Problems and Parables of Law: Maimonides and Nachmanides on Reasons for the Commandments* (Albany: State University of New York, 1998).

Specifically, on the function of prayer, see Marvin Fox, "Prayer and the Religious Life" in his *Interpreting Rambam: Studies in Methodology, Metaphysics, and Moral Philosophy* (Chicago: University of Chicago Press, 1990), and Abraham Joshua Heschel, *Man's Quest for God: Studies in Prayer and Symbolism* (New York: Crossroad Publishing, 1954).

3.   *Genesis Rabbah,* 33:6, 65:1 and 33:12. Rashi brings all these sources, thus "canonizing" Esau as an anti-saint.

4.   m. *Menachot* 13:11.

5.   Rabbi Bunam, in *Itturei Torah*, ed. Aharon Yakov Greenberg (Tel Aviv: Yavne Publishing House Ltd., 1996), 1:44.

6.   For an introduction to the characteristics of Hasidism, see Martin Buber, *Hasidism and Modern Man*, trans. Maurice Friedman (New York: Horizon Press, 1958), Yoram Jacobson, *Hasidic Thought*, trans. Jonathan Chipman (Tel Aviv: MOD Press, 1998), and Abraham Joshua Heschel, *A Passion for Truth* (New York: Farrar, Straus and Giroux, 1973). Heschel explores two poles of Hasidic thought represented by the joyous Baal Shem Tov and his foil, the Rebbe of Kotzk. On Hasidism and prayer, see Arthur Green and Barry W. Holtz, *Your Word is Fire: The Hasidic Masters on Contemplative Prayer* (New York: Paulist Press, 1977).

7.   See Augustine, *City of God*, bk. 16, chap. 27. The dogma is mitigated in the Eastern Orthodox Church as articulated by Athanasius (early 4 c.) For a full discussion, see Tatha Wiley, *Original Sin: Origins, Developments, Contemporary Meanings* (New York: Paulist Press, 2002).

8.   See Gen. 15:19 and Num. 24:21f. For a summary and refutation of this view, see Umberto Cassuto, *A Commentary on the Book of Genesis*, trans. Israel Abrahams (Jerusalem: Magnes Press, 1961–64), 179–184.

9.   James Kugel, "Cain and Abel in Fact and Fable: Genesis 4:1–16," in *Hebrew Bible or Old Testament? Studying the Bible in Judaism and Christianity*, ed. Roger Brooks and John J. Collins (Notre Dame: University of Notre Dame Press, 1990), 167–190.

10.   I John 3:10–12 makes this connection implicitly as do comments in the Zohar, e.g., 1:54a.

11.   Rashi on Gen. 4:1.

12.   This reading, only tentatively suggested by Radak, is supported by a contemporary biblical scholar. Ziony Zevit, "Invisible and Unheard in Translation: How New Discoveries in Hebrew Grammar Affect Our Understanding of TANAKH," *Conservative Judaism* 55, no. 2 (Winter 2003): 38–48. A very good grammar text is Marc Zvi Brettler, *Biblical Hebrew for Students of Modern Israeli Hebrew* (New Haven: Yale University Press, 2002).

13.   Cf. *Genesis Rabba* 22:9.

14.   *Messengers of God: Biblical Portraits and Legend*, trans. Marion Wiesel (New York: Simon & Schuster, 1976), 44.

15. One medieval philosopher, Joseph Albo, does suggest that Abel was guilty of a sin and thereby lost Divine protection. *Book of Principles*, 3:15.

16. This verse, even for the Rabbis, was among the most inscrutable in the entire Torah. See *Genesis Rabbah* 80:6.

17. Judith Bleich paints the background for the specific case of Malbim in "Rabbinic Responses to Nonobservance in the Modern Era," in *Jewish Tradition and the Nontraditional Jew*, ed. Jacob J. Schachter (Northvale, N.J.: Jason Aronson, 1992). See also Yaakov Geller, "The Malbim: Leadership and Challenge," in *Studia et Acta Historiae Iudaeorum Romaniae* (Bucharest: Editura Hasefer, 2002), 176–82.

18. *Tales of the Hasidim*, ed. Martin Buber (Schocken Books, 1991), 2:308.

19. *Itturei Torah*, 1:44.

20. Many ancient translations, like the Greek Septuagint and the Latin Vulgate, use a similar technique.

21. See, for example, Josephus, *Jewish Antiquities* 1:54. This pun was noted by the Rabbis in *Sifre*, Numbers 78:1, but they refrained from applying the linguistic connection to Cain.

22. The word, *hevel*, meaning something that has no permanence, reflects Abel's fate in our story. The word frequently appears in Ecclesiastes and is translated by NJPS as *futile*.

23. b. *Megillah* 29a and b. *Brachot* 6a.

24. 1 Kings 8:27, Isa. 6:3 and *Pesikta Rabbati* 5:7.

25. b. *Sanhedrin* 37a.

26. There is yet another exegetical problem that Cain taking his sister as a wife addresses. In Leviticus 20:17, we have an unusual description of brother-sister incest characterized as *hesed*, usually translated as mercy, but in this one instance NJPS translates it as *disgrace*. The Rabbis connected this verse to Cain procreating with his sister and populating the world. They understand this particular act of incest to be an act of mercy. *Sifra*, Kedoshim 11:11.

27. The Israeli Torah teacher, Nechama Leibowitz, emphasized this point.

28. Hebrews 9:11–26.

29. *Avot d'Rabbi Natan*, chaps. 4 and 11. m. *Yoma* 8:9.

30. The Rabbinic way of calling somebody a "dirty Greek philosopher" was to call him an Epicurean, or an Apikorus. For us in the West, Epicureanism suggests the promotion of sensual pleasures; for the Rabbis, it denies God's intervening role in the world.

31. m. *Sanhedrin* 10:1 frames similar ideas in a halachic setting.

32. "God, freedom, and immortality . . . are founded upon the moral use of reason, while speculation could not find sufficient guarantee even of their possibility." Immanuel Kant, *Critique of Practical Reason*, trans. Lewis White Beck, 3rd ed. (New York: Macmillan Publishing Company, 1993), 5.

33. This statement itself is a riff on I Corinthians 10:23.

34. Recent scholarship serves as a reminder to qualify these historical assertions since our scanty knowledge about these sects derives from polemical literature. Shaye J.D. Cohen, *From the Maccabees to the Mishnah* (Philadelphia: Westminster Press, 1987) offers a very readable history of the period. Menachem Kellner writes on the question of belief in *Must a Jew Believe Anything?* (Oxford: Littman Library of Jewish Civilization, 2006).

35. *Cain & Abel: Finding the Fruits of Peace* (Woodstock: Jewish Lights Publishing, 2001), 18.

36. Wiesel, 56ff.

37. Translation from Greek by F. H. Colson and G. H. Whitaker (Cambridge: Harvard University Press, 1958), 319.

38. At least one of the traditional commentators, the *Tanhuma*, accuses Cain of insincerity.

39. Giovanni Garbini attempts to resolve these curiosities with a historical theory rather than a religious one. *Myth and History in the Bible* (Sheffield: Sheffield Academic Press, 2003), 19–21.

Abraham B. Yehoshua offers a moral assessment of the story that reveals a significant punishment for Cain. "What Was the Real Punishment Inflicted on History's First Murderer?" in his collection of essays, *The Terrible Power of a Minor Guilt*, trans. Ora Cummings (Syracuse: Syracuse University Press, 2000), 3–16.

40. For the laws and philosophy of *teshuvah*, see Rambam, Laws of Repentance, *Mishneh Torah* and Rav Abraham Isaac Kook, *The Lights of Penitence, The Moral Principles, Lights of Holiness, Essays, Letters, and Poems*, trans. Ben Zion Bokser (New York: Paulist Press, 1978).

Chapter 4

THE HEBREW SLAVE

These are the rules that you shall set before them: ²When you acquire a Hebrew slave, he shall serve six years; in the seventh year he shall go free, without payment. ³If he came single, he shall leave single; if he had a wife, his wife shall leave with him. ⁴If his master gave him a wife, and she has borne him children, the wife and her children shall belong to the master, and he shall leave alone. ⁵But if the slave declares, "I love my master, and my wife and children: I do not wish to go free," ⁶his master shall take him before God. He shall be brought to the door or the doorpost, and the master shall pierce his ear with an awl; and he shall then remain his slave for life.

—Exodus 21:1–6

³⁹If your kinsman under you continues in straits and must give himself over to you, do not subject him to the treatment of a slave. ⁴⁰He shall remain with you as a hired or bound laborer; he shall serve with you only until the Jubilee year. ⁴¹Then he and his children with him shall be free of your authority; he shall go back to his family and return to his ancestral holding.—⁴²For they are My servants, whom I freed from the land of Egypt; they may not give themselves over into servitude.

—Leviticus 25:39–42

¹²If a fellow Hebrew, man or woman, is sold to you, he shall serve you six years, and in the seventh you shall set him free. ¹³When you set him free, do not let him go empty-handed: ¹⁴Furnish him out of the flock, threshing floor, and vat, with which the LORD your God has blessed you. ¹⁵Bear in mind that you were slaves in the land of Egypt and the LORD your God redeemed you; therefore I enjoin this commandment upon you this day.

[16]But should he say to you, "I do not want to leave you"—for he loves you and your household and is happy with you—[17]you shall take an awl and put it through his ear into the door, and he shall become your slave in perpetuity. Do the same with your female slave.

—Deuteronomy 15:12–17 (JPS TANAKH)

If a rose by any other name smells just as sweet, is bondage just as bitter? The subject of this chapter is the Hebrew slave. Or is it the Hebrew serf, or, perhaps, the Hebrew servant?[1] Our translation of Leviticus uses *slave* in verse 39 and *servant* in verse 42. One commentator, Rabbeinu Bahya, points out that the Hebrew term, *'eved*, is ambiguous. There are no distinct words in Hebrew to differentiate between a slave and a servant, or anything in between. *'Eved* is used to describe the Israelites in Egypt as well as the person whom Rabbeinu Bahya likens to a hired hand and for whom the master pays upfront. Nevertheless, this "hired hand" can be forced to play the stud and provide his master with a fresh stock of hands to perpetuate the system.

Regardless of the terminology, the Hebrew Bible and the world from which it emerges recognized slavery as a social reality. Even in the 14th century, when slavery was still the norm, we sense that Rabbeinu Bahya felt defensive about its existence in the Torah. I, too, cannot help but being defensive and apologetic about the laws regulating the sale and treatment of human beings. Given the dissonance between the Bible's posture toward slavery and our own, this subject affords a fascinating case study of Jewish interpretations of the Hebrew Bible with the verses in Exodus serving as our central focus. (One should not confuse these *interpretations*, however, with the social reality of Jews in post-biblical times.[2]) Before beginning with the content of the laws themselves, though, our commentators ask more general questions.

First Impressions

1. Why are these civil laws adjacent to the previous chapter's laws regarding the altar? This tells you to put the high court of law near the Temple.

(Rashi, 1040–1105, France)

Rashi slides between the literary geography of this chapter and the literal geography of the Temple in Jerusalem that housed both the sacrificial altar and the Sanhedrin, the High Court. One of Rashi's many commentators, Judah Loew ben Bezalel of Prague (c. 1525–1609), spells out what is implicit in Rashi's comment: "Just as the sacrificial altar establishes peace between the individual Jew and God, the civil laws establish peace in the world." The altar is the venue for addressing wrongs committed against God, while the court is the venue for addressing wrongs between people. The compartmentalization we sometimes experience, and perpetuate, between the sacred and mundane is artificial. The literary style of the Torah and the sacred structures of Judaism both point to the unity of ethics and monotheism.

2. *There's nothing in the world more difficult for a man than to be under the authority of someone like himself. That's why the civil laws begin here.*
(Abraham ibn Ezra, 1089–1164, Spain)

3. *The first law begins with the Hebrew slave because sending out the slave in the seventh year is reminiscent of the exodus from Egypt mentioned as the first utterance of the Decalogue (Ex. 20:2).*
(Ramban, 1194–1270, Spain)

Ibn Ezra focuses on the psychology of the slave. It is humiliating to lose one's freedom, and ibn Ezra emphasizes that the master is not of a different order of man than the slave. As the prophet Malachi says, "Have we not all one Father?"(2:10). Whatever the name we use, being under the control of anyone else chafes.

Ramban, like Rashi, sees the placement of the law of the Hebrew slave more in terms of literary structure than psychology. The previous chapter of Exodus contained the Decalogue which begins by God introducing himself to the Israelites as their liberator from the house of bondage in Egypt. Ramban sees parallels between the elements of the Decalogue and subsequent commandments. In this case, we learn from God's actions; we follow in God's ways (Deut. 8:19). Just as God liberated the Israelites from their bondage, so should every Israelite do the same. Ramban, unlike ibn Ezra, points out that the thrust of our verses is not about slavery, but about setting the slave free. The obligation to release the slave in the seventh year already distinguishes this form of slavery from many others. But, beginning with the Rabbis, how the slaves were treated in those six years furthers the distinction.

Defining Terms

4. *"And when your brother sinks down (in poverty) beside you, and sells himself to you, you shall not make him serve the servitude of a serf"* (Fox

*translation, Lev. 25:39). "'My brother'?! Does this mean I need to treat him
fraternally? He's still called a slave in our verse in Exodus!"*

You must treat him fraternally; but he is to consider himself a slave.

(from *Sifra*, Behar 7, 3rd century, Land of Israel)

The *Sifra* highlights the paradox: he's your brother *and* your slave. It's an uncomfortable situation best negotiated by clear rules. And since the parties do not share equal authority, the Rabbis placed the burden of restrictions on the master.

The *Sifra*, a halakhic midrash on Leviticus, also raises another issue: the laws of the Hebrew slave are articulated in three different sections of the Torah. What's more, the sections contain different terms of service and terminology. For instance, the passage in Leviticus stipulates that Hebrew slaves be freed at the Jubilee, which occurs every fifty years, not in the seventh year as our verse from Exodus states. The Rabbis, reading the Torah as a perfect, unitary document, could not abide by the thought that there were contradictions between sections. Therefore, much of the Rabbinic program will be to reconcile what modern biblical scholars consider to be disparate documents voicing different treatments of the Hebrew slave.

In addition to these different treatments of the Hebrew slave, the Torah is quite clear that there are different kinds of slaves, namely the Hebrew slave (*'eved ivri*) and the non-Hebrew slave (*'eved cena'ani*). Rabbinic tradition understands that the slave from our verses in Exodus is a Hebrew and not an alien slave acquired from a Hebrew. All codes of ancient laws make the distinction, as do many contemporary ones, between outsiders and insiders, affording preferential treatment to the latter. Israelite law is no exception. Leviticus 25:44–46 confirms this two-tiered system whereby the alien slave could be worked harder and kept as inheritable chattel.

Even within the category of Hebrew slave, though, there were distinctions. A halakhic midrash on Exodus, the Mekhilta D'Rabbi Yishmael, deliberates on which kind of slave is being described in our verses.

5. This slave was sold by a court because he stole something and then, when caught, could not make restitution.

But maybe it's talking about someone who sold himself?

No. That case is covered in Leviticus when it says, "And when your brother sinks down (in poverty) beside you, and sells himself to you . . ." (25:39). Therefore, this case must be about the one sold by the court.

(Mekhilta, 3rd century, Land of Israel)

Although the Mekhilta doesn't come right out and say it, Rashi does, which is why he is nearly indispensable for understanding the Rabbinic Torah. The next chapter of laws discusses a thief who is sold when he can't pay back the value of the theft plus the penalty (Exod. 22:2). The case in Leviticus has the person selling himself on account of his impoverished state. Our thief doesn't sell himself of his own volition; he is sold on account of his theft. One implication of this distinction is that the person who sells himself is not necessarily released in the seventh year. He can negotiate, should he desire, for a longer period of servitude up to the occasion of the Jubilee year. With this distinction between the two types of Hebrew slaves, the tension between our passage in Exodus and Leviticus dissolves. The six years of Exodus applies to the Jewish thief; the 49 years of Leviticus to the Jewish pauper.

Why Six and Which Seventh?

6. Perhaps the reason for six years corresponds to three acts of thievery: the person's money, the person's trust, and the Almighty's trust. The thief gets one year for each act of thievery and the penalty is then doubled to six years, as it says "he shall pay double" (Exod. 22:3). But there are others who claim that this falls into the pattern of sevens that were chosen for rest as a reminder of the renewal of the world, like Shabbat, the Shmittah and the Jubilee, since all sevens were chosen for rest. This is more correct.

(Shlomo Ephraim of Lunschitz, 1550–1619, Prague and Poland)

Shlomo Ephraim points out that every crime against one of God's creatures is also a crime against God. In our case, the thief has stolen not only the person's property, but also his trust in the society and its rules. Since all criminals violate the terms of the covenant with God, those three acts are then doubled, as the law in Exodus 22 stipulates, to arrive at the number of years which the thief must serve as a slave.

Clever. Perhaps it was too clever, and Shlomo Ephraim felt such a calculation was artificial. His second suggestion, toward which he leans, is rooted in the very structure of the world. Sevens are respites. The seventh day, when God ceased world-creating activity, Israelites similarly refrain from creative work (Exod. 20:7–11). The seventh year, the *Shmittah*, is a year of release when all agricultural fields in the Land of Israel lie fallow and debts are forgiven (Lev. 25:3–5 and Deut. 15:1–3). Seven cycles of seven years culminates in the advent of the fiftieth year, the Jubilee. To mark this occasion, family and tribal units return to their ancestral holdings (Lev. 25:13). And, as we have seen, slaves are manumitted (Lev. 25:39–40). After forty-nine years of family dislocation, alienation from the tribe, and the vagaries of personal misfortune, entropy is reversed. Things are brought back to their initial equilibrium. The poor stop getting poorer and the rich richer. God created a world which was very good, and the Israelites are enjoined to prevent the world from sliding into social injustice by the elimination of those initial boundary conditions.[3] Just as the people of Israel were meant to inhabit the Land of Israel, people were meant to be free. It is no accident that on the Sabbath, which the sages describe as a taste of the coming world when Israel shall again dwell securely in its borders, the accidental disparities between the slave and the master are temporarily leveled.[4] The slave, too, rests on Shabbat (Exod. 20:10).

Shlomo Ephraim also mentions that this pattern of sevens is a reminder of the renewal of the world. The greatest single point of contention in the Middle Ages between those with a religious worldview and those with a philosophic or scientific worldview concerned the origin of the world. The philosophers, following Aristotle, maintained the world was eternal. It is now as it always was and always will be. Nature never changes its course. Religious thinkers in Judaism, Christianity, and Islam denied this assumption and maintained that God created the world as we know it. Jewish liturgy refers to God as daily renewing acts of creation. The idea of continual renewal is that creation has not been relegated to a historical drama but is an ongoing process. The existence of the world depends on continuous Divine infusion. God does change the course of nature, and this connection between God and the world is solace for those longing for their own plights to be transformed. As the psalmist writes, "You turned my lament into dancing, you undid my sackcloth and girded me with joy" (Ps. 30:12). The renewal of the world allows the future, as Jean-Paul Sartre said, to be virgin, and not entirely determined by the past.

7. Why the seventh year? Since there's no plowing, sowing, reaping, or harvesting, there's less work.
    (Joseph Bechor Shor, 1130–1200, France; cf. *Targum Pseudo-Jonathan*)

Bechor Shor's assumption is that the slave is released in the *Shmittah* year regardless of when the sale occurred. There is a certain logic that when there's less work to be done, there's less need for slaves. Furthermore, the law in Leviticus stipulates that the slave is to be freed at the Jubilee, which occurs on a fixed cycle of 50 years. Since the Leviticus slave is liberated according to a fixed calendar, the Exodus slave should be, as well. (Like the Jubilee, the *Shmittah* years fall according to a fixed seven-year cycle.) There's also a literary parallel. The language describing the *Shmittah* in Exodus 23:11 is the ordinal number, seventh. It's the same in our verse. Theoretically, either verse could have read, "And after six years." Bechor Shor combined the logic of the agricultural cycle, the fixed period of manumission in Leviticus, and the linguistic parallel with the seventh year to conclude that the Hebrew slave is to be released in the *Shmittah* year.

The problem with the logic is two-fold, as the Rabbis recognized. First of all, it hardly seems just to have thieves' periods of enslavement vary depending on when they committed their crime. If this were the case, crime rates might spike in the period preceding the *Shmittah*! In addition to this logical problem, there's a textual one: "He shall serve six years" (Exod. 21:2). The Rabbis understood that justice to the text, and to one thief compared to his brother, required a six-year term.[5]

Bechor Shor was a younger contemporary of, and in the same school as, the Rashbam. As we will see, both of these *pashtanim* were willing to interpret the Torah independently of how the Rabbis determined the *halakhah*. In this case, Bechor Shor was well aware that his understanding of *the seventh* was not consistent with Jewish law. But the intrinsic value of *peshat* does not vitiate the centrality of the *halakhah*. In Rashbam's introduction to our laws, he writes, "I have not come to explain the *halakhah* even though they are the essential things . . . I have come to explain the *peshat* of the verses." Bechor Shor would agree.[6]

Terms of Enslavement

8. *"He shall serve six years." I might understand this to mean any kind of service. But, the Torah says, "Do not subject him to the treatment of a slave" (Lev. 25:39). From this verse, the Rabbis said, "A Hebrew slave may not wash the feet of his master, nor put on his shoes, nor carry his things in front of him when the master goes to the bathhouse. . . ."*

I might understand "He shall serve six years" to mean disgraceful work. But, the Torah says, "as a hired laborer" (Lev. 25:40). Just as you cannot force a hired laborer to change his profession, you can't force a Hebrew slave. From this verse, the Rabbis said, "His master may not put him to work serving the public. For example, he may not serve as a well attendant, a barber, a tailor, or a cook. . . ." Also from this verse we learn that just as a hired laborer works during the day but not during the night, so, too, does the Hebrew slave work during the day but not the night.

(Mekhilta, Nezikin)

On a technical level, the Rabbis are applying the more merciful conditions of Leviticus to the situation in Exodus. In other words, the pauper and the thief get the same treatment! While contemporary Bible scholars may see these sources as independent traditions, the Rabbis perceived a Divine unity which required read-ing each in the light of the other. Morally, the Rabbis here demonstrate concern for the dignity of the slave. His work is not to be demeaning. His disgrace is not to be paraded publicly. And his labor is not to be exploited.[7] The Rabbis, "bear-ing in mind" that they are descendants of slaves from Egypt (Deut. 15:15), are struggling to make this socially tolerated system of slavery as humane as possible.

> *9. It has been taught, "'And [the Hebrew slave] is happy with you' (Deut. 15:16). With you in food and with you in drink. Don't you eat fine flour while he eats inferior flour, or drink aged wine while he drinks young wine, or sleep on a mattress while he sleeps in straw." Because of this teaching, the sages said, "Anyone who acquires a Hebrew slave is like one who acquires a master for himself."*
>
> (Gemara, *Kiddushin* 22a, 6th century, Babylonia)

The Gemara here is particularly interesting because the clause it *derashes* is taken from a description of the slave who wants to stay with his master and have his ear pierced. The Rabbis extrapolate that all slaves should be treated so well. They are members of the household, sharing the same vintage and sleeping on the same thread count even to the extent of resting on the Sabbath and holi-days. More than even a member of the household, it's as though the slave is the master's guest—a provocative model of criminal rehabilitation! A commentary on the Talmud asks the question, "What if the master has only one mattress?" The answer is that the slave gets the mattress while the master gets the straw; otherwise, the master would be in violation of the slave being "happy with you."[8] The Gemara's statement, that one who acquires a Hebrew slave is like one who acquires a master, is understandable, yet paradoxical. Theoretically, one only becomes a slave when one is lacking means and either steals or sells himself. If one had the means, why would one want to acquire a master? A Hasidic teach-ing suggests that the acquisition has been arranged by the Master of masters.

> *10. It's obvious that the slave has some deficiency; otherwise he wouldn't have stolen in the first place. But the master also has a deficiency—he believes that he is solely responsible for his own success. Furthermore, he believes that his material well-being is the ultimate good. The master's arrogance blinds him to the reality that all is from God and that nothing happens without God. Ultimate good is beyond the ability of humans to attain; it lies with God.*
>
> *Once the master experiences the worry and struggle to provide for his slave, he'll realize that he is a conduit connecting God's goodness to the*

slave. God is providing for the slave through the human master. The master will then come to understand that his own wealth was similarly due to the grace of God, and that ultimate goodness lies at the conclusion of a long life dedicated to blessing others with his gifts.

(from Yakov Leiner, 1828–1878, Poland)

It's easy to imagine a person of wealth, seemingly on top of the world, sneering at those beneath him, ignoring God above him, and unwilling to see himself as one member in a larger community. "Beware lest your heart grow haughty and you forget the LORD your God . . . and you say to yourselves, 'My own power and the might of my own hand have won this wealth for me'" (Deut. 8:14,17). The Beit Yakov, as Leiner is called after the title of his Hasidic commentary, suggests that the person who acquires a Hebrew slave needs a lesson in humility and community. And God, who is the author of all reality, has written the lesson into the master's life. When the master quips how good his slave has it, only working for a few hours a day and being taken care of by the master, he will realize that he, the master, is no different. He also is being provided for. His wealth is not a reflection of his own power, but of God's (Deut. 8:18). Moreover, the slave works for his master. But what does the master do for God? It is at this point that our Hasidic master, concerned not with legal formalities but with religious psychology, imagines that the slave master understands that his mission is to become a vehicle to distribute those gifts with which he has been temporarily entrusted by God's munificence and grace. "Furnish him out of the flock, threshing floor, and vat, with which the LORD your God has *blessed you*" (Deut. 15:14).

A cynical reading of this teaching might see a synagogue appeal for funds from the congregation's wealthy members. Perhaps. But I suspect that the Beit Yakov is pointing out that we all need each other; the ecology of the human community is symbiotic. The master could not have discovered his own deficiency without the slave. The Talmud says that more than the calf needs to suckle, the heifer needs to nurse.[9] When you have so much to give, holding back is harmful, whether you know it or not.

Caveat Emptor

11. Even if the slave was sick and the master incurred great expenses to heal him, the slave owes the master nothing, as the Torah says, "In the seventh year he shall go free, without payment."

(Rambam, 1180, Egypt; *Mishneh Torah,* Laws of Slaves, ch. 12, end; cf. *Sifre, Re'eh,* 65)

Buyer, beware! First of all, "without payment," in its immediate context, may very well mean that the slave does not have to redeem himself
from slavery. After his time is served, he is free to leave. But the Rabbinic
tradition has understood this term to mean that in almost all imaginable
circumstances, even if the slave was incapacitated for more than three
years, he owes the master nothing. What's more, since the master is
responsible for the slave's well-being, the master is liable for the slave's
medical treatment. So, one could find oneself in a situation where one is
saddled with a sick slave and medical bills instead of a productive pair of
hands. One wonders if it might not be more prudent to hire a day worker,
especially when the coup de grace is that, following Deuteronomy's charge,
the master has to provide the liberated slave from his own stock. Not
only does the slave go free, without paying the master, the master actually
pays him!

All in the Family

*12. Rabbi Shimon said, "If he was sold, was his wife sold, too?! From her
inclusion in the Torah we learn that the master is responsible for feeding
the slave's wife." [A similar strategy is used on the verses in Leviticus 25 to
learn that the master is also responsible to feed the slave's children.]*

(Gemara, *Kiddushin*, 22a)

The bump for Rabbi Shimon is that the Torah mentions the slave's wife at
all. She wasn't sold as a slave like her husband. Isn't it obvious that she's free
to go with her husband? The Rabbis' perception of the Torah is that it would-
n't bother to state the obvious. Therefore, it intends to teach us something,
in this case that it is the master's responsibility to feed his slave's wife and
children.

In our country, when a man is imprisoned, his family is not maintained by
the government. One can imagine that the slave's family would similarly be
left to their own devices. The Rabbis could not imagine such a thing. The
wife and the children should not be punished for the crimes of the man.
(Even more so if the Hebrew slave sells himself because of poverty.) The master may acquire the work of the male slave, but he acquires responsibility for
his entire family.

The Slaves Demand Their Due

There was a great famine in the land of Russia. The leaders of the community wrote to Rabbi Aryeh Leib, the Shpoler Zeide of Ukraine (1724–1811), to intercede on their behalf. He instructed them to convene a tribunal of ten leading rebbes or tzaddikim.

"The Almighty is negligent of His responsibilities," began the Shpoler Zeide. "If the Jewish people are His children, it is the obligation of the father to provide the needs of the children. Why does the Creator of the Universe not provide them with food, thereby preventing their death from hunger?"

The Shpoler Zeide continued, "And if we are slaves as the Torah says, 'For the Israelites are My slaves,' Jewish law teaches that a master is required to provide for his slaves, as well as the wife and children of his slaves. Can the Almighty violate His own Torah so blatantly?!"

The tzaddikim who comprised the tribunal, after fitful deliberation, found God guilty of dereliction of duty. The Almighty was enjoined to provide for the Jews of Russia. Three days later, news of a huge shipment of wheat from Siberia reached the town. The price of grain immediately plummeted, and the famine was relieved.

(Hasidic legend)

13. Rabbi Nachman bar Yitzchak said this: "If the Hebrew slave has a wife and children, then the master can give him a gentile slave woman. If he has no wife or children, then his master does not give him a gentile slave woman."

(Gemara, *Kiddushin* 20a)

When we initially read verses 3 and 4 of Exodus 21, we naturally read them as independent of one another. Regardless of whether or not the Hebrew slave is married (v. 3), the master can give him a slave woman (v. 4). Rabbi Nachman bar Yitzchak reads verse 4 as dependent upon the final clause of verse 3: if and only if the slave comes in married can the master give him a gentile slave woman in order to sire more slaves.

This reading of the verses, with which our medieval *pashtan*, Rashbam, cannot concur, severely limits the number of slaves able to perpetuate the institution of slavery. But there's an additional reason that the sages may have legislated that single men could not serve as studs—they might enjoy it! If a single man, a thief, suddenly finds himself a family man, he might be tempted to remain in that position even after his six-year term is over. The Rabbis wanted to remove any incentive for an Israelite to remain a slave and, therefore, prohibited the single man from being the recipient of a gentile slave woman.[10]

14. There are those who say that the reason that the master can give a gentile slave woman to the married Hebrew slave is because, after all, the master is responsible for feeding the slave's wife and children. If the master couldn't get more slaves out of the relationship, no one would want to incur such liabilities.

(from Shlomo Ephraim of Lunschitz)

A voice of fiscal prudence. Shlomo Ephraim speaks not only for the masters in society who need to get their value from their purchase; he is also speaking for the victim of the initial theft. If the demand for Hebrew slaves falls because of all the liabilities attached to such a purchase, so does the thief's sale price. Then the victim of the slave's theft might not receive the funds due him. The ironic byproduct, therefore, of compensating the Israelite victim from a crime perpetrated by another Israelite is to increase the number of gentile slaves. (The children of a gentile slave woman are themselves gentile slaves.)

Shifting Perspectives

15. The laws of the Hebrew slave begin in Exodus 21:2 in the second person: "When you acquire a Hebrew slave. . . ." By verse 4, the text has shifted to the third person: "If his master gave him. . . ." The institution of slavery is unconscionable and we respond with disgust by distancing ourselves from the thought.

(Meshi, contemporary, United States)

Meshi reads himself into the text: "When *you* acquire a Hebrew slave." He recoils from the thought of treating another human being, an image of God, as a commodity. "Me? Acquire a slave? Unimaginable!" The chasm that opens up between Meshi and the Torah, as he reads the text, is indicated by the shift from the immediacy of the second person to the distant third person.

Of Sound Minds

16. The Rabbis taught: " 'But if the serf should say, yes, say . . .' (Fox transla-
tion, Exodus 21:5). He must say it twice, at the beginning of the sixth year
and at the end."

(from Gemara, *Kiddushin* 22a)

The slave must declare his desire to stay with the master when he knows
exactly what it means to be a slave *and* while he is still a slave. The rule seems
reasonable enough, especially if your intent is to minimize such occurrences as
was clearly the Rabbis' goal. The Talmud insists if the slave's words do not
conform to this timing, his ear is not to be pierced.

If you are following in the NJPS translation, the Rabbis' law would be
mystifying. "How did they come up with having to say it twice?" The Fox
translation, as awkward as the English is, gives the answer. The Hebrew uses a
grammatical form called the *infinite absolute* that adds emphasis. The Hebrew
itself uses *says* twice. From this emphatic doubling, the Rabbis learn that the
slave must be equally emphatic about committing to permanent slave status.
Although not all Rabbis accepted the principle that *infinite absolutes* are always halakhically available for *drashing*,[11] in this particular instance, there was
no opposition.

17. Both the slave and the master must have a wife and children, both must
be healthy, and the affection and attachment must be mutual. [These condi-
tions are all from Gemara, Kiddushin 22a.] If we imagine the absence of
even one of these conditions, the decision to stay may well have been made
in haste. If the master is now single, and later on a wife and children enter
the home, or if the slave is now single and later on a wife and children enter
the home, the conditions could easily become unbearable. If either of them
is sick, the decision may have been made out of a feeling of weakness or
dependence which would pass when he regains his health. . . . If the feeling
of affection is not reciprocated, the decision is considered unnatural and
indicative of a perverse emotional state. Such consequential decisions
should not be made in such a state of mind.

(from Samson Raphael Hirsch, 1808–1888, Germany)

Rabbinic Judaism is paternalistic. It won't let you make too big a mistake.
For instance, when you're buying or selling an object, it must be within one-
sixth of the market price, otherwise you can reverse the transaction.[12] In our

case, the Gemara in *Kiddushin* prohibits the slave from having his ear pierced unless a number of requirements are all fulfilled. (These requirements are all *derashed* from our various verses and summarized in the concluding chart.) Samson Raphael Hirsch explains the logic of the Gemara in a way which makes the Rabbis seem psychologically astute to his nineteenth-century audience of enlightened Jews. The choice to stay with the master may have seemed like a good idea at the time, but the Rabbis, and their Torah, know better. This, after all, is a decision with momentous consequences for all involved.

The Mishnah offers another example of such paternalism. If Ploni believes he is about to die, gifts all his property to Almoni, and then Ploni recovers—the gift is invalid. But, if Ploni holds on to a little something for himself, the gift is valid. The Rabbis understand that had Ploni been of sound mind, he would have taken into account that he might recover and then be left with absolutely nothing. Since he didn't account for that possibility, he must not have been of sound mind, and, therefore, his gift is invalidated.[13] Interestingly, as the Gemara turns this case over and over, it arrives at the scenario of Ploni gifting all his property to his slave, Almoni. Since Almoni is part of Ploni's property, such a gift includes Almoni's own manumission. When Ploni recovers, he gets his property back, but Almoni remains a free man. Regained freedom is irrevocable, or so the Rabbis insisted on legislating.[14]

Who Do You Love?

18. *Sefat Emet adds a comment on the slave's words: "I love my master." He sets this against the Commandment, "You shall love God." Effectively, the slave is proclaiming an easier way of loving God, through love of the master and of all the provisions of his slave status. He prefers the indirect form of religious life. This, however, represents a regressive mode, a failure, essentially, of the ear.*

In this passage, the Chasidic writer attaches the largest value to the faculty of hearing. The destiny of the Jewish people, he claims, lies precisely in their openness to the continual revelation of the not-yet-revealed. The already-revealed is to be obeyed; but beyond that, and closer to the heart of the spiritual life, is the constant quest indicated by [listening for God]. The slave becomes a prototype of a stupefied existence, which confines itself to correct behavior. In such an existence, what is loved is the "master," not God. . . .

The slave in love with slavery has offended against the ear, in a way that no specific violation of the law can match. He has "deafened" himself to

the voice that speaks each day and makes Revelation a daily affair. Indeed,
the words that the slave uses, "I do not wish to go free" —lo etze—*jars*
against the primary theme of Exodus. In a book where "going out of Egypt"
is the thematic premise, "I shall not go out" resonates demonically.

(Aviva Zornberg, contemporary, Israel)[15]

Aviva Zornberg, among the most perceptive of contemporary Torah commentators, frequently cites the Hasidic masters. In this passage, she brings the
comments of Rabbi Yehudah Leib Alter of Ger (1847–1905), author of the
Sefat Emet. By way of explaining why the ear is pierced as a sign of perpetual
slavery, the Sefat Emet zeroes in on the slaves' own words—he loves his
master. Fox's translation captures the problematic better—he loves his *lord.*
The Hebrew is *adon,* which is used for both the human and Divine lords. Our
Hebrew slave has decided to love the LORD through loving his lord and
that represents an abdication of responsibility. The slave is content to be
told how to worship God without "keeping himself alert to further and finer
intimations of God's will."[16] He has replaced the yoke of the Kingdom of God
with the yoke of the slave master.

The Sefat Emet's comments may well have been targeting those in his
own Hasidic world. The leadership structure of Hasidism involve many
Hasidim under the guidance of a single, charismatic figure called the *tzaddik.*
Some tzaddikim (pl. of tzaddik) were critical of those followers who relied on
their masters for their spiritual connection. Each of us has to do our spiritual
work ourselves, according to this school of Hasidic thought, which included
the Sefat Emet. The critique, of course, might apply to any figure or structure
that serves as an intermediary between the individual and God, be it a priest,
rabbi or even the *halakhah.* Zornberg emphasizes that not wishing to go free,
preferring the lazy comfort of spiritual slavery to hearing the Lord for oneself,
has demonic overtones. As Jesus said, "No servant can serve two masters"
(Matt. 6:24).[17]

The Boring Details

Our final verse begins with the master taking the slave before God. Almost all
the commentaries agree that this expression means the judges who are God's
representatives. The Mekhilta raises the possibility, only to reject it, that the
slave was brought to the gates of the town, where the judges sat, and had his
ear pierced in full public view. Such a public piercing was considered by the
Rabbis to be degrading and, therefore, they argued that after the slave was

brought to the judges for consultation, he was then taken back to the master's home where the piercing was done in private. Both Abraham ibn Ezra and Rashbam agree that the text here is speaking of a public piercing. In other words, these medieval *pashtanim* rehabilitate as the *peshat* precisely what the Rabbis of the Mekhilta rejected. Assuming then, with the Rabbis, that the door in question is that of the master's home, the question now posed is why a door rather than a wall or some other surface.

> 19. Rabbi Shimon bar Yochai derashed this verse as an allegory: Why are the door and doorposts different from anything else in the house? The Holy One, blessed be He, said, "The door and the doorposts were my witnesses in Egypt at the time that I passed over the doors, and I said, 'The Israelites are my slaves' (Lev. 25:55), not slaves of slaves. I took them from slavery to freedom and this one went and got himself a master—let him be pierced before them!"
>
> (Gemara, Kiddushin 22b)

The doors in Egpyt were a symbol of God's new relationship with the Israelites (Exod. 12:23). In a bit of an anachronism that underscores what Jon D. Levenson calls the "literary simultaneity of Scripture,"[18] our *darshan* pulls from Leviticus, the third book of the Torah, to explain the details of a law from Exodus, the second book of the Bible. But what is Rabbi Shimon's real point? The piercing is a punishment, a stigma for swapping one Lord for another. (The repetition of the word *adon* in verse 6 reinforces the exchange.) Shlomo Ephraim of Lunschitz makes this explicit. He links the doorpost to the words of the Shema (Deut. 6:4–9) written in the mezuzah that is affixed to the doorpost of Jewish homes. It's almost as if the master is dragging the slave by the ear and pulling the ear up to the doorpost so the slave can hear the words of the Shema—"Hear, O Israel! The LORD is our God, the LORD alone. You shall love the LORD your God with all your heart and with all your soul and with all your might." Since he refuses to hear, to be whole-hearted in his love for God, his ear is marked as defective. Our *pashtan*, Rashbam, has a more prosaic explanation for why the door is singled out—it's made out of wood, so the awl can easily penetrate the ear and the door.

> 20. Why is the ear singled out to be pierced? Rabban Yochanan ben Zackai said it was like an allegory: "The ear that heard 'Do not steal,' (Exod. 20:13) went and stole. Let it be pierced!"
>
> (Mekhilta)

This midrashic explanation ties two strings together. First of all, it links our chapter with the previous chapter in which the commandment prohibiting theft appears in the Decalogue. Secondly, it reinforces the Rabbinic interpretation that the slave we are dealing with in this chapter is the thief who cannot afford to make restitution. Rabban Yochanan brings these threads together as an explanation of why it is that the slave's ear is pierced rather than some other part of the body.

But what of the slave who sells himself but has not stolen? He, too, is prescribed to have his ear pierced if he chooses to remain a slave. But he did not violate the commandment against stealing. So, why bore his ear? Rabban Yochanan ben Zackai suggests yet another allegory.

21. God said, "The ear that heard my voice at Mount Sinai when I said 'The Israelites shall be my slaves' (Lev. 25:55) and not the slaves of slaves, but who then went and took another master for himself—let his ear be pierced!"

(Gemara, Kiddushin 22b)

In both cases, Rabban Yochanan understands the Torah to be telling us something about the slave. He has, allegorically or symbolically, hollowed himself out. Aviva Zornberg brings the Sefat Emet to emphasize that the offense against the ear is the decision to stop listening to God and for God. The punishment is measure for measure: just as the (future) slave has partially removed God from his consciousness, he will have his ear, the organ of perception, partially removed. The principle of being God's exclusive slaves, articulated in Leviticus, informs Rabban Yochanan's understanding of the halakhah in Exodus. But, in the case of one who sells himself and exchanges one master for another, isn't there a problem with the chronology of this explanation?

22. Why don't we pierce his ear immediately after he sells himself? At the time, he's in dire straits and unaware of the degradation attendant to slavery. But after he has tasted slavery and still refuses to be a free man, let him be pierced and carry with him the sign of slavery for the rest of his days.

(Torah Gems, Divrei Peninim; cf. Sefat Emet)

Judaism, more than any other ancient law code, distinguishes between different states of mind. The halakhah has different consequences for those who violate a commandment knowingly and unknowingly. Even in the latter category, there's a different consequence for those who unintentionally break the law out of ignorance and those who inadvertently break a law they know about. ("I didn't know that was illegal" versus "I didn't mean to do that precisely because I know that is illegal.")

The *Divrei Peninim* explains the time delay for piercing the ear as a result of the change in the slave's awareness. The piercing is not for initially selling oneself in order to stave off starvation; it's for continuing to serve as a slave after experiencing the humiliation of being in someone else's control. The piercing is for not recognizing God as the exclusive Lord after six long years of experience with a human master.

The story of Exodus, as Zornberg reminds us, is the movement from being Pharoah's slaves to being free to serve God (Exod. 7:16). The traditional prayer service begins each morning by thanking God that we are not slaves who are unable to fully dedicate ourselves to worshipping God.[19] It concludes each evening by praising God who delivered Israel from Egypt to everlasting freedom. We recount the exodus from Egypt every year at Passover in order to reinforce that psychological shift from slavery to freedom. The Passover *haggadah*, the holiday's skeletal script, says, "In each and every generation one must see himself as if he left from Egypt." The one who has himself pierced reverses the gains of the exodus.

All these explanations, as Rabban Yochanan says, are by way of reading our text allegorically, as if the external piercing reflects the internal emptiness. Academic bible scholars, who use other ancient Near-Eastern texts to help them understand the Bible, teach us that according to the Laws of Hammurabi and Middle Assyrian Laws, piercing a slave's ear or cutting it off altogether was the standard punishment for rebellion.[20] Thus, Rabban Yochanan's non-allegorical reading would be that "the piercing of the ear is indeed a punishment imposed upon a [Hebrew] slave who has rebelled against his true master, the Lord of all Israel."[21] On a more functional level, the piercing is a sign of slavery, like a branding. Our medieval precursor to contemporary Bible scholars, Rashbam, says as much.[22]

Forever Yours

The law in Exodus and Deuteronomy says that after the piercing, the slave remains with the master forever. The law in Leviticus, however, says that the slave shall serve until the Jubilee year. The Leviticus text makes no mention of release after six years. The Rabbis, in an effort to reconcile these contradicting traditions, claim that all slaves must be released upon the occasion of the Jubilee.

23. "Forever"—until the Jubilee. Or, maybe it means literally "forever"? But the Torah says, "You are to hallow the year, the fiftieth year, proclaiming freedom throughout the land and to all its inhabitants; it shall be Homebringing for you, you are to return, each-man to his holding, each-man to his clan you are to return" (Lev. 25:10, Fox translation).

(Mekhilta)

Competing claims and competing values. One can imagine that thieving slaves would be exempt from the release of the Jubilee. That could have been the decision. But, given the values of the Rabbis, if there was a way to circumvent the law of both Exodus and Deuteronomy, which says the slave is to be held forever, the Rabbis will do so. The text in Leviticus proclaiming freedom (which Bible scholars might say has nothing to do with our text in Exodus) does have each man returning to his holding.

But to promote a "values" influenced reading at the expense of exegesis would be to do a disservice to the Rabbis. After all, what is the Jubilee? It's the time when property returns to its initial owner. Remember, the slaves had to sell themselves in order to repay the victim of their theft. If they could have afforded to indemnify the owner for the object, plus the penalty, the thief would not have become a slave. In other words, slavery is not exclusively punitive. The primary purpose of the court selling the thief is to compensate the owner for his lost property. The thief is compelled by the court to sell himself in order to recompense the owner. Then in the Jubilee, just as real estate returns to its original owner, so do slaves.[23]

24. "Forever"—According to the peshat, it means all the days of his life.

(Rashbam)

Once again, Rashbam is unconcerned about opposing the traditional, Rabbinic understanding of the verse that has been accepted as the *halakhah*. *Forever* means *forever* not in the philosophical sense of eternity, but in the sense of one's own personal forever, which is why our translation renders the Hebrew as *for life*. In other words, a truly literal reading of this term might lead into the world after this one. This is the direction that Hayim ben Attar, a mystical commentator, takes this verse. Rashbam, however, does not read the term literally. Nor does he look to other biblical laws outside of our verses in Exodus, as the Rabbis do, in order to interpret the word. His *peshat* methodology favors narrow, contextual readings. The resort to comparisons within the larger Hebrew Bible, for Rashbam, is only necessitated by a lack of clarity with the words or verses under investigation in the immediate context.

Rashbam, whose self-appointed task is the elucidation of the *peshat*, even when it conflicts with the *halakhah* which he accepts as binding, sees no reason here to question the natural sense of language.[24]

A Jeremiad on Slavery

> 25. *Truly, we find an explicit opinion which claims that Israel was commanded about the release of slaves prior to their departure from Egypt. The verse reads: "So the* LORD *spoke to both Moses and Aaron in regard to the Israelites and Pharoah king of Egypt, commanding them to deliver the Israelites from the land of Egypt" (Exod. 6:13). The Jerusalem Talmud says, "About what were they commanded? The laws concerning the release of slaves" (y. Rosh Hashana 3:5). The commandment to Israel was similar to the commandment to Pharaoh. Just as Pharaoh was commanded to send forth his slaves, so Israel was commanded to send forth their slaves, and their command comes before his. Only if the Israelites accept the responsibility to respect the freedom of every person in their midst will they merit to emerge into freedom themselves. Heaven forbid they should impair the freedom of those in their midst, they're liable to lose their national freedom.*
>
> (Yehudah Shaviv, contemporary, Israel[25])

Rabbi Shaviv is actually commenting upon the *haftarah*, or concluding reading, to our Torah portion. (There is no etymological relationship between the two words. *Haftarah* is spelled with a tet and *Torah* with a tav.) A *haftarah* is a relatively small selection read from one of the prophetic books after the Torah portion is read on the Sabbath. The institution of reading a prophetic passage may have come about toward the end of the Second Temple period as a response to the Samaritans who rejected the sanctity of any text besides the Pentateuch. The *haftarah* always has some sort of connection to the Torah portion, sometimes linguistic, sometimes conceptual. In our case, the *haftarah* for the laws of Exodus comes from the Book of Jeremiah (34:8–22, 33:25–26).

Rabbi Shaviv summarizes that the *haftarah* from Jeremiah envisions Israel being sent into exile because they had re-enslaved those they had previously freed. Since they violated their covenant with God, God will suspend his covenant of protection with them. What Rabbi Shaviv adds to the *haftarah* is that the Israelites, according to a creative reading in the Jerusalem Talmud, agreed to free their people *before* God liberated them from Egypt. Our commitment to each other's freedom is a prerequisite for national liberation. If we backslide on that commitment to one another, to protecting each other's fundamental freedoms, we expose ourselves to the incursions of outsiders, as happened with King Nebuchadnezzar of Babylonia in the sixth century BCE. Rabbi Shaviv's comment may resonate ominously to his Israeli audience struggling with their neighbors as well as with themselves.

> *26. It's not only the Book of Exodus that is about the Divine liberation of the Israelites, it's the central motif of Judaism. We recount it in our daily prayers, we reference it every Sabbath as we sanctify the day with wine, and we retell the story every year at Passover. It's the central motif because the redemption from Egypt is the precedent for our future redemption. If we didn't believe that God has the power to redeem, we'd despair and settle complacently into our lives in exile.*
>
> *The Rabbis, or their predecessors, selected Jeremiah as the haftarah to "conclude" the laws of slavery introduced in the Torah portion. When King Zedekiah proclaims liberty, he proclaims it for all time: "Everyone should set free his Hebrew slaves, both male and female, and no one should keep his fellow Jew enslaved" (Jer. 34:9). The Book of Exodus bowed to the social reality that included slavery. King Zedekiah issued an emancipation proclamation as a royal decree. Walking in God's ways (Deut. 28:9) demands that we release the captives just as God did (Ps. 146:7). King Zedekiah, whose name means God's justice, understood that logic, and the Rabbis promoted his words as the haftarah.*
>
> (Meshi, contemporary, United States)

Meshi suggests that the Rabbis chose the *haftarah* to conclude (or finish) the institution of slavery, at least among Jews. One contemporary Israeli bible scholar concurs.[26] Before examining that claim in particular, let us explore Meshi's unstated assumption that sometimes the *haftarah* serves as a critique of the Torah portion. In other words, the *haftarah* selection is sometimes a Rabbinic commentary on the Torah![27]

Take the case of Phineas, the grandson of Aaron, who demonstrated his *zeal for the* LORD (Num. 25:10) by spearing an Israelite man through the innards and Moabite woman who were fornicating within the holy precincts. God rewards Phineas for his act of zealotry with a covenant of priesthood for himself and his descendants. The *haftarah* for Phineas, 1 Kings 18:46–19:21, offers a linguistic connection. The prophet Elijah says that he, too, is zealous for the LORD (1 Kings 19:10). He had demonstrated his zealotry by having 450 prophets of Baal slaughtered (1 Kings 18:40). As a "reward" for this act of zealotry, Elijah has the distinction of being the only prophet fired from his job. But before

Elijah is removed from his post, God gives him a lesson in prophetic leadership. The famous passage of God not appearing in the great and mighty wind or the earthquake or the fire is, for the Rabbis, not only a revision of the Mount Sinai tradition (1 Kings 19: 11–12). It's also a lesson for Elijah that God's word can sometimes be most effective when it is still and small, as opposed to Elijah's zealotry. By appending this selection to the account of Phineas, the Rabbis are critiquing such lethal acts of zealotry. But what of Meshi's claim that in our case the Rabbinic selection of the *haftarah* served a similar critiquing function?

Meshi begins by explaining why salvation from slavery is central to the Jewish mind: it serves as the precedent and paradigm for future salvation. As a contemporary commentator influenced by the Hasidic tradition, Meshi understands slavery in psychological terms as well as in physical terms. Anything that distances us from the Messianic age when we are at peace within ourselves, with one another, and with God is, by this understanding, tantamount to enslavement to false gods, or exile.

But if the Rabbis interpreted Jeremiah as a blanket emancipation proclamation for all times, it seems strange that they would not say as much explicitly. Perhaps they interpreted King Zedekiah's proclamation as "beyond the letter of the law" of Exodus.[28] This category, which straddles the divide between highly recommended and compulsory,[29] may have emboldened the Rabbis to attempt to legislate slavery into oblivion such that when one acquires a slave it is as if one acquires a master.

The Legislative Leap

By most accounts, the *peshat* of Exodus 21:2–6 is quite distant from its Rabbinic *derash* and the subsequent *halakhah*. Looked at in isolation, the laws of Exodus seem to allow a master to force his unmarried slave to sire children with whom the slave will maintain no filial connection, leave after a six-year period of servitude without payment, or opt to remain a slave for life. The Rabbinic *derash* codified in the *halakhah* insists only a slave with a family can be forced to play the stud, the master must generously provide for the slave's transition to freedom at the end of six years, and in any case, the slave must be released at the Jubilee. Furthermore, the conditions under which the slave serves would be the envy of many contemporary laborers. How do we understand this legislative leap?

27. *The language used in the written Torah is so skillfully chosen that often by the use of a striking expression, an unusual or altered construction, the*

position of a word, a letter, etc., a whole train of ideas of justice and human rights is indicated. After all, it was not out of this book that the law was to have been acquired. This book was to be given into the hands of those who were already well informed in the law, simply as a means of retaining and of reviving ever afresh this knowledge which had been entrusted to their memories.

The written Torah is to the Oral Torah, also given at Mount Sinai to Moses, like class notes on a full lecture, sufficient to bring back to one's mind the whole subject of the lecture. If one hadn't heard the lecture, the notes would be useless. The wisdom, the truths, which the initiated reproduce from them, but do not artificially produce out of them, are sneered at by the uninitiated as being merely a clever or witty play of words and empty dreams without any substantial foundation.

(from Samson Raphael Hirsch, 1808–1888, Germany[30])

Hirsch's defensiveness is obvious. He's under attack by both Jewish reformers and non-Jewish biblical scholars who agree that Rabbinic midrash is an exceedingly unnatural reading of the Hebrew Bible. Hirsch understands why they think so: they missed the full lecture and are just reading the class notes. The Oral Torah, deriving from the same source and time as the written Torah, contains the full expression of the Divine will as reproduced from the linguistic oddities of the written Torah. Those oddities were skillfully embedded in the text to stimulate our memory, but the laws are not derived from the written Torah.

Hirsch's position gets at the heart of the dispute between traditionalists and contemporary thinkers by asking whether it is legitimate to use later evidence to understand earlier phenomena. Hirsch's argument relies on the Rabbinic claims of an Oral Torah, claims that are conspicuously absent from the written Torah. Contemporary scholars are dismissive of those Rabbinic claims as the fabrications of later Jews to lend authority to their idiosyncratic interpretations of Torah. Hirsch refuses to see the written Torah in isolation from the Oral Torah of the Rabbis. For Hirsch, the Rabbinic *derash* is the *peshat* of Sinai.[31] Other traditionalists, however, preferred a different approach.

28. For many of the verses in our Torah portion, their clear meaning is totally different than, and sometimes even opposes, the halakhah which is obligatory for all Jews through the generations. The Vilna Gaon (Rabbi Elijah ben Solomon Zalman of Lithuania, 1720–1797) does not tolerate far-fetched explanations. He says, as others said before him, "'The halakhah uproots scripture.' This is the greatness of the Oral Torah which is halakhah to Moses from Sinai." It's not that the details are halakhah to Moses from Sinai, but the essential nature of the oral Torah itself is halakhah to Moses from Sinai. That is, the authority that was given to Torah scholars and teachers to legislate the halakhah for Israel.

(from Yeshayahu Leibowitz, 1903–1994, Israel)

Leibowitz allied himself with the greatest Talmudist of the 18th century, the Vilna Gaon, to challenge Samson Raphael Hirsch. It's obvious that the *halakhah* sometimes opposes the biblical *peshat*—that's its glory! Elsewhere, Leibowitz refers to "the relation between the Bible and *halakhah* as one of feedback: the *halakhah* of the Oral Torah, which is a human product, derives its authority from the words of the living God in Scripture; at the same time it is the *halakhah* which determines the content and meaning of Scripture."[32]

For this school of halakhic philosophy, the sages do not uncover or reveal the *halakhah*, they decide the *halakhah* through the authority vested in them by the written Torah (Deut. 17:10–11). Such a theory helps to neutralize charges against the artificiality of halakhic midrash by Jewish reformers and biblical scholars. The problem, of course, with such a claim is that the Rabbis usually portray the *halakhah* as being the product of midrashic exegesis and not as independent laws deriving from the authority of the sages.

Accounting for the Contradictions

29. To paraphrase this from God's point-of-view: "I'm going to take this people, a people that can only conceive of a society based on a stratified view of human worth, and try to bring them My dynamic of freedom. I'll trust that this current formulation of My truth will point beyond itself. The contradiction between the law and its principles will prevent the tradition from becoming rigidified. It may take centuries or even millennia, but the dynamic I am revealing will eventually explode in the consciousness of this people. . . ."

God's Will unfolds over time . . . Halakhah is the result of God's Will in relationship with concrete realities. . . .

(Benjamin Edidin Scolnic, contemporary, United States[33])

Rabbi Scolnic, a Conservative Rabbi, is not addressing the legislative leap between the biblical material and the Rabbinic *halakhah*. In his essay, he is primarily concerned with the internal contradictions of slave laws within the Bible itself. As we've seen, the Rabbis utilized those inconsistencies, say between Exodus and Deuteronomy, in order to generate their exegesis. Thus Scolnic's argument is relevant to our discussion of the legislative gap.

His point, a standard trope of Conservative Judaism, is that law changes over time as we come to understand God's Will more clearly. As we experience slavery, perhaps from both sides, God's revelation clarifies itself to us in the light of "concrete realities." In Deuteronomy (23:16–17), there is a prohibition against returning a runaway slave. The Code of Hammurabi, by comparison, punishes someone who does *not* return a runaway slave! At least one contemporary Jewish philosopher reads the Torah's prohibition as an attempt to abolish involuntary servitude.[34] The Torah's law here certainly provides a dramatic counterpoint to America's Fugitive Slave Law of 1850 and the Dred Scott case of 1857, both of which were much closer in spirit to Hamurrabi's Code than to Deuteronomy's.

The Conservative movement accepts the premises of biblical criticism. Thus there is a willingness to concede or even embrace the contradictions within the Torah. Rabbi Scolnic suggests that there are various voices within the Torah, and Meshi would add the later books of the Hebrew Bible, trying to reconcile the social reality which they inherited with the biblical principles that we are all, equally, created in the Divine image and have only one Lord. When the Rabbis stepped back from our specific verses in Exodus and framed those laws within the broader context of the more enlightened legislation and principles throughout the Torah, they tried to legislate slavery out of existence by creatively combining those more enlightened biblical voices with their own.[35]

As a final exegetical nail in the coffin of slavery, they ask, "Is one allowed to acquire a Hebrew slave today?" No, say the Rabbis. The ability to have a Hebrew slave depends on the Jubilee so we know when to free him. Since there has not been a Jubilee since the destruction of the First Temple in 586 BCE, one is prohibited from acquiring a Hebrew slave.[36] With impressive legal acumen and moral sensitivity, the Rabbis have prohibited slavery until the reinstitution of the Jubilee, ostensibly when redemption is at hand and the LORD shall be King over all the earth (Zech. 9:14 and 14:9) and no human will suffer any other lord.[37]

Summary of Comments

Comment	Problem	Resolution	Textual Mechanism	Historical Circumstance
1.	What's the connection between these civil laws and the sacrificial laws that came before them?	We build the High Court next to the Temple since they serve the same function within a religion of ethical monotheism	Juxtaposition of texts	None
2.	Why start with the laws of the Hebrew slave?	Because there's nothing more difficult than slavery	None	Later standard of morality
3.	Why start with the laws of the Hebrew slave?	That's how the Decalogue opens	Parallels between Decalogue and subsequent laws, and emphasis in our text on manumission	None
4.	Is he a brother or a slave?	Both	Reconciling two slave texts	Rabbinic standard of morality
5.	What kind of a Hebrew slave is he?	A thief who can't repay his debt	Comparing texts in Exod. 22 and Lev. 25	None
6.	Why six years of slavery?	3 thefts plus the doubling penalty/ sevens are respites	Breaking down the act of thievery into three violations and combining it with Exod. 22:3/ patterns of seven as respites with Shabbat, *Shmittah* and Jubilee	None
7.	The seventh year of the *Shmittah* cycle or from the sale?	*Shmittah*	Other instances of "on the seventh year" refer to *Shmittah* and Leviticus law liberates slaves on the fixed, Jubilee cycle	Medieval acceptance that *peshat* is not always the *halakhah*
8.	What service can the Hebrew slave perform?	That akin to a hired hand	Reconciling our text with Leviticus 25	Rabbinic standard of morality

Comment	Problem	Resolution	Textual Mechanism	Historical Circumstance
9.	How is the Hebrew slave to be treated?	The same as you treat yourself	Emphasizing *with you* from Deut. 15 and applying it to all slaves	Rabbinic standard of morality
10.	If the master has so many responsibilities, what does he gain from having a slave?	It provides a lesson in humility and community	Looking at the psychological effects of Rabbinic exegesis	Religious psychology of Hasidism
11.	In which cases does the slave go out without payment?	In almost all cases, including ill health	Reading "without payment" not as a rejection of redemption money, but as nearly unconditional	Rabbinic standard of morality
12.	Why mention his wife and children at all?	To indicate that the master is responsible for their well-being	Since wife and children are mentioned, we learn of the master's responsibility toward them	Rabbinic standard of morality
13.	Who can be given a gentile slave woman?	Only the Hebrew with a wife and children	Read verse 4 as dependent on the second half of verse 3	Rabbinic standard of morality
14.	Why is the master allowed to use the slave as a stud?	To compensate the master for his acceptance of the liability of maintaining the slave's family	Explaining our verse in light of Rabbinic exegesis	None
15.	Why does the text shift from 2nd person to 3rd person?	To mirror the distance that is generated by the text	The text shifts from 2nd person to 3rd person	Modern standard of morality
16.	Why the infinite absolute?	To tell us that the slave must say the formula twice	The use of the infinite absolute	Rabbinic standard of morality
17.	Under what conditions may the slave say he wants to remain with the master?/Why the exclusions?	Both must be married and have children, both must be healthy, and the affection must be mutual/Rabbinic paternalism and insight into relationships	Family—Deut. 15:16 and Exod. 21:5 Health—Deut. 15:16 Affection—Deut. 15:16	Rabbinic standard of morality/Emphasis that the laws are vehicles to express psychological insights and protect humans from their own short-sightedness

continued

Comment	Problem	Resolution	Textual Mechanism	Historical Circumstance
18.	Why does the slave use that particular language?	He demonstrates that he prefers to love God through the love of the slave master	Juxtaposing our verse with Deut. 6:5 and different meanings of *adon*	Religious psychology of Hasidism/Critique of the role of the tzaddik
19.	Why a door or doorpost?	Doors were witnesses in Egypt that Israel is to be God's slaves, not slaves of slaves	Repetition of *adon* in verse 6 and combining verses from Exod. 12 and Lev. 25	None
20.	Why pierce the ear of the thief?	He heard the command not to steal and disobeyed	Juxtaposition of our text with the Decalogue	None
21.	Why pierce the ear of the one who sells himself?	He heard that the Israelites were to be God's slaves and he took another master	Repetition of *adon* in verse 6 and juxtaposition of our text with Lev. 25	None
22.	Why wait until the slave declares his intention to stay with the master?	It is only after he tastes slavery that he can be held accountable for prolonging his servitude	None	Religious Psychology of Hasidism
23.	What does "forever" mean?	Until the Jubilee year	The language and logic of the Jubilee (Lev. 25:10) suggest a return of *all* property	Rabbinic standard of morality
24.	What does "forever" mean?	Until death	None	Medieval acceptance that *peshat* is not always the *halakhah*
25.	Why Jeremiah as the *haftarah*?	To remind us of the dire consequences of reneging on our commitment to one another's liberty	Thematic connection with Jeremiah which concludes in the Babylonian exile	Israeli political tensions
26.	Why Jeremiah as the *haftarah*?	As King Zedekiah proclaimed, slavery should be abolished	King Zedekiah releases the Jewish slaves	Rabbinic standard of morality/ Contemporary disgust with slavery
27.	What accounts for the differences between *peshat* and *derash*?	The written Torah is like class notes to the full lecture of the Oral Torah	None	Jewish Reformers and bible scholars deriding the artificial interpretations of Rabbinic midrash

128

continued

Comment	Problem	Resolution	Textual Mechanism	Historical Circumstance
28.	What accounts for the differences between *peshat* and *derash?*	The license that the Torah gives Jews to legislate anew	Leaders can decide law, Deut. 17:8–11	Jewish Reformers and bible scholars deriding the artificial interpretations of Rabbinic midrash
29.	What accounts for the differences between the various slave laws in the Torah?	God's will becomes revealed and refined over time	Internal contradictions with the Torah	Emphasis on development of law and unfolding of Divine Will in the Conservative movement

NOTES

1. Fox prefers *serf*. The Jewish Publication Society translation, from 1917, uses *servant*.

2. Catherine Hezser has written extensively on this topic in *Jewish Slavery in Antiquity* (Oxford: Oxford University Press, 2005). An anthology of Black-Jewish relations (hence, not related to the laws of the Hebrew slave) edited by Jack Salzman and Cornel West, *Struggles in the Promised Land* (New York: Oxford University Press, 1997) has several relevant essays including David Goldenberg's "The Curse of Ham: A Case of Rabbinic Racism?" and David Davis' "Jews in the Slave Trade." A similar anthology, *Strangers & Neighbors: Relations between Blacks and Jews in the United States*, ed. Maurianne Adams and John Bracey (Amherst: University of Massachusetts Press, 1999) has pertinent essays by Seymour Drescher, "The Role of Jews in the Trans-Atlantic Slave Trade," Jayme Sokolow, "Revolution and Reform: The Antebellum Jewish Abolitionists," and two articles by Bertram Wallace Korn, "Jews and Negro Slavery in the Old South" and "The Rabbis and the Slavery Question." Jon D. Levenson has an informative essay combining history and Bible in his *The Hebrew Bible, the Old Testament, and Historical Criticism* (Louisville: Westminster/John Knox Press, 1993). For comparisons to Catholic doctrine, see John T. Noonan Jr.'s *A Church That Can and Cannot Change* (Notre Dame: University of Notre Dame Press, 2005). For comparisons to Islam, see Jacob Neusner and Tamara Sonn, *Comparing Religions through Law: Judaism and Islam* (New York: Routledge, 1999), 158–168.

3. Arthur Waskow writes movingly about the spirals of seven in the Torah. See his contributions in the second volume of *Torah of the Earth* (Woodstock: Jewish Lights Publishing, 2000) and the last section of *Down to Earth Judaism* (New York: William Morrow & Co., 1995).

4. The *Sefer Hachinuch (Book of Education)*, a medieval commentary on the 613 commandments, explains that we should have mercy on the slave because we, or our children, might one day be in the position of a slave (Mitzvah 344).

5. Mekhilta, *Nezikin*.

6. Sara Japhet has written on "The Tension between Rabbinic Legal Midrash and the 'Plain Meaning' (*Peshat*) of the Biblical Text—An Unresolved Problem?: In the Wake of Rashbam's

Commentary on the Pentateuch," *Sefer Moshe — the Moshe Weinfeld Jubilee Volume*, eds. Chaim Cohen, Avi Hurvitz, and Shalom M. Paul (Winona Lake, IN: Eisenbrauns, 2004), 403–425.

7. Not only does this prohibition prevent the master from reaping a windfall, it also prevents the master from driving down the market rates by forcing his slave to undersell the competition.

8. *Tosafot, Kiddushin* 20a.

9. b. *P'shachim* 112a.

10. See Hizkuni and Gur Aryeh.

11. b. *Kiddushin* 17b.

12. b. *Baba Metzia*, chap. 4.

13. m. *Baba Batra* 9:6.

14. b. *Gittin* 9a.

15. *The Particulars of Rapture: Reflections on* Exodus (New York: Doubleday, 2001), 308ff.

16. Ibid., 308.

17. Arthur Green has translated and commented upon excerpts from the Sefat Emet's commentary as well as providing an illuminating introduction to his life and thought in *The Language of Truth* (Philadelphia: The Jewish Publication Society, 1998). Green has also written on "Typologies of Leadership and the Hasidic Zaddiq," in *Jewish Spirituality*, vol. 2 (New York: Crossroad, 1994).

18. *The Hebrew Bible, the Old Testament, and Historical Criticism*, 62–81.

19. The Conservative Movement has modified the language of that blessing to thank God for making us free people. There are two essays in the front matter of *My People's Prayer Book*, vol. 5, ed. Lawrence A. Hoffman (Woodstock, Jewish Lights Publishing, 2001) that concern the blessing for not making us a slave.

20. See Victor (Avigdor) Hurowitz, "'His Master Shall Pierce His Ear With an Awl' (Exodus 21:6)—Marking Slaves in the Bible in Light of Akkadian Sources," *Proceedings — American Academy for Jewish Research* 58 (1992): 47–77.

21. Ibid., 67.

22. See, also, Hurowitz, 76. Benno Jacob, a modern Jewish commentator, suggests that the piercing is a sign of love.

23. See Nahum M. Sarna, "Zedekiah's Emancipation of Slaves and the Sabbatical Year," in *Orient and Occident* (1973): 143–149.

24. Jonah ibn Janah, from the first half of the 11th century, anticipated Rashbam by a century in this interpretation of *forever*.

25. *Between the Haftarah and the Torah Portion* [Hebrew] (Jerusalem: Reuven Mas, 2000), 83.

26. Moshe Weinfeld, "Sabbatical Year and Jubilee in the Pentateuchal Laws and their Ancient Near-Eastern Background," in *The Law in the Bible and its Environment*, ed. Timo Veijola, Göttingen: Vandenhoeck & Ruprecht, 1990), 41.

27. For those interested in the connections between the Torah portions and the *hafatara*, see Michael Fishbane, *The JPS Bible Commentary: Haftarot* (Philadelphia: The Jewish Publication Society, 2002). Fishbane's work can also be found in *Etz Hayim* (Philadelphia: The Jewish Publication Society, 2001).

28. On this reading, see Malbim.

29. b. *Baba Metzia* 30b.

30. Translation based on that of Isaac Levy for Exod. 21:2.

31. See Harris for Hirsch's innovative understanding of the Oral Torah, 223–228.

32. *Judaism, Jewish Values, and the Jewish State*, ed. Eliezer Goldman, trans. Eliezer Goldman, et. al. (Cambridge: Harvard University Press, 1992), 12. Avi Sagi has written extensively on Yeshayahu Leibowitz. A relevant article is "Contending with Modernity: Scripture in the Thought of Yeshayahu Leibowitz and Joseph Soloveitchik," *Journal of Religion* 77, no. 3 (1997): 421–441. Harris treats these different schools of thought in chaps. 7 and 8 of *How Do We Know This?*

33. "How To Read the Torah's Laws of Slavery," *Conservative Judaism* 47:3 (1995), 40–41.

34. Lenn Evan Goodman, *God of Abraham* (New York: Oxford University Press, 1996), 294, fn. 5.

35. Elliot N. Dorff has collected the spectrum of theories on *halakhah* within the Conservative movement in his *The Unfolding Tradition: Jewish Law after Sinai* (New York: Aviv Press, 2005). Also, Jon D. Levenson has an important essay on the significance of contextualizing biblical traditions, "The Eighth Principle of Judaism and the Literary Simultaneity of Scripture," in *The Hebrew Bible, the Old Testament, and Historical Criticism*.

36. b. *Arachin* 29a and 32b. But see *Tosafot* on the bottom of b. *Gittin* 36a.

37. *Seder Eliyahu Zuta* 22:2 and b. *Rosh Hashana* 26a.

Chapter 5

KORAH
AND HIS GANG

Now Korah, son of Izhar, son of Kohath, son of Levi, betook himself, along with Dathan and Abiram, sons of Eliab, and On, son of Peleth—descendants of Reuben — ²to rise up against Moses, together with two hundred and fifty Israelites, chieftains of the community, chosen in the assembly, men of repute. ³They combined against Moses and Aaron and said to them, "You have gone too far! For all the community are holy, all of them, and the LORD is in their midst. Why then do you raise yourselves above the LORD's congregation?

⁴When Moses heard this, he fell on his face. ⁵Then he spoke to Korah and all his company, saying, "Come morning, the LORD will make known who is His and who is holy, and will grant access to Himself; He will grant access to the one He has chosen. ⁶Do this: You, Korah and all your band, take fire pans, ⁷and tomorrow put fire in them and lay incense on them before the LORD. Then the man whom the LORD chooses, he shall be the holy one. You have gone too far, sons of Levi!"

(JPS TANAKH) Numbers 16:1 – 7

In the chapters exploring both the creation of humanity and the laws of the Hebrew slave, there were examples of how the commentators contended with parallel texts in tension with one another. The redactor of the Torah included two stories of creation (Gen 1:1–2:4a and Gen 2:4b-24) and three sets of laws about slaves (Exod. 21:2–6, Lev. 25:39–40, and Deut. 15:12–17) that present contradictory details. Another opportunity for exegetical ingenuity arises when an editor combines two or more disparate accounts of similar events and braids them into a single narrative. There is scholarly consensus that our version of Korah was the result of braiding two or more distinct challenges to Moses' and Aaron's leadership during their sojourn in the desert. References to these multiple strands of rebellion are unavoidable; but they will only be considered here as they arise in the commentaries on this paradigmatic account of rebellion. The main problem for the commentators is the charge of the rebels: that the entire community is holy. Why would such a claim, even if not true, elicit such a lethal response?

For the Taking

1. "Taking" always means "drawing with supple speech." Korah drew all the giants of Israel and the courts after him.
(*Tanhuma*, an early medieval compilation of Rabbinic material; Rashi)

Although the NJPS translation has Korah taking himself, the phrase in Hebrew has no direct object. We simply do not know what Korah took. *Tanhuma* solves the mystery by suggesting that Korah's co-conspirators were taken in by him. (In English, we also use *taken* to mean deceived.) He was charismatic, eloquent, and offered speciously compelling arguments. In short, he was a demagogue. *Tanhuma* does offer an explicit example of where "taking" is associated with speech (Hosea 14:3.) But, our comment might be as interested in highlighting Moses' weakness, and thus his vulnerability, as explaining Korah's strength.[1]

Not once, but twice, does Moses refer to his own ineloquence (Exod. 4:10 and 6:12). It's not clear if Moses had a speech impediment (stuttering or a lisp?), an anatomical irregularity (cleft palate?), or simply lacked the gift of gab. Another possibility is that Moses spoke just fine, but either out of modesty (Num. 12:3) or a negative self-image, Moses described himself as a bumbler. In any case, where the Torah emphasizes Moses' difficulty with locution, the midrash emphasizes Korah's rhetorical prowess. *Tanhuma* is sounding a warning to its readers not to be taken in by the undeniable power of rhetoric. Those who were swept away by Korah's hortatory power were ultimately swept away altogether (Num. 16:31–33).

2. What is written in the preceding passage? "Speak to the Israelite people and instruct them to make for themselves fringes on the corners of their garments throughout the ages; let them attach a cord of blue to the fringe at each corner" (Num. 15:38). Korah jumped and said to Moses, "You say to put a cord of blue on the fringes. If the garment is entirely blue shouldn't

*it be exempt from the blue cord?" Moses responded, "It is still required."
Korah retorted, "A garment that's entirely blue is not exempt, but four
strings exempt it? . . . You were not commanded these things. You fabri-
cated them yourself!"*

(*Tanhuma* and Rashi)

More in keeping with the common usage of "take," Korah takes a garment. This comment really is an extension of the first comment from *Tanhuma*. Korah is using the blue garment as a prop. The reader, or listener, can almost see Korah holding up this big, blue garment and challenging Moses: "You mean to tell me four little blue strings fulfill a commandment that the entire blue garment cannot?" Korah is still a demagogue, but now he's a demagogue with a visual aid.

Tanhuma is employing the common exegetical strategy of linking consecutive passages. There is no logical connection between the laws of wearing fringes and Korah. Yet the Rabbinic assumption of the Torah's perfection denies that these passages could have been arranged haphazardly. *Tanhuma*, therefore, provides the connection while simultaneously solving the grammatical problem of a missing direct object. Korah took what had just been discussed in the previous passage, a garment.

The choreography of *Tanhuma* has Korah jumping. He was waiting, impatiently, for the right moment to challenge Moses' leadership. His claim that the entire community is holy (v. 3) parallels his query to Moses about a garment which is entirely blue. Why does the garment still need a single blue cord on each corner? Why does a holy community need a single person for priestly and political leadership? The answer, in both cases, is that God has so decreed.[2]

It is precisely the issue of the Divine will that is at stake in this midrashic confrontation. Korah accuses Moses of fabricating certain laws himself. While the Torah's version of the rebellion focuses on the political, *Tanhuma* shifts the attention to the theological. Korah is not claiming that all the commandments are Mosaic rather than Divine, just the ones that don't seem to make any sense, including, perhaps, the selection of Moses' brother to be High Priest.

During the early Rabbinic period, there was a group of Jews who similarly believed that not all the commandments in the Torah were from God. They, too, accused Moses of fabricating laws and attributing them to God. This group later became known as the Christians. As early as the first-century Gospels, there are claims that the Torah is partially Mosaic in origin and partially Divine (see Mark 10:29). A second-century Valentinian Christian,

Ptolemy (fl. 136–180), concurs: "Now, first you must learn that, as a whole, the law contained in the Pentateuch of Moses was not established by a single author, I mean not by God alone: rather, there are certain of its command-ments that were established by human beings as well."[3]

We will also encounter Jewish groups who saw themselves as the spiritual descendants of Moses while pointing to their opponents as the sons of Korah. Indeed, since our story is about an insider gone bad, the history of commen-tary on Korah is one long hall of mirrors for the schisms punctuating Jewish history. For *Tanhuma*, wrapping Korah in a garment highlights the specious-ness of his arguments. In the section on fringes, the Torah says: "That shall be your fringe; look at it and recall *all* the commandments of the LORD and observe them, so that you do not follow your heart and eyes in your lustful urge" (Num. 15:39). Korah couldn't see the fringe for the garment as his lust for power led his heart astray.

> 3. *Korah, Dathan, and Abiram took many people, to the point that there were 250 who rose up against Moses.*
>
> (Rashbam, c. 1085—c. 1174, France)

Rashbam lives up to his reputation as a *pashtan*, a seeker of *peshat*. He contends that the direct object is implied in verse 1 and made explicit in verse 2. There is one difference between Rashbam and the NJPS translation worth noting. Rashbam understands that Korah isn't the only one involved in taking the 250 men—it was a conspiracy led by Korah, Dathan, and Abiram. The NJPS translation has Korah taking Dathan, Abiram, "together with" (v. 2) the 250 Israelites. But, that "together with" does not appear in the Hebrew. For NJPS, Korah is spearheading the rebellion alone. Given the conflation of rebel-lion stories, Rashbam is probably correct in having Dathan and Abiram as active co-conspirators rather than victims of Korah's manipulations.

In both understandings, though, Korah took men. This type of taking is not a physical taking in one's hand like *Tanhuma*'s Korah who took a garment. Rashbam's taking, though, is a common usage of the term, and he offers an example of where the term is used in exactly that sense (Gen. 12:5). What our first comment from *Tanhuma* may have attempted is *to assume* that Korah took the men with him to challenge Moses. *Tanhuma* then went a step further and asked *how* did Korah manipulate these princes of Israel to challenge Moses' leadership. For *Tanhuma* (Comment 1), Korah took the men with supple words. It is sometimes the case, as I believe it is here, that the *peshat* is so simple (*pashut* in Hebrew!) that the Rabbis assume what the medieval *pashtan* will spell out explicitly. But, the Rabbinic commentator will go on to address a deeper problem in the text.

> *4. Onkelos translates "Korah took" as "Korah separated himself." The sages say: "A person must reflect, when will my deeds connect with the deeds of my ancestors?" Rabbi Simcha Bunem of Przyscha (1765–1827) explained that in the deeds of every Jew there must be a seamless, binding connection and striving toward the deeds of the ancestors, that is toward the beautiful deeds that ensure the succession of generations. And that was Korah's sin. Korah took, he separated himself. He took a different road that had no connection to the past. He severed the links to the ancestors.*
>
> (Yehudah Leib Alter of Ger, 1847–1905, Poland)[4]

When Onkelos translated "took" by using a reflexive verb, he probably meant that Korah was taking himself away from the rest of the Israelites. The JNPS translation has largely followed Onkelos' early second-century translation of this verse: Korah betook himself. For the Torah, Korah separated himself from those around him; for Yehuda Leib Alter of Ger, usually known as the Sefat Emet, he separated himself from those who came before him.

Both the Sefat Emet and Simcha Bunem were Hasidic masters in Eastern Europe during the 19th century. They were struggling to keep Judaism relevant and attractive for a population that had unprecedented opportunities to leave the traditional Jewish lifestyle and explore new ways and new ideas. Many Jews took advantage of their newfound freedoms and separated themselves from the communities in which they were raised. Some became free thinkers, socialists, Zionists, and a few converted to Christianity. (Remember Tevya's daughters from *Fiddler on the Roof*?) The Sefat Emet is trying to preserve tradition, and casts Korah as one who severs himself from the chain.[5]

The Sefat Emet has an agenda, but he also represents glimmerings of a 20th-century sense of pluralism. The biblical Korah didn't just take a different road, he took a bad road, and it led to Hell. In this teaching, the Sefat Emet withholds value judgments on non-Jewish roads; his charge is simply that they're not Jewish. When the Torah commands the Israelites not to follow in the ways of the Egyptians or Canaanites (Lev. 18:3), Rashi tells us how depraved those folks were. Ibn Ezra, on the other hand, says we should keep away from their ways because they're not *our* ways. Like ibn Ezra, the Sefat Emet restrains the perhaps natural inclination to vilify the other. In modernity, all paths are for the taking. Without disparaging other paths, the Sefat Emet argues that Jews should remain on the path of tradition.

Why *Now?*

Many traditional translations of our first verse, including the NJPS, begin with "Now Korah took."[6] But, there is no time marker in the Hebrew. Nevertheless, as we saw in the second comment by *Tanhuma*, one question about the rebellion is: why now? *Tanhuma* links Korah's timing to the preceding passage dealing with the laws of fringes and portrays Korah as lying in wait for the opportunity to incite the leaders against Moses' leadership. Ramban offers a different scenario.

> 5. *When Israel was in the wilderness of Sinai, nothing bad happened to them. Even after the great and infamous sin of the Golden Calf, only a few people died. The people were saved by Moses' intercession when he prayed on their behalf for 40 days and 40 nights (Deut. 9:25). Thus they loved Moses as themselves and obeyed him. Had someone rebelled against Moses then, the people would've stoned him. Therefore Korah suffered the greatness of Aaron and the firstborns suffered the status of the Levites and all the deeds of Moses. But when they came to the wilderness of Paran and the camp was burned in Tavera (Num. 11:1–3), and many died in Kibroth-hattaavah (Num. 11:33–34), and when after the sin of the spies (Num 13:17–33) Moses did not pray on their behalf so that the decree against them was not annulled, and the princes of all the tribes died in a plague before the LORD, and it was decreed that the entire people would be consumed in the wilderness, and there they will die (Num. 14:35), then* the disposition of the people became bitter. They said to themselves that mishaps occur to them due to Moses' words. Then Korah found an opportunity to dispute Moses' deeds thinking that the people would listen to him.
>
> (Ramban, 1194–1270, Spain)

Like *Tanhuma*, Ramban has Korah waiting for the opportune moment to strike against Moses and Aaron. But, Ramban's context is larger than *Tanhuma's*. Indeed, widening the focus is characteristic of medieval commentary. Whereas Rabbinic commentary tends to focus on small units, such as letters, words, or the relationships between consecutive verses or episodes, the medievalists often looked at larger narrative patterns. Here, Ramban offers a penetrating psychological analysis of the community's initial loyalty to Moses and then their increasing disaffection.

Only once does the Torah tell us that the Israelites had faith in Moses, or faith in God, for that matter (Exod. 14:31). Immediately upon salvation, seeing the Sea of Reeds open up and swallow the Egyptians, does the Torah tell us of that faith. But "faith" in this context does not mean belief; it means trust. Seeing is trusting. Once the Israelites no longer saw God's saving grace, they complained about the bitter water in the desert (Exod. 15:23). Their complaints continued in the desert (Num. 11:1 and 14:1), and Ramban suggests that with every additional mishap, the people's susceptibility to Korah's charges grew. After the Israelites allowed their fears and insecurities to be confirmed by the report of ten of the twelve returning spies, God condemned that slave generation to die in the wilderness. Their error was not that they believed the spies about the challenges before them in conquering the Land of Canaan, but that they doubted their ability to meet those challenges. "We looked like grasshoppers to ourselves (in comparison to the inhabitants of the Land)" (Num. 13:33). Korah's demagoguery, then, fed on the Israelites' desperation. Not only does Ramban explain the timing of the attempted coup, but he helps us understand how a people can turn against their leaders and against their own best interest.

Casting Aspersions

Even before the rebellion unfolds, our commentators offer brief biographies of the cast.

> 6. It's known that the Kabbalists have said that Korah is the reincarnation of jealous Cain and that Moses is the reincarnation of Abel. And in Korah's death, we see the principle of measure for measure: just as the earth opened its mouth to swallow the blood of Abel (Gen 4: 11), so did the earth open up to swallow Korah (Num. 16:32).
>
> (from Isaiah Horowitz, Shnei Luchot Habrit, 1565–1630, Poland)

Just as the rebellion of Korah becomes the archetype for all future acts of sedition, the Kabbalists see our narrative as a recapitulation of the original act of fratricide.[7] But the recapitulation involves retribution; God's justice is set straight. Cain got away with murder once, but his later incarnation was justly punished. This Kabbalistic tradition might be betraying a discomfort with the seemingly disproportionate punishment Korah receives in the Torah. Cain (now Korah) was given another chance to support his brother and he failed to do so. Moreover, from this reading we know that Korah's challenge to Moses and Aaron was a function of his jealousy of their Divine election, since Cain is the root of Korah, and not out of genuine concern for the equal holiness of all the Israelites.

In this reading, there is nothing necessarily incorrect about Korah's charges against Moses and Aaron, except his intention. As we will see, the mystical tradition actually rehabilitates Korah and his argument in some ways. Horowitz inherited a Rabbinic tradition that understands Korah to be jealous of the status that Moses bestowed upon their mutual cousin, Elizaphan (Num. 3:30). Korah reasoned that since his father was older than Elizaphan's father was, although younger than Moses and Aaron's father, his position should be higher than that of Elizaphan.[8] The Zohar, the central text of Jewish mysticism, understands Cain's motives to be similarly rooted in jealousy which is hinted at by the similarity between his name, *Kayin*, and the Hebrew word for jealousy, *kinah*.[9] Horowitz combines these traditions with the mystical doctrine of reincarnation. The later shepherd, Moses, is able to execute justice on behalf of the former shepherd, Abel. The law of retribution in Genesis reads: "Whosoever sheds the blood of man, by man shall his blood be shed" (9:6). A Kabbalistic reading of that law might be: "Whoever sheds the blood of man, by (that same) man shall his blood be shed." Horowitz ties together his Kabbalistic belief in reincarnation, the literary parallels between Cain/Korah and Abel/Moses, and the linguistic parallels of the earth's mouth opening up.[10] In doing so, he explains Korah's motivation and punishment while, at the same time, preserving the potential veracity of Korah's claim that all the community is holy.

> *7. Rabbi Yochanan said in the name of Rabbi Shimon bar Yochai: Wherever* nitzim *(quarreling) or* nitzavim *(standing) is mentioned, the reference is to Dathan and Abiram.*
>
> (Gemara, Nedarim, 64b)

What the Talmud here offers us is a literary example of the transitive property of Rabbinic logic, the *g'zerah shavah*.[11] Early in Moses' life, he ventures out of his protected environment in the Egyptian palace. He sees an Egyptian slave master beating a Hebrew slave and he responds to that injustice by killing the Egyptian (Exod. 2:12). According to Horowitz, that Egyptian, too, is a reincarnation of Cain. In Moses' next encounter, he sees that internecine conflict is not restricted to them (the Egyptians) versus us (the Hebrews). Two of "us" are quarreling (*nitzim*), and Moses, once again, acts on his sense of justice to support the oppressed party (Exod. 2:13).[12] The response of the Hebrew bully to Moses' intervention is: "Who made you chief and ruler over us?"

Rabbi Shimon bar Yochai hears the echo of that complaint in our episode: "Why then do you raise yourselves above the LORD's congregation?" (Num. 16:3) But, Rabbi Shimon's comment is not only predicated on the literary echo, but on the linguistic similarity between *nitzim* (quarreling) and the verb describing Dathan and Abiram later in the chapter, *nitzavim* (standing) in verse 27. Usually a *g'zerah shavah* operates on the identical word, but in this case, the Rabbis make the connection between this pair (in Egypt and in the wilderness) based on the similar sound. The Rabbis dislike biblical anonymity, and through this *g'zerah shavah*, they not only name the protagonists of Moses' encounter in Egypt, they also explain the later antagonism of Dathan and Abiram to Moses in the wilderness.

While a *peshat* reading of the Exodus narrative suggests that one Hebrew was being wronged by an "offender" (Exod. 2:13), a midrashic rereading of this verse has them equally culpable. Rashi's running commentary on this story, drawn from Rabbinic sources, further suggests that it was Dathan and Abiram who informed Pharaoh that Moses had killed the Egyptian (v. 15). Thus, when Dathan and Abiram challenge Moses in the wilderness, for the Rabbinic reader, there is a history to the confrontation. There was motivation for this quarreling pair to avenge Moses for having officiously intruded in their affairs. The Torah warns us against seeking revenge and holding grudges (Lev. 19:18). Through this *g'zerah shavah*, Rabbi Shimon shows us the deep downside of holding on to negative experiences from the past: "They went down alive into Sheol" (Num. 16:30).

> 8. Rav said: On, the son of Peleth, was saved by his wife.
>
> (Gemara, *Sanhedrin*, 109b)

The Talmud goes on to describe how On's wife first tried to persuade him and finally disabled him from continuing his association with the other rebels. The next chapter will feature Rabbi Nathan exclaiming that women's power is greater than men's, and Rav's statement above seems to agree. Contrary to other religious traditions that speak of women submitting graciously to their husbands, biblical literature is replete with stories of wives who control, and sometimes manipulate, their environments. Also in Rabbinic literature, women are described as having significant influence. In one particularly telling scene, the elders of the Sanhedrin, the ancient Jewish tribunal, offer the presidency to young Rabbi Elazar ben Azaryah. Rather than accepting, he beseeches the sages for time to consult with his wife.[13]

The textual problem that gives rise to this comment is On's appearance in the first verse and disappearance from the rest of the story. Where did he go? Contemporary bible scholars point to On's initial presence as evidence that multiple rebellion stories have been braided together to form this chapter. In some cases, the details of the story just don't fit together. For example, in verse 8, we have the jarring statement: "Moses said further to Korah: 'Hear me, sons of Levi.'" To whom is Moses speaking, Korah or the sons of Levi? It is clear to many commentators, including the medievals, that Korah has a different complaint than do Dathan and Abiram. The former wants greater priestly power, while the latter seek political authority because they are descendants of Reuben, the firstborn of Jacob. The braiding of these different insurrection accounts provides material for the commentators to flesh out the biographies of the cast. Most of the insurgents are vilified as habitual offenders, but On's wife is praised for her virtuous manipulation.

> 9. *Together with 250 Israelites, the most distinguished in the community,* chosen in the assembly, *they knew how to intercalate the year and establish the months.*
>
> (Gemara, *Sanhedrin,* 110a)

The Talmud is giving us a hint about whom those 250 rebels were. The biblical phrase *chosen in the assembly* can also be read, with a slight change of vowels, as *callers of times.* The Talmud then suggests that this group of rebels joining with Korah were experts in determining when the month begins and when extra days or months are needed to keep the calendar's agricultural holidays in sync with the appropriate season. (The Rabbinic calendar is a hybrid: 7 out of every 19 years have 13 lunar months rather than twelve. *Intercalation* is the process of adjusting the calendar.)

One contemporary theory links this group to those Jews who were responsible for writing the Dead Sea Scrolls.[14] They had a different calendrical system than Rabbinic Jews. The issue of holy time is often a source of contention within religious schisms. The Roman Catholic Church and Eastern Orthodox Church have also adhered to different calendars for many centuries. Given that the issue of calendar-keeping is completely absent from the biblical story, the Talmud may very well have been pointing to contemporary schismastics who were well known for their calendrical concerns.[15]

On the previous page of Talmud, there is a dispute as to whether Korah and his gang will have a share in the world to come. Rabbi Akiva maintains that they will not. Rabbi Yehuda ben Beteyra objects: "They are like a lost article which is sought, as it says, 'I have strayed like a lost sheep; search for Your servant, for I have not neglected Your commandments" (Ps. 119:176). Rabbi Yehuda acknowledges that these lost ones are not neglecting the commandments. How different is this depiction of Korah and his gang from *Tanhuma's*, claiming that certain commandments are not Divine! The Dead Sea community maintained a rigorous approach to Jewish law, especially concerning matters of ritual purity. Rabbi Yehuda may be conceding that the separatists who formed the Dead Sea community are lost to this world, but he insists that their dedication to God's commandments, even though improperly understood and performed, will earn for them a portion in the world to come.

Interestingly, the Dead Sea Scrolls themselves contain references to Korah that one scholar sees as pointing to an early schism within their own community.[16] The same scholar, James M. Scott, demonstrates that the plasticity of our biblical narrative allowed the early Christian community to use the text as a literary template of the true Israel versus the impostors, such that Korah became a symbol of opposition within the early Church. In particular, Paul and Timothy are likened to the challenged figures of Moses and Aaron who are attempting to restore authority in Corinth.[17] As we have seen in earlier comments, the Korah template was also used to finger the early Christian community and the modern, assimilating Jewish community. The identities of Moses and Korah depend on who is holding the mirror of Torah.

Holiness Is in the Eye of the Beholder

10. "For all the community are holy, all of them! They all heard at Sinai, 'I am the LORD your God.'"

(*Tanhuma* and Rashi)

What constitutes holiness? Is it inherent or achieved? Is it temporary or permanent? Besides God, what else can be holy: people, land, time? A twentieth-century German theologian and scholar of religion, Rudolf Otto, suggested that to be holy meant to be separate. The ancient Rabbinic commentary on the Book of Leviticus, *Sifra*, suggests the same thing in its explication of the verse: "You shall be holy, for I, the LORD your God, am holy" (Lev. 19:2). Just as God is separate, so, too, should the Israelites. The context of this charge in Leviticus is within a series of laws. In other words, the placement in Leviticus suggests that holiness has something to do with behavior.

Tanhuma's Korah, alternatively, understands that the entire community is holy by virtue of a single experience, having heard God's revelation at Mount Sinai. Nothing that the community did or will do affects their holy status for Korah. The experience of God has forever conferred upon the entire community a holy status. Since the entire people shared the experience, no single individual is holier than any other. Hence, Korah claims, Moses' holier than thou posture is arrogant and a violation of the universal aristocracy that God has bestowed upon the entire community. Korah's claim that all of Israel experienced Divine revelation at Mount Sinai is incontrovertible. Indeed, immediately prior to that event, the Torah has God telling Moses to inform the Israelites that they are to be "a kingdom of priests and a holy nation" (Exod. 19:6).

11. "Come morning, the Lord will make known who is His for Levitical service *and who is holy* for the priesthood.*"*
(Rashi, 1040–1105, France)

Rashi's comment changes our story from rebellion to tragedy. Rashi fills in the meaning of Moses' response to Korah: holiness is functional, not essential. The Levites and the priests were selected by God to perform certain functions involving the sacrificial system in the Tabernacle. Holiness, as Moses understands it, has nothing to do with the experience of revelation which somehow transformed the essence of each Israelite. Of course, the entire community witnessed revelation, but that is totally irrelevant to the issue of leadership. Rashi's comment also addresses the potential redundancy in Moses' response. Moses is informing Korah and his gang that God appointed both the Levites, the attendants in the Tabernacle, as well as the priests, those who actually offered the sacrifices.

The tragedy is that Moses and Korah were miscommunicating. Perhaps had Moses engaged Korah in dialogue, the terms of their dispute could have been clarified and loss of life avoided. Moses, however, feels personally attacked and reacts to Korah as an adversary. An onlooker to their exchange senses that something is amiss, since Korah and Moses are obviously using the word *holy* to mean different things. Korah says the entire community is holy, while Moses responds that God will choose the holy one (v. 7). Like Otto, Moses understands holiness to mean being separated or designated for a certain task. For Moses, holiness is more a responsibility than a privilege.

12. The entire community was by no means holy already. They were called upon to become holy by dedicating themselves exclusively to God.
(from Samson Raphael Hirsch, 1808–1888, Germany)

Hirsch makes a fine Talmudic distinction. The Israelites were charged with being a holy people, not described as having yet attained that status. Thus, Korah's argument was flawed. Hirsch, in keeping with Rashi, reasons that when Moses responds to Korah, he uses *holy* in a slightly different sense. For Hirsch, human holiness is a goal achieved by ensuring that all actions and emotions, both personal and political, are directed to God. In his commentary on loving the LORD with "the whole of your heart, and with the whole of your soul, and with the whole of your resources" (Hirsch's translation of Deut. 6:5,) he emphasizes that "everything that you think and feel, everything that you strive for and desire, and everything that you possess, should serve only as a means for you to get near to God and for bringing God near to you. But not vice-versa. Do not seek God in order to attain and preserve what you think about, yearn for, possess, or would like to possess."

As we saw in chapter two, Hirsch, the father of modern Orthodoxy, sought to portray Judaism as far more than dry legalism. Being holy and loving God are two appropriate platforms upon which he can preach the value of going above and beyond any legal requirements in order to fully dedicate oneself to God. This dedication, this holiness, is theoretically attainable by all people, regardless of status, religion, or nationality. Equal opportunity for holiness is an important marker of modernity. Anticipating later German Jewish philosophers, like Herman Cohen and Martin Buber, who denounce using others as a means for one's own ends, Hirsch claims that our only goal should be communion with God. God is not a marriage broker, a securities trader, or a fire insurance salesman. Turning this verse in Deuteronomy on its head, Hirsch implies that anything we love with all our heart, soul, and resources is, for us, a god.

Martin Buber, like Hirsch, understands that holiness is a goal to be achieved through relentless pursuit, rather than a status conferred through Divine grace. Our next commentator, Yeshayahu Leibowitz, develops that distinction and claims that throughout Jewish history, there have been well-meaning, pious Jews who have been on both sides of this debate.[18] Leibowitz reads the Torah as religious literature devoid of historical or scientific information. Therefore, when the Torah says that "sons of Korah did not die" (Num. 26:11), which is in tension with the earlier verse (16:32) that all of Korah's people were swallowed alive, he claims that Korah's argument that holiness is inherent in all the people of Israel is a claim that has lived on.

13. Korah's conception of holiness is not that of a goal but of a given status. This "holiness" grants to the individual self-assurance, since he belongs to a holy people and he has similarly been guaranteed all the goodness in this world and the world to come. This type of consciousness exempts the believers from all responsibility. More than that, it induces an arrogance and sense of entitlement. This line of thinking can be traced from Rabbi Yehudah Halevi through the Maharal of Prague to the teachings of Rav Kook and his followers.

(Yeshayahu Leibowitz, 1903–1994, Israel)

It's very easy to be smug if you think you're holy. (Of course, if you are smug, it's a good indication you're not holy.) One of the reasons that Mordecai Kaplan, the founder of Reconstructionist Judaism, abandoned the idea of the Jews being the chosen people was precisely because he felt it led to inappropriate feelings of condescension. Leibowitz rails against this concept of holiness, because it works against the goal of striving for holiness through Divine worship. Leibowitz takes aim at the mystical tradition and its conception that Jews are inherently holy. The idea that Jews are somehow essentially superior to gentiles can be traced back to Ezra's polemics against inter-marriage with the Babylonians during the exile (Ezra 9:2). That smugness can lead to violations of what Leibowitz perceives are fundamentals of *halakhah.*[19]

What Leibowitz likely has in mind includes the Israeli possession of the West Bank of the Jordan River. After the 1967, 6-Day War in which Israel acquired that territory from Jordan, Leibowitz immediately appealed to the Israelis to withdraw. The followers of Rav Kook and his son, Tzvi Yehuda Kook, understood the Israeli victory as a further sign that the period of messianic redemption had begun. They spearheaded the settlement of the West Bank. Their sense of Divine promise for their ongoing possession of the entire biblical Land of Israel leads them to circumvent both democratic and halakhic processes, according to Leibowitz. When you're on a mission from God, it is tempting to ignore conventional protocols.

14. It is customary that when criticizing someone who is not particularly pious and doesn't keep the Torah and commandments, he will retort: "I have a Jewish heart, and deep down I'm a good Jew." That was Korah's claim: "Even though my people's behavior isn't always meticulous, God is in them. Deep down, they're good Jews."

(Eliezer Valdman, Divrei Eliezer, fl. 1898–1905)[20]

The Divrei Eliezer is reading Korah's claim that "God is in their midst" literally to mean that God is inside of them. The Divrei Eliezer is writing at the turn of the 20th century when the traditional Jewish lifestyle and observance of the *halakhah* are breaking down. What we today refer to as cultural Judaism has its roots in this period, when Jews maintain their identity through food, literature, and fellowship, but not through traditional religious observance. As for Leibowitz, what matters to the Divrei Eliezer are deeds, not whatever may or may not be deep down.

Ups and Downs

The final part of Korah's charge against Moses was arrogance. The Meshi asks how anyone could think that Moses, described as the most humble man on earth (Num. 12:3), could be perceived as arrogant.

> *15. Sometimes we are cast in roles in which, to be effective, we must adopt postures which are not entirely natural. Moses did not ask to be the leader. He resisted. He was humble. We, the readers, know that. But Korah does not. He sees an imperious ruler who appointed his own brother as High Priest. The weight of Korah's charge—"Why do you raise yourself above us?"—brings Moses to his knees. It's true that he is above this people, but not due to his own ambition. As Samson Raphael Hirsch has pointed out, there's no way to verbally convince Korah of the purity of his deeds. Moses stays on his knees, demonstrating his humility, while looking Korah straight in the eyes. He then explains the ordeal that will settle Korah's charges by recapitulating, with a twist, Moses' fiery call to leadership.*
>
> (Meshi, contemporary, United States)

Meshi's comment addresses several issues. The first is the occasional incongruity between role and reality. In order to succeed, people tend to behave according to their rank. Professors don't generally consult with their students about which questions should appear on the final exam. Although professors may value democracy as much as their students, the classroom environment has elements of a dictatorship. But if the students were to evaluate their professors strictly on the basis of their classroom behavior, those students might conclude that their professors were arrogant dictators. It works in the reverse, too. A professor shouldn't conclude that students are in agreement with him or her simply because no opposition is voiced in class. Students tend not to contradict their professors to their face. Meshi makes the point that Korah's claim, while uncharitable, is not necessarily unreasonable.

Meshi also explains why Moses fell on his face. Korah and his gang rose up against Moses (v. 2) and accused him of raising himself above the people (v. 3). The language here suggests that Korah was projecting on to Moses the sin for exactly which Korah was guilty. By lowering himself, in front of all the rebels, Moses was showing Korah that the charges against him were misguided in a way that words could not. How can you *tell* someone that you are really very humble? Furthermore, Meshi explains why Moses' response to Korah seemingly ignores the substance of Korah's charges. The only way to resolve the issue of leadership was to make what had been a private affair into a matter of public record. God's selection of Moses, originally involving an unconsumed burning bush, would now be reconfirmed through the consumption by Divine fire of Korah's 250 men (Num. 16:35).

> *16. Moses was shaken from this dispute since it was already their fourth offense and he had defended them each time before this. But now, he fell on his face, thinking, "How many times can I pester God on their behalf?"*
>
> (from *Tanhuma* and Rashi)

For Meshi, Moses fell to his face as a sign of humility; for *Tanhuma*, Moses fell in exasperation. As the defender of the people, Moses had intervened when God wanted to punish the people after the incident of the Golden Calf (Exod. 32), after the Israelites complained about conditions in the wilderness (Num. 11), and after the pessimistic report of the spies (Num. 14). According to *Tanhuma*, Moses felt that he had only so much credit with God and couldn't continue to request leniency for these stubborn transgressors.

Tanhuma's comment, therefore, highlights Moses' character development. This stiff-necked people (Exod. 34:9) has worn down Moses. He's no longer the leader he once was. He's weakened. We have no reason to think that God, "forgiving iniquity and transgression" (Num. 14:18), would feel harassed by Moses' repeated petitions on behalf of his people. Rabbinic tradition tends to distinguish between Noah and Abraham on precisely that issue. Noah didn't put up a fight when informed about the impending flood (Gen. 6:22). Abraham, however, showed himself to be a veteran of the Middle Eastern *souk* by bargaining with God over the destruction of Sodom and Gomorrah (Gen. 18:16–33). While in the past, Moses had acted with Abrahamic strength, after the long desert sojourn, the *Tanhuma*'s Moses is feeble.

> *17. Moses fell on his face in prayer. And there it was said to him what he then told Korah.*
>
> (Rashbam)

Rashbam points out the consequences of his grandfather Rashi's commentary. If Moses had fallen to the ground out of exasperation, then the ordeal which he commanded, which killed hundreds of people including the rebels' wives and children, was of his own devising. It's one thing for God's anger to blaze forth, quite another in the case of Moses. For *Tanhuma* and Rashi, God goes along with Moses' plan. As the midrash says, "When the righteous make a plan, God upholds it."[21] In this case, Moses' plan and its consequences reflect bitterness and despair. Of all the options available, including a test that culminated in almond blossoms (Num. 17:16–24), Moses chose capital punishment for the offenders and all their families.

Rashbam, however, is explicit that the bloody ordeal was conceived by God. Moses fell to the ground in prayer and, thereafter, he immediately outlined the ordeal. Rashbam makes a logical connection between verses 4 and 5: what Moses received from God in one verse, he transmitted to Korah in the next. In exculpating Moses from the effects of the ordeal, Rashbam might also be limiting the authority of Moses. Moses could not have answered Korah on behalf of God without first receiving a prompt. When Moses speaks in the Torah, he relays God's messages; he does not innovate his own. In every generation, there are those who claim to speak on God's behalf. The issue which separates Rashi and Rashbam highlights for their readers how difficult it is to know the source of those who claim to speak on God's behalf.

18. Since Moses seemingly could have responded immediately to Korah, why did he fall on his face? Moses feared that this question from Korah was really coming from above and Korah was simply the intermediary. Thus, Moses fell on his face to contemplate. Was there any haughtiness in him? After a scrutinizing search, he found there was not even a trace of pride. Then he understood that Korah was no heavenly intermediary but only a contentious man. Moses then responded to him.
    (from Rebbe Schneur Zalman of Liadi, 1745–1812, Poland/Russia)[22]

Rebbe Shneur Zalman was the founder of the Chabad-Lubavitch group of Hasids. Like other Hasidic masters, he is acutely aware of the psychology of the Torah's characters. In this case, as a religious leader himself, he has particular insight into the mind of Moses. He understands how easy it is for authority to corrupt. His Moses is not only introspective, but amazingly receptive to constructive criticism. Although the Torah commands us to "reprove your kinsman" (Lev. 19:17), it is often difficult to hear such proof from a stranger or foe. Part of the Rebbe's message is that to be like Moses, we need to open ourselves up to self-improvement regardless of where the criticism springs forth. Constructive criticism is ultimately Divine.

It seems that the Rebbe might also be bothered by Moses' response to Korah. Although Moses conceived of the ordeal on his own, he did so because he understood that Korah was trying to divide the community with his false charges. In such a case, when the unity of the Jewish people is at stake, the Rebbe seems to suggest, Moses was entitled to stage a dramatic verification of his own rightful leadership. There are exigencies in life when drastic measures must be taken, and the *halakhah* recognizes that sometimes laws must be broken in order to preserve the greater good.[23] In a stunning rereading of Psalm 119:126 ("It is time to act for the LORD, for they have violated Your Torah"), Rabbi Natan exclaims: "It is time to act for the LORD: violate your Torah!"[24]

The Timing, the Test and the Taunt

19. Moses said to himself, "This is the time of day when people indulge in drinking and eating and maybe that's why they're saying such things." Therefore, Moses called the ordeal for the following morning in the hope that in the interim they would repent.

(*Tanhuma* and Rashi)

Why doesn't Moses stage the test immediately upon the challenge? According to this reading, he recognized that at the time the rebels rose up against him, they may have been emboldened by alcohol after having been charged up at a venting session over a communal table. Moses was hoping that cooler heads would prevail the following morning. Moses may have learned from serving as God's agent to Pharaoh the strategy of warning the victim to allow him an opportunity to repent.[25] Although the strategy was not successful with Pharaoh, Moses may have hoped that Korah was less hardhearted. *Tanhuma's* Moses is both perceptive and merciful. He senses the bravado of Korah and his gang and provides them with an opportunity to fade into the night without losing face or being killed. According to the Talmud, On's wife makes good use of this window of opportunity. Moses, here, is a model of how to react to challenges without being reactive.

In this section of Rashi's Torah commentary, he relies heavily on the *Tanhuma* and says so at the beginning of his comments. One would not expect an anthology of Rabbinic comments, like the *Tanhuma*, to be internally consistent. So, for instance, there are several different explanations for what Korah took. One might expect, however, that Rashi ought to be consistent throughout his commentary. But, Rashi's medieval anthology of Rabbinic comments displays the same characteristic plurality as the earlier anthologies. Therefore, in our comment, Rashi cites the *Tanhuma's* explanation for why Moses delayed the test until the following day by suggesting that Moses wanted to provide the rebels with an opportunity for *teshuvah* (repentance). Yet in comment 16, Rashi cites a comment from *Tanhuma* which portrays a less patient Moses. Of course, one could reconcile these two comments and temper Moses' impatience with Korah and his gang. But Rashi's agenda, unlike many of the later medieval commentators, was not internal consistency. He sought to preserve those Rabbinic statements that shed light on the Torah in meaningful ways and which crystallized a Rabbinic reading of the Torah. His emphasis on the authority of the interpreters of Torah can be seen in the following comment: "You shall act in accordance with the instructions (*torah*) given you and the rulings handed down to you; you must not deviate from the verdict that they [the priests or the magistrates] announce to you either to the right or to the left" (Deut. 17:11). Rashi's addition: "Even if he says to you that the right is the left or that the left is the right."[26] Perhaps Rashi's commitment to communal authority helps explain his acquiescence of Moses devising the test for Korah on his own.

> 20. *The true argument of the rebellion is that in the world of the law what has been inspired always becomes emptied of the spirit, but that in this state it continues to maintain its claim of full inspiration; or, in other words, that the living element dies off but that thereafter what is left continues to rule over living men. And the true conclusion is that the law must again and again immerse itself in the consuming and purifying fire of the spirit, in order to renew itself and anew refine the genuine substance out of the dross of what has become false. This lies in the continuation of the line of that Mosaic principle of ever-recurrent renewal.*
>
> *As against this comes the false argument of the rebels that the law as such displaces the spirit and the freedom, and the false conclusion that it ought to be replaced by them.*
>
> (Martin Buber, 1878–1965, Germany and the Land of Israel)[27]

Buber's Korah has a problem with externally imposed laws. Since we are all holy, on what basis can anyone "give orders or issue prohibitions to anybody else"?[28] Buber recognizes that communities require laws, promulgated by a few inspired people, which obligate all its members. The problem is not with the Law; it's with certain laws that no longer pulse with the Divine spirit. The solution is not to abandon the Law, and certainly not to replace the Law with men who have only their interests at heart; the solution, as Moses shows us in literary fashion in verse 6, is to constantly renew the law through the purifying "fire of the spirit."

Buber's Korah is Immanuel Kant and those who followed him, Jewish and non-Jewish, in denigrating heteronomy, or externally imposed laws. Buber rejects the critique, though he is sympathetic to the question of all legal systems: when does a law no longer embody the spirit through which it was initially drafted? Buber speaks of the "Mosaic principle of ever-recurrent renewal" as the solution to this problem, one that he sees symbolically in the test that Moses assigns to Korah and his gang. Buber regards the Torah as religious literature while rejecting the traditional notions of Divine dictation or Divine authority mediated through Rabbinic *halakhah*. In this comment, Buber places himself in that liminal space between theoretical acceptance of *halakhah* as an attempt to embody the Divine will, and practical rejection of the authority of Rabbinic *halakhah* because of its failure to live up to the Mosaic principle of ever-recurrent renewal.[29]

Martin Buber and those who share his religious ideology, in turn, become the Korah for traditional halakhic adherents.

21. Korah was committed to the doctrine of religious subjectivism, which regards one's personal feelings as primary in the religious experience. . . . The mitzvah [commandment] is an external form of a spiritual experience . . . What follows from this reasoning is that the mitzvah may be modified according to changing times or even according to the individual tempera-ments of different people. There is, to him, no inherent redemptive power in the mitzvah beyond its therapeutic effects, its capacity to evoke a subjective experience. . . . This kind of ever-changing worship, which responds to vary-ing sensations, is basically idolatrous.
(Rav Joseph B. Soloveitchik, 1903–1993, Lithuania and United States)[30]

Rav Soloveitchik begins his essay on Korah by presenting the *Tanhuma*'s scene where Korah takes an entirely blue *tallit* to Moses and asks him whether it still requires a blue cord. Common sense would suggest that Korah was right. How could a single thread fulfill a mitzvah that all the threads in the *tallit* could not? Rav Soloveitchik's point is precisely that the world of *ha-lakhah* is not one of common sense. Halakhic reasoning involves a system of logic, much like mathematics or physics, that is sometimes counterintuitive. Only people trained in *halakhah* are competent to make halakhic judgments. Korah's claim that all the community is holy may be correct, but it does not qualify them to make halakhic decisions on their own.

Rav Soloveitchik is targeting all those in the Jewish world, particularly the leaders of Reform Judaism, who claim the authority to make halakhic decisions themselves based on their common sense rather than halakhic training. His fear is that this religious subjectivism will lead to religious anarchy with "everyone doing as they please" (Judges 21:25). Worse, from the Rav's standpoint, is that such anarchy is tantamount to idolatry. Just as *Tanhuma's* Korah denied that some commandments were Divine, contemporary religious subjectivists neglect some commandments because the performance of those commandments leaves them empty. In some cases, non-Orthodox Jews reject certain traditions because they're perceived to be unethical. In both cases, the individual places their own "common" sense of the Divine over and above what the halakhic tradition has authorized. Worshipping God by "following your heart" (Num. 15:39, immediately preceding the Korah passage) is the Torah's definition of idolatry.

> *22. The holy One, blessed be He, said to Moses, "The stick with which you struck them will be used to strike you. You said to them, 'You have gone too far,' and tomorrow you'll hear from Me, 'You have gone too far'"* (Dt. 3:26).
> (*Numbers Rabbah* 18, a medieval compilation of Rabbinic midrash)

The literary parallels are striking. First, Korah says to Moses that he has gone too far (v. 3). Moses throws it back in Korah's face (v. 7). He's the one who has gone too far by challenging Moses' position as a leader. The midrash, however, points out that this phrase is echoed later in the Book of Deuteronomy. There, Moses pleads with God to allow him to cross over the Jordan River and enter the Land. For forty years Moses has led the Israelites through the wilderness after having taken them out of Egypt. He is now in sight of his goal, and God denies Moses the ultimate sense of closure with the words: You have gone too far. The *darshan* hears the echo and draws the conclusion that God is reminding Moses of why he will not be allowed into the Land. Measure for measure: as Moses threw Korah's words back in his face, so does God throw the same words back in Moses' face.

Within the Bible itself there is an explanation for why Moses does not gain entry into the Land. He lost his temper and struck a rock (Num. 20:2–13). Perhaps our *darshan* is bothered by this rather innocuous slip leading to Moses' death on the east side of the Jordan. Both stories share the theme of Moses being confronted by rebels and reacting unkindly. Leaders have the burden to maintain the dignity of their office. Moses, as God's chosen representative, had the additional burden of behaving in a godly way. Our *darshan* seems to be extending that line of midrashic reasoning that Moses was exhausted. He no longer had the patience, the long-suffering kindness to lead his people into the Land.

Disputes for Heaven

Our story becomes incorporated into the Rabbinic paradigm for disputes. The Mishnah, though almost entirely halakhic, has one tractate that is exclusively aggadic, *Avot*. Toward the end of the tractate is an enigmatic mishnah: "Any dispute which is for the sake of Heaven, its end will endure. But if it's not for the sake of Heaven, its end will not endure. Which is a dispute for the sake of Heaven? That's the dispute of Hillel and Shammai. And which isn't for the sake of Heaven? That's the dispute of Korah and all his gang" (*Avot* 5:19).

What does "its end will endure" mean? If we say that the dispute will be resolved once and for all, then that means that the dispute of Korah and all his gang will *not* be settled once and for all. Alternatively, if we understand that clause to be referring not to the resolution of the dispute, but to the dispute itself, then the dispute of Hillel and Shammai will go on and on, while that of Korah and all his gang will not. In either case, what seems to define the dispute is not the argument as much as the intention of the disputants. Maimonides, in his commentary on *Avot*, maintains that the desire for truth motivates Hillel and Shammai. Maimonides takes his cue from Rabbinic traditions which posit that the words of both Hillel and Shammai are the words of the living God, and that identify God with truth.[31] But those same Rabbinic traditions usually resolve the dispute in favor of Hillel. If so, how can the dispute endure?

> 23. *"Any dispute which is for the sake of heaven, its end will endure,"* means that people will always persist in raising the issues of the dispute, sometimes concerning this point, and sometimes concerning another. Over the course of time, disputants will add to the argument. A dispute that's not for the sake of Heaven, its end will not endure. *Only the original dispute will be mentioned, and it will be finished and there it'll die, like the dispute of Korah.*
>
> (Rabbeinu Yonah, d. 1263, Spain)

It's not only a good story that can be turned over and over again, a good dispute can be, as well. Rabbeinu Yonah, once a foe of the philosophizing Rambam, came to change his mind later in life. He knows the value of dispute; it can illuminate previously hidden aspects of reality. Any adversarial system, be it the courts of Israel or those of the United States, believes that the best method for approaching truth is through dispute. The arguments of Hillel and Shammai live on through the spirited debate of Torah students. Isaac Luria, the great sixteenth-century Kabbalist of Safed, even suggests that in the coming era, the *halakhah* will be decided according to Shammai. An argument like Korah and his gang isn't about truth, it's about blind ambition and power. Our next commentator, influenced by Isaac Luria, adds further light on our disputants.

> *24. Since the mishnah's wording places Hillel against Shammai, shouldn't the parallel construction at the end place Korah against Moses? But it places Korah against all his gang. The mishnah is telling us that there was internal dissension and everyone involved in the rebellion was in it for his own glorification. Thus we see that their intention was not for the sake of Heaven.*
>
> (Jonathan Eybeschutz, *Ya'arot Dvash*, 1690–1764, Prague)

According to Maimonides, the mishnah was telling us that Korah and his gang were in it for themselves. For Eybeschutz, the mishnah is telling us that each was in it for himself. Many a revolutionary movement has foundered for lack of internal cohesion. Conflicting agendas, driven by megalomaniacs who put their self-interest ahead of their ostensible cause, undermine the legitimacy of their communal goals. Eybeschutz may be picking up on the braiding of our story—there are multiple agendas being pursued in this text. They each fail and Eybeschutz draws the appropriate conclusion.

In the process, though, he salvages Korah's claim in two ways. First of all, the problem is not with Korah's argument; it's with his intention. Neither the mishnah nor Eybeschutz seem to have a problem with Korah's claim that all the people are holy. But if so, by what right does Korah have to lead the congregation? The mystical tradition, as we have seen, straddles the fine line between rejecting Korah and preserving his claim of universal Jewish holiness. Meshi makes explicit the second way in which Eybeschutz subtly promotes Korah.

> *25. Eybeschutz emphasizes that the dispute between Korah and all his gang is not for the sake of Heaven. The implication is that the dispute between Korah and Moses is for the sake of Heaven.*
>
> (Meshi)

By one measure, Meshi is surely right. Aspects of Korah's rebellion have been mulled over by generation upon generation of Torah students. Korah may not have taken charge of the Israelites in the wilderness, but he certainly captured the attention and imagination of future commentators. But Meshi's point, and perhaps Eybeschutz's as well, is theological, not historical.

Isn't there some sense in which the entire community is holy? Notwithstanding the objections by commentators like Hirsch, Buber, and Leibowitz, the

Book of Deuteronomy does call the Israelites holy and chosen by God as a special possession.[32] As much as many modern, liberal Jews might want to claim that the traditional concept of the chosen people is all just a misunderstanding, that's not entirely honest. Whether being chosen involves distinction (as in Otto's definition of holiness as separation) or superiority (as in the mystical tradition's understanding), is itself the subject of dispute in the Jewish tradition.

Korah's claim, once cleansed of his selfish stain, has echoed through the history of Jewish thought. Modern liberals, like Meshi, might want to strip the question of its biblical racialism. Are humans holy, and, if so, in what sense? Hasidic teachings tell us that of course we're holy. Hasidism, after all, is based on the mystical teachings of Judaism which emphasize the Divine immanence in all aspects of reality. But the principle of Divine immanence is dangerous. One might come to believe erroneously in his own holiness. That's what happened to Korah. All things in their isolated parts participate in the Divine, yes; but only as a unified whole are things holy. Korah spoke a truth he didn't fully understand. *All the community is holy*—as a community, as a whole, but not as individuals.

Summary of Comments

Comment	Problem	Resolution	Textual Mechanism	Historical Circumstance
1.	What did Korah take?	He took in (deceived) the leaders	*Take*, in Hosea, means deceive	None
2.	What did Korah take?	A *tallit* (prayer shawl)	Juxtaposition of chapters	Christian challenges to divinity of all commandments
3.	What did Korah take?	250 men	Direct object, implied in verse 1, explicit in verse 2	None
4.	What did Korah take?	He took himself away from the ways of his ancestors	Based on Onkelos' translation of Korah separating himself from the community	Assimilation and acculturation in Europe at the turn of the 20th century
5.	a. The timing of the rebellion b. How could Korah manipulate the leaders of the people?	The people were desperate and susceptible to Korah's demagoguery	The narrative context of increasing punishments	Medieval concern with larger narrative units

continued

Comment	Problem	Resolution	Textual Mechanism	Historical Circumstance
6.	Why did Korah rebel?	Jealousy—Korah was the reincarnation of Cain	Similarity of motives between Cain and Korah and literary parallels between stories	Kabbalistic doctrine on reincarnation
7.	Why did Dathan and Abiram rebel?	They disliked Moses for having high-handedly intruded on their argument in Egypt	G'zerah shavah	None
8.	What happened to On?	His wife disabled him from joining the insurgency	Biblical and Rabbinic context of wives influencing husbands	None
9.	Who were the 250 men of the assembly?	They were experts in determining the calendar	Vowel change turns men of assembly into callers of times	Challenge of Dead Sea community in late antiquity
10.	What does holy mean?	For Korah, holiness is a product of the experience of revelation	Context of revelation	None
11.	What does holy mean?	For Moses, holiness is a function of being appointed by God for a specific task	Frequent meaning of holiness in Torah involves separating for special role	None
12.	What does holy mean?	Dedicating yourself wholly and exclusively to God	Being holy is a commandment, not a description of a state achieved	Modern emphasis on equal opportunity and reaction to Kantian charges of legalism
13.	Who are the sons of Korah who did not die?	Those who maintain Korah's sense of inherent holiness—contemporary Hasids and nationalist followers of Tzvi Yehuda Kook	Verses 16:32 and 26:11 in tension	Inner-Israeli debate about the future of the West Bank

continued

Comment	Problem	Resolution	Textual Mechanism	Historical Circumstance
14.	What does Korah mean by God being in our midst?	God is inside of us	The Hebrew, *b'toch*, can be read as *in the midst* or as *inside*	Assimilation in modernity
15.	Why does Moses fall on his face? What's the relationship between Korah's charge and Moses' response?	To demonstrate humility, since words would be ineffective. Similarly, only a demonstration could determine whom God desires to lead	Moses responds to the charge of raising himself by falling on his face.	None
16.	Why does Moses fall on his face?	He was exasperated	He is not praying on their behalf as he had other times the people sinned	None
17.	Why does Moses fall on his face? Whose idea was the ordeal?	He was praying. The ordeal was revealed to Moses in prayer.	Juxtaposition of falling on his face and explaining the ordeal	None
18.	Why does Moses fall on his face?	Introspection	None	Hasidic concern with religious psychology
19.	Why does Moses wait until the morning?	To provide an opportunity for the rebels to repent	Biblical context—Moses offered Pharaoh opportunities to repent	None
20.	What's the real test?	To purify the law in the fire of the spirit	Putting the incense in the fire is understood symbolically	Kantian denigration of heteronomy
21.	What's Korah's argument?	Since all are holy, each is equally competent to determine the law	Extending the *Tanhuma*'s reading of Korah taking an all-blue *tallit*	The predominance of non-halakhic Jews and Judaisms in modernity
22.	Why wasn't Moses allowed to enter the Land?	He was short-tempered and sarcastic to Korah	God uses the same words that Moses had used to Korah	None

continued

Comment	Problem	Resolution	Textual Mechanism	Historical Circumstance
23.	What does the mishnah's "its end will endure" mean?	The dispute will continue to be disputed	"its end" refers to the dispute rather than the resolution	Rabbinic value of dispute
24.	Why is there seemingly no parallelism in the mishnah?	The dispute in question is between Korah and his gang	There is parallelism	None
25.	What else does the mishnah's parallelism tell us?	The dispute between Korah and Moses is for the sake of Heaven	Eybeschutz's emphasis on parallelism	None

NOTES

1. On Korah's rhetorical ability, see Louis Feldman, "Josephus' Portrait of Korah," *Old Testament Essays* 6:3 (1993): 399–426.

2. *Chatam Sofer.*

3. *Epistle to Flora*, in *The Gnostic Scriptures*, trans. Bentley Layton (New York: Doubleday, 1987), 309. Cited in Steven D. Fraade, "Moses and the Commandments: Can Hermeneutics, History, and Rhetoric be Disentangled?" in *The Idea of Biblical Interpretation: Essays in Honor of James L. Kugel*, ed. Hindy Najman and Judith H. Newman (Leiden: Brill, 2004), 399–422, 418. Fraade devotes several pages to the Rabbinic midrashim on Korah, 413–415.

4. *Itturei Torah.* Cited in *Sparks Beneath the Surface: A Spiritual Commentary on the Torah*, ed. Lawrence S. Kushner and Kerry M. Olitzky (Northvale, N.J: Jason Aronson, 1993), 189.

5. Arthur Green has an introductory essay on Rabbi Yehudah Leib Alter of Ger in *The Language of Truth* (Philadelphia: The Jewish Publication Society, 1998).

6. Some contemporary translations, including Robert Alter's *The Five Books of Moses* (New York: W. W. Norton & Co., 2004) and Richard Elliott Friedman's *Commentary on the Torah with a New English Translation* (New York: HarperCollins, 2001) do not include "now." Interestingly, they also both preserve the grammatical problem of what Korah took.

7. Robert Alter makes a similar connection in his analysis of the Korah episode. *The Art of Biblical Narrative* (New York: Basic Books, 1981), 133–137.

8. *Tanhuma.*

9. Zohar, Genesis 54a.

10. For more on reincarnation in the mystical tradition, see Gershom Scholem, chap. 5, *On the Mystical Shape of the Godhead* (New York: Schocken Books, 1991).

11. The *Steinsaltz Reference Guide* (New York: Random House, 1989) explains and provides examples of Talmudic terms and principles, like *g'zerah shavah*.

12. Moses' circle of concern for those outside of his ethnic group is further widened in the episode immediately following this one when he defends the daughters of Reuel against the shepherds (Exod. 2:16–17). The principle is further extended and enshrined, repeatedly, in Mosaic legislation: "You shall not wrong a stranger or oppress him, for you were strangers in the land of Egypt" (Exod. 22:20). See also Exod. 23:9, Lev. 24:22, and Num. 15:16. Nehama Leibowitz develops this theme in her *Studies in* Exodus, trans. Aryeh Newman (Jerusalem: World Zionist Organization, 1981).

13. b. *Brachot* 27b.

14. J. A. Draper, "'Korah' and the Second Temple," in *Templum Amicitiae: Essays on the Second Temple Presented to Ernst Bammel*, ed. William Horbury (Sheffield: JSOT Press, 1991), 150–174.

15. See Geza Vermes, *The Complete Dead Sea Scrolls in English* (New York: Penguin Classics, 2004), 78ff. See also Rachel Elior, *The Three Temples: The Emergence of Jewish Mysticism* (Oxford: Littman Library of Jewish Civilization, 2004).

16. James M. Scott, "Korah and Qumran," in *The Bible at Qumran*, ed. Peter W. Flint (Grand Rapids: William B. Eerdmans Publishing Company, 2001), 182–202.

17. *New International Biblical Commentary: 2 Corinthians* (Peabody, MA: Hendrickson Publishers, 1998).

18. For an examination of modern Jewish thinking on the role of the commandments, see Arnold Eisen, *Rethinking Modern Judaism: Ritual, Commandment, Community* (Chicago: Chicago University Press, 1998).

19. Leibowitz's approach to Judaism is succinctly presented in the first essay of *Judaism, Human Values and the Jewish State*, ed. Eliezer Goldman (Cambridge: Harvard University Press, 1992). For more on Kaplan's rejection of chosenness, see chap. 13 of *The Future of the American Jew* (New York: Macmillan Company, 1948).

20. *Itturei Torah*, 5:100.

21. *Numbers Rabbah* 14. Fraade deals with this issue in his article cited above.

22. *Itturei Torah*, 5:101.

23. Ramban also understands Moses is operating on his own due to the exigencies of the moment and that God will fulfill Moses' plan.

24. b. *Brachot* 54a.

25. My student, Jennifer Emsley, helped me understand how this statement could be something more than a naked attempt by the Rabbis to promote *teshuvah* (repentance). Although one would be hard-pressed to clearly see the theme of *teshuvah* in our verses, in the broader context of Moses' life it is certainly a strong motif. See Deut. 30:8. In other words, though *Tanhuma*'s comment seems to be an unlikely *peshat* in the immediate context of our chapter, the comment gains plausibility as we look at Moses' character throughout the Pentateuch.

26. *Sifre* 154.

27. *Moses* (Oxford: East and West Library, 1946), 188.

28. Ibid., 186.

29. Buber draws out the distinctions between religion and religiosity in "Jewish Religiosity," chap. 5, *On Judaism*, ed. Nahum N. Glatzer (New York: Schocken Books, 1995).

30. "The 'Common-Sense' Rebellion against Torah Authority," in *In Reflections of the Rav* (Jerusalem: Department for Torah Education, 1979), 139–49.

31. b. *Eruvin* 13b and b. *Yoma* 69b.

32. Deut. 7:6 and 14:2.

Chapter 6

THE DAUGHTERS OF ZELOPHEHAD

T HE TORAH CAN be a difficult piece of literature for contemporary feminists. Although the women of Genesis and Exodus are usually portrayed as strong and perceptive, the legal sections of the Torah tend to treat women as the inferior other. Prior to the moment of God's revelation at Mount Sinai, for example, Moses directs his words of preparation only to the men (Exod. 19:15).

Yet women's subordinate legal status is counterbalanced by a commitment to justice and equity. The story of the daughters of Zelophehad demonstrates the Torah's flexibility concerning unprecedented cases that might result in an injustice were the law not amended. While many important women go unnamed in the TANAKH, our story is remarkable in that it names the five sisters who respectfully appeal to Moses to change the Torah's law of inheritance. And the law is changed. And, then, at the very end of the Book of Numbers, the law is changed yet again.

> The daughters of Zelophehad, of the Manassite family—son of Hepher, son of Gilead, son of Machir, son of Manasseh, son of Joseph—came forward. The names of the daughters were Mahlah, Noah, Hoglah, Milcah, and Tirzah. ²They stood before Moses, Elazar the priest, the chieftains, and the whole assembly at the entrance to the Tent of Meeting, and they said, ³"Our father died in the wilderness. He was not one of the faction, Korah's faction, which banded together against the LORD, but died for his own sin; and he has left no sons. ⁴Let not our father's name be lost to his clan just because he had no son! Give us a holding among our father's kinsmen!" ⁵Moses brought their case before the LORD. ⁶And the LORD said to Moses, ⁷"The plea of Zelophehad's daughters is just: you should give them a hereditary holding among their father's kinsmen; transfer their father's share to them."
>
> (Numbers 27:1–7)

Lovers of Zion

*1. Just as Joseph loved the Land of Israel, so too did the daughters of
Zelophehad.*

(Sifre, Numbers 133, compilation of midrash halakhah
on Numbers, 3rd century, Land of Israel)

The Torah is very concerned about tracing family lines. Indeed, in the
previous chapter, Numbers 26, the bulk of the text is dedicated to genealo-
gies. To historians and attorneys, lengthy lists of family lines might prove
useful; but to readers expecting to find God's words, these inventories of
who begat whom quickly become tiresome. In our case, the genealogy found
in our first verse and previously in Numbers 26:29–33 are nearly identical
and exceptional, since usually women remain in the background. Even if we
reluctantly agree that such bookkeeping was necessary in order to allocate
the Land of Israel properly among the tribes of Israel, why do we need this
repetition?

The *Sifre* notices that in this verse, unlike in the previous chapter, the genealogy extends back to Joseph. This connection suggests to the *Sifre* that it is
the similarity of values held by Joseph and the daughters of Zelophehad that
warrants this near repetition. On his deathbed, Joseph makes his brothers
swear that his bones will be taken to the Land of Israel when the Israelites
eventually leave Egypt (Gen. 50:25). On the surface, our comment links
Joseph's love of the Land and the daughters' love of the Land as they plead before Moses for their father's share.

The *Sifre* was well aware that several of the Israelite tribes, including descendants of Joseph in the tribe of Menasseh, opted to settle in the greener
pastures on the east side of the Jordan River (Num. 32:33). In other words,
not all of Joseph's descendants loved the Land of Israel so much that they
were willing to settle in it. And as the *Sifre* subtly points out, neither did
Joseph. Although as viceroy of Egypt he certainly could have ascended to the
Land of Israel, if only to retire, he chose to be buried there instead. Joseph and
his descendants may love the Land of Israel, but only some, the descendants
of Zelophehad's daughters, love it enough to live there.[1]

Mercy, Sexism, and Thinking with Women

*2. When the daughters of Zelophehad heard that the Land was being
divided among the tribes to the men, but not to the women, they all came*

together to take counsel. They said, "The mercies of flesh and blood are not
like the mercies of the Omnipresent. The mercies of flesh and blood are
greater for men than women, but the One who spoke and the world came
into being is not like that. Rather, His mercies are on men and women. His
mercies encompass all, as it says, 'Who gives food to all flesh' (Ps. 136:25),
and 'Who gives the beasts their food' (Ps. 147:9), and 'The LORD is good to
all, and His mercy is upon all His works'" (Ps. 145:9).

(Sifre)

The NJPS translation has the daughters coming forward, ostensibly to
Moses. But the *Sifre* reads the predicate in our first verse (*vatikravna*) as
though the women drew near each other rather than near to Moses. After all,
the predicate in the second verse clarifies that they're in front of Moses.
Given the assumption of the Rabbis that the text is pregnant with Divine
meaning, the first predicate *must* be telling us more information than what we
would know from the predicate in verse 2.

The Rabbis of the *Sifre* tend to paint very flattering portraits of the
daughters. In this comment, we see that the women are paying attention to
communal events. Immediately before we are introduced to Zelophehad's
daughters, there is a census taken for the purpose of apportioning the Land.
The women then realize that only men will receive allocations of property.
Upon discovering the patriarchal system of allocation, they confer. What's
more impressive, from a Rabbinic perspective, is that their discussion employs
biblical verses. They are not merely lamenting their fate as the subordinate
sex, they're pointing out that the rules of inheritance do not conform to the
religious principle and biblical descriptions of a merciful God who does not
discriminate according to gender (or species).

The *Sifre's* comment is quite radical. While in the biblical text the daughters couch their argument in terms of their father's loss of a name, here the
argument is simply one of gender equality. Ancient Israelite and Rabbinic
societies, as well as many of their laws, were patriarchal; and the Rabbis, by
"thinking with women" and putting their words in the mouths of Zelophehad's daughters, admit as much.[2]

Speculating on Sins and Sons

Once the daughters mention their father's death, they immediately distance
him from Korah, whose gang also died in the desert. The daughters are
explicit that Zelophehad died "for his own sin," but they are tantalizingly

silent about what that sin was. Some commentators cannot resist the temptation to satisfy our curiosity.

> 3. Our Rabbis taught: The wood gatherer was Zelophehad. Just as it says, "Once, when the Israelites were in the wilderness, they came upon a man . . ." (Num. 15:32) Further on it says, "Our father died in the wilderness." Just as there it was referring to Zelophehad, so here, too. These are the words of Rabbi Akiva.
>
> Rabbi Yehudah ben Beteyra responded: "Akiva, whether you're right or wrong, you'll have to give an accounting for that in the future. If you're right, the Torah concealed his identity and you revealed it! If you're wrong, you've slandered a righteous man!"
>
> (Gemara, Shabbat, 96b, 6th century, Babylonia)

As the ensuing Talmudic discussion suggests, but then rejects, it seems as though Rabbi Akiva was employing a g'zerah shavah, a common Rabbinic principle of biblical interpretation. In our verse, the expression *in the wilderness* is used. The same expression appears in the earlier story of the wood gatherer on Sabbath who is killed for violating a Sabbath prohibition. This identical term, *in the wilderness*, is the connective tissue that allows for a g'zerah shavah, the transitive property of Rabbinic logic. The transitive property says, if a equals b and b equals c, then a equals c. In our case, if wood gatherer equals wilderness in Num. 15 and wilderness equals Zelophehad in Num. 27, then, using the transitive property of Rabbinic logic (g'zerah shavah), the wood gatherer of Num. 15 equals Zelophehad of Num. 27. In different language, in one case in the wilderness we know the man's name but don't know why he died (Zelophehad); in the other case in the wilderness, we know why he died but don't know his name (the wood gatherer). The g'zerah shavah allows the Rabbis to learn something from two seemingly unrelated stories connected by a word or phrase. But according to the Rabbinic rules of interpretation, a g'zerah shavah cannot be innovated by a student; it needs to have been passed down to a student from his teacher.[3]

Rabbi Yehudah rebukes Rabbi Akiva for a transgression of the tongue.[4] Who are *we* to reveal what the Torah has chosen to conceal? If God wanted to protect the wood gatherer's anonymity, why speculate on his identity? Some even suggest that the wood gatherer was a martyr who intentionally transgressed in order to impress upon others the centrality of Shabbat and, thereby, raise the level of religious commitment within the community.[5]

What's even more interesting is that, according to Rabbi Yehudah, if Rabbi Akiva is wrong, he has slandered a righteous man. Rabbi Yehudah is calling Zelophehad righteous even though the daughters admit that he died for his own sin. Apparently, some transgressions are worthy of death but don't vitiate a person's righteousness. Perhaps Rabbi Yehudah understood that the daughters' passion for a portion of the Land of Israel must have been inherited from their father. Indeed one anonymous rabbi (Rabbi Yehudah?) suggests that the sin of Zelophehad was overzealousness. He waged war prematurely against the Canaanites and Amalekites without God's blessing (Num. 14:44).[6]

4. The cantillation mark over "our father" resembles a serpent with its tail in its mouth. Zelophehad died because of improper speech.
(from Zohar 205b/206a, late 13th century, Spain)

Although not written in the Torah scrolls themselves, many printed editions of the Torah contain cantillation marks. (The Yiddish word for these signs is *trop*, and the Hebrew is *t'amim*.) These symbols indicate the melody to which each word of the Torah is traditionally chanted in synagogue services. Although the Talmud claims that the cantillation was given at Mount Sinai along with the Torah,[7] the Masoretes fixed the musical notations in the Land of Israel between the 6th and 10th centuries, though undoubtedly there were already traditional melodies earlier.[8]

The Zohar's comment reflects the mystic's sensitivity to visual stimulation. Cantillation signs can certainly function as interpretation. Take, for instance, Joseph's response to the sexual advances of his master's wife. The Torah, in typically clipped fashion says, "He refused" (Gen. 39:8). The cantillation mark over that single Hebrew word (*vay-ma-en*), however, involves going up and down the scales three times. In other words, according to the cantillation, Joseph wavered and wavered again before finally mustering the resolve to refuse her.[9] The Zohar's comment on our verse, though, is not about the melody, but about the shape of the sign itself. The symbol, a *shalshelet*, is wavy and it triggers an association for the author of the *Zohar* with the serpent in the garden of Eden who beguiles Eve through his words.

Not only does the scroll of the Torah contain no cantillation signs, it has no vowels either. The Masoretes were also responsible for establishing the vowels of the Torah. The Zohar reconfigures the vowels of *ba'midbar* (in the wilderness) to arrive at *b'm'daber* (through speaking). The Zohar retains the cantillation sign of the Masoretes, but modifies their vowels. Zelophehad's sin, and therefore the cause of his death, was speaking to Moses with a lack of regard for Moses' position as the leader of the Israelites. The mystics were particularly concerned with behavior that transcended halachic requirements and rose to an ethical ideal.[10] The Book of Numbers is filled with people complaining to Moses; but the daughters of Zelophehad are the only ones in the entire Torah who bring a complaint to Moses without being adversarial. The Malbim says that the daughters were righteous because they didn't emulate their father's bad traits. Of course, it also takes much wisdom to know which of your parents' traits *are* worthy of emulation.

> 5. *Dying without sons was punishment for his sin.*
>
> (Rabbi Yehudah Halevi, 1080–1145 [as cited by Rabbi Abraham ibn Ezra, 1089–1164, Spain])

> 6. *His only punishment for his sin was that he would die, not that his possessions would be lost to his heirs.*
>
> *(S'forno, 1475–1550, Italy)*

We shouldn't let our curiosity about Zelophehad's sin distract us from the fact that his daughters said, in public no less, that their father sinned. That's not very respectful, and honoring your parents (Exod. 20:12) is considered quite a virtue in the Jewish tradition.[11] What could possibly explain the daughters' disrespect?

Rabbi Yehudah Halevi explains the daughters' comment as a necessary preamble to their request. He connects the phrase "died for his own sin" to "he has left no sons," giving us the following reading for the second half of verse 3: "because of his sin, he [both] died and has left no sons." The Hebrew word, *ki*, which appears before *his sin* (*b'cheto*) in verse 3, can mean both *but* (as *NJPS* has it) and *because*. In other words, he was already punished for his sin, and he shouldn't be punished any more by losing the association of his name with a territorial holding in the Land. For Halevi, having the daughters mention both Zelophehad's sin and punishment is a necessary condition for Moses to understand the reasonableness of their request.

S'forno's reading of verse 3 is that for his sin, he died. Period. No more punishment for Zelophehad. And that also explains why the daughters specifically mentioned that Zelophehad was not part of Korah's band. For their rebellion against Moses, Korah and his gang lost their property. S'forno adduces this law from what Moses says following the rebellion: "Move away from the tents of these wicked men and touch nothing that belongs to them, lest you be wiped out for all their sins" (Num. 16:26). For a rebellion against the state, as it were (and as we see explicitly in 1 Kings 21:11–16), the rebel's property is confiscated by the state. But for other crimes, the death penalty suffices. And that's S'forno's point. Zelophehad paid for his sin with his life. His name, though, deserves to be preserved, and his daughters needed to let Moses know enough of the story for him to understand that. Both Rabbi Yehuda Halevi and S'forno answer another question about the text. Why, since the daughters mention their father's sin, don't they say what he did? The daughters do not divulge what their father's sin was because it was unnecessary for their claim and would, therefore, be disrespectful.

> 7. *He died* with *his sin*. Zelophehad committed the transgression for the sake of heaven. He thought he was doing right and therefore he never made confession over his sin.
>
> (Rav Y. Y. Trunk, 1820–1893, Poland)[12]

For Rav Trunk, a Hasidic Rabbi, Zelophehad died in denial. Even though Zelophehad was acting with the best possible intention, for the sake of heaven, he was never able to admit to himself that he had, nevertheless, committed a transgression. He held on, defiantly, to the rightness and righteousness of his act until his dying day. The Rabbis recognize a category of transgression that is done with good intentions, but the Rabbis recognize it as a transgression—apparently, for Rav Trunk, Zelophehad never did.[13] The only way to live morally is to recognize our past misdeeds and to steel ourselves against repeating them. In other words, the only way to live morally is to be open to the possibility of *teshuvah*, returning to being in right relation with God and God's creatures.

Rav Trunk's interpretation hinges on a *bet*. The preposition, *bet*, in *b'cheto* (for his own sin) is translated by NJPS as *for*, but Trunk understands it as *with*. Prepositions are plastic, especially in Hebrew. With Rav Trunk's rereading of the verse, the daughters may have been telling Moses that they were worthy of inheriting the Land because they understood the importance of *teshuvah* in leading a righteous life. With this reading, we again don't know exactly what Zelophehad's sin was. Alternatively, we can *combine* Rav Trunk's comment with a plain sense reading to arrive at the following suggestion: Zelophehad's death was the result of obstinately, sinfully denying that his past misdeed was transgressive. His initial misdeed was not worthy of being punished by death. But the sin of self-righteously holding on to it demonstrated his stubborn refusal to live and, therefore, condemned him to death.

Stage Presence

> 8. Why does the verse repeat "he had no son" after it already said "he has left no sons"? This shows us that the daughters were both sages and

exegetes. The women are really saying, "If Zelophehad had a granddaughter through a son, we wouldn't make such a claim."

(*Sifre*)

In verse 4, we're seemingly given the same information as offered previously in verse 3: Zelophehad died without a male heir. An uncharitable commentator might suggest that the speaker was flustered in her legal debut before Moses and simply repeated herself. But the *Sifre* credits the daughters with providing Moses all the information he needs to decide the case. According to the logic of the *Sifre*, had the daughters only revealed to Moses that Zelophehad died without a male heir, Moses would have needed to ask, "Did Zelophehad have a son who died before him?" If, according to Rabbinic law, Zelophehad had been predeceased by a son who himself had a child, then Zelophehad's inheritance would pass to the son's child, even if the child were a daughter![14] According to the *Sifre's* reading, the daughters disclose to Moses not only that Zelophehad left no sons upon his death, but that he had no sons during his life. The *Sifre* exploits a textual redundancy to extol the women's wisdom of Rabbinic *halakhah* and their ability to engage in exegetical reasoning; they're not just citing simple verses from Psalms as in comment two.

The *Sifre* accounts for the seeming redundancy, but there is still the issue of who is speaking in our verses. Verse 2 says, "they said." Does that mean they spoke in unison? Did they elect a spokeswoman to represent them all? Jill Hammer, a contemporary commentator who gives voice to Hoglah, offers a third option.

9. The crowd begins to quiet. Mahlah walks forward with delicate steps. Her head is as high as a pillar of cloud. Mahlah speaks before Moses: "Our father died in the wilderness. He was not one of the rebels, Korah's faction, who banded together against God, but died for his own sin. He has left no sons."

Silence. Mahlah cannot say more. Tears fall from her cheeks and make dark spots on the ground. Noah clears her throat but says nothing. A chieftain mutters something under his breath. My heart is pounding. Inside my body a gazelle runs from a lion, but I am the gazelle and I am the lion. I step forward without feeling my feet.

"Let not our father's name be lost to his clan just because he had no son! Give us a holding among our father's kinsmen!"

(Jill Hammer, contemporary, United States; cf. Yalkut Shimoni)[15]

Rabbi Hammer presents an anxious Mahlah whose words are unscripted and sentences staccato. The daughters have good reason to be nervous; after all, they are confronting God's chosen prophet and political leader in front of the whole assembly. Hammer's staging of the confrontation between the daughters and Moses clarifies for us why the language of verse 2 suggests that more than one daughter was speaking. Hammer takes the grammatical plurality and envisions a team effort. Furthermore, having multiple speakers on the stage makes it easier to understand the repetition that Zelophehad had no son.[16]

Staking Their Claim

10. The daughters of Zelophehad were wise and righteous women. What shows their wisdom? They spoke at the appropriate moment just when Moses was dealing with the issue of inheritance, "The land will be apportioned to these . . ." (Num. 26:53). They said to Moses, "If we are like male children, we should inherit like male children; if not, our mother should undergo levirate marriage."

(*Numbers Rabbah*, 9th century, Land of Israel; cf. Baba Batra 119b)

Not only did the daughters demonstrate appropriate timing, but they combined their knowledge of Rabbinic law with their own logical reasoning to infer that their situation demanded legal remedy. The daughters are referencing the law of levirate marriage, in which a woman whose husband dies prior to the birth of a male heir should marry the deceased husband's brother. The first male issue of that union then stands in the place of the deceased (Deut. 25:5–10).

According to Rabbinic law, a widow is exempt from levirate marriage regardless of whether she has a son or a daughter.[17] The daughters, ostensibly knowing this piece of Rabbinic interpretation, argue that if they are considered "children" for the purposes of levirate marriage, then they should similarly be considered children for the purposes of inheritance. If they are not considered children for the purposes of levirate marriage, then their mother should be married to one of Zelophehad's brothers in order to secure a male heir to inherit Zelophehad's portion in the Land of Israel.

Numbers Rabbah portrays the daughters acting altruistically. They seem to be indifferent as to whether they inherit or their mother undergoes levirate marriage. The issue for them is that their father's name not be lost as a result of his property being inherited by his brothers. The biblical text agrees that the daughters are concerned with perpetuating their father's name, but they want that accomplished through their own inheritance, not via levirate marriage. Our next comment explains their insistence on receiving the inheritance themselves.

> 11. *Inheritance is not just a legal matter, but also a deeply emotional matter, having deep spiritual and psychological meaning. Being "part of the loop" of succession paves the way, we know, for healthy grieving.*
>
> (Pamela Wax, contemporary, United States)[18]

Although *Numbers Rabbah* suggests that Zelophehad's wife is still alive and of child-bearing age, the Torah itself gives us no indication of her status. It very well may be that she is dead. After all, until quite recently in human history, childbirth was often lethal. If the daughters, at the time of their appeal to Moses, are bereft of father and mother, that makes Rabbi Wax's comment all the more poignant. The daughters are groping for something to hold on to from their parents. They want to perpetuate his name, yes. But they also need to be the vehicles through which that perpetuation takes place in order for them to feel as though they are legitimate links in the family chain.

Women of Valor

The daughters of Zelophehad have pled their case. From the following Rabbinic comments, one has the impression that even if the law had not been found in their favor, the daughters, and the women they represent, would have been upheld as exemplary.

> 12. *In that generation, the women maintained boundaries that the men broke through.*
>
> (Numbers Rabbah)

> 13. *Rabbi Nathan said: Women's strength is greater than men's. Men say, "Let us head back to Egypt" (Num. 14:4). But the women say, "Give us a holding among our father's kinsmen!"*
>
> (Sifre)

Our commentator in *Numbers Rabbah* gives the Golden Calf (Exod. 32) as an example of the men transgressing while the women remained steadfast in their loyalty to God. Similarly, when the spies returned from their reconnoitering trip to Canaan, they try to convince the men that any attempt to conquer Canaan would be folly (Num. 14). The men balked, but the women believed. Hence, the men, and only the men, were punished by not being able to enter the Land.[19] The women of the Exodus generation were examples of faithfulness to God and His promises.

There is an admission here, on the part of the Rabbis, that women's faith and strength is more than simple obedience to authority. *Numbers Rabbah* speaks to self-control, what the Mishnah describes as the characteristic of a mighty person, a hero.[20] It's also a characteristic of the Rabbinic God who restrains himself from acting on impulse.[21] In the most Divine (and, hence, most important) sense, the women of that generation were mightier than the men.

What the *Sifre* adds to this composite picture of women is their clarity of purpose and their ability to attain their goals effectively. The men are shaken and want to return to the security of slavery. They die in the wilderness. The women stand firm (verse 2) and seek a holding in the Promised Land. They get it. Rabbinic Judaism was not always fair to women. The Rabbis themselves admit as much in comment two. But in this case, the Rabbis take the opportunity to acknowledge that women possess the virtues of piety, self-control, perspicacity and tenacity that make them indispensable role models of the righteous life.

The *Supreme* Court

14. Why is there a large nun *in the word* mishpatan *(their case)? This is a hint to a sage who is great in Torah and has learned the teaching of manners that a person should not render judgment in the presence of one who is greater than he. Rather, he needs to bring the case before him. This is what Moses did. He did not want to rule in the case of Zelophehad's daughters until he inquired of the Holy One, blessed be He.*

(Rabbeinu Bahya, 1263–1340, Spain; cf. Numbers Rabbah)

Look at the Hebrew of our story and you'll notice that in verse 5 there is a letter larger than all the rest. It appears larger in the Torah scroll as well. Within the TANAKH, there are roughly thirty instances of large and small letters.[22] Another example of large letters is in the *Shema*: "Hear, O Israel! The LORD is our God, the LORD alone" (Deut. 6:4). In that single verse there are two large letters, an *ayin* (the last letter of *hear*) and a *dalet* (the last letter of *alone*), which together spell '*ed*, the Hebrew word for witness. Thus the articulation of the verse calls us to witness the monotheistic faith according to one commentator.[23]

For some of these unusually sized letters, there are theories to explain their distinctiveness. For example with the *Shema*, if the *ayin* were an *aleph*, although the pronunciation would be nearly identical, it would spell the Hebrew word for *maybe* instead of *hear*. That's not good for a declaration of faith. And if the *dalet* were mistaken for a *resh*, which it closely resembles, it would spell *another*, which is not good for monotheism! But, for some letters, including our *nun*, biblical scholars have no explanation.

Rabbeinu Bahya, writing under the assumption that everything in the Torah has a Divine purpose, explains two anomalies at once. Within the Torah, there are four instances where cases arise that are not covered by the initial legislation, and Moses has to seek counsel with God.[24] Since our verse is one of those four occasions, the infrequency of such a phenomenon is used as the explanation for the similarly unusual phenomenon of a large letter. Rabbeinu Bahya extols Moses' humility (Num. 12:3) and etiquette. When there is someone greater (as hinted at by the large *nun*) than you, you should defer to their judgment.

> 15. *Moses knows this is a "hot issue." We can imagine that women have grumbled about this before, have questioned their role in land distribution, ever since the census counted them out. Some of those now joined with the Israelites in the desert come from cultures in which women had the right to inherit, and they feel cheated. . . . Even though the daughters of Zelophehad petition only for themselves, Moses hears in their protest the voices of other women, and does not want to answer the challenge himself."*
>
> (Elyse Goldstein, contemporary, United States)[25]

For Goldstein, Moses' response to the daughters is not motivated by etiquette, but by politics. If the answer from God were to come back in the negative, Moses could shrug his shoulders and say, "Sorry, ladies, I did the best I could."

Goldstein's comment brings up two interesting issues. The first is that there were other cultures which did grant daughters the right to inherit. More often than not, the Torah contains legislation that is progressive compared to earlier Near Eastern legal codes. For example, in the case of the suspected adulteress, the Torah prescribes that she drink from a cup of bitter waters to determine her guilt or innocence (Num. 5:11–31). In Hammurabi's Code of ancient Babylonia (c. 18 c. BCE), a suspected adulteress would be thrown in a river to make such a determination. Both cultures put women through ordeals involving water, but only in the Israelite version did the woman stand a fighting chance.

But on the issue of female inheritance, the Torah was less enlightened than the surrounding cultures, from our perspective. According to Jacob Milgrom, "the concession made by the Bible to Zelophehad's daughters was anticipated in Mesopotamia by a millennium."[26] Moreover, in ancient Elam (southwest Iran), even when sons were living, in matters of inheritance all children were equal.[27] So when the daughters of Zelophehad stood before Moses and all the elders, there is good reason to suspect that Moses understood that it was critical not only that justice be done, but that justice be perceived to be done. As Moses would later say, "Observe them [these laws and rules] faithfully, for that will be the proof of your wisdom and discernment to other peoples" (Deut. 4:6).

Goldstein also points out that when the Israelites escaped from Egypt, they weren't the only ones to run away. The "mixed multitude" ('erev rav) joined the exodus once the prison gates were flung open (Exod. 12:38). They, along with the ethnic Israelites, stood at Sinai and committed themselves to the covenant with God. Throughout Jewish history, there has been a tendency among some to blame this 'erev rav for lapses in the covenant. Who instigated the idolatrous orgy around the Golden Calf, for example? The 'erev rav.[28] In the modern period, the Ultra Orthodox blame the 'erev rav for the acculturating tendencies of the Modern Orthodox.[29]

What Goldstein does is to transform this motley crew that had traditionally been used as a whipping boy into a force for redemption.[30] These women, standing silently behind the daughters of Zelophehad, are happy to be joining the Jewish people, but they do not want to diminish the legal rights and personal status that they had enjoyed in their native cultures. Goldstein, a contemporary rabbi, is not embarrassed to admit that Judaism can profit from embracing what is best in other religions and cultures. In the pre-modern period there was greater reluctance to admit the strengths of other religions. Today, the rehabilitation of the 'erev rav from a racist theory to a justification for fuller inclusion of proselytes and a degree of self-conscious religious syncretism would be an appropriate legacy for the daughters of Zelophehad.

16. Moses, also, is faced with an unprecedented situation. The daughters of Zelophehad are barred by law from inheriting. They appeal outside of the law, upon the simple human merits of the case.

Inherent in their plea is the understanding that codified law exists only as an attempt to provide justice and mercy; that, as a human construct, it must be imperfect; and that a system which does not allow final appeal (to that human impulse which gave rise to the code) is an abomination. . . .

Moses realized that he was unable, in conscience, to perform as ordered, and he brought his problem to God.

(David Mamet, contemporary, United States)[31]

How to respond to the unprecedented? It's so much easier to rely on the well-worn rules of the game, whatever they may be. It's dangerous to open up the rulebook to revision. Where will it stop? What David Mamet, the play-wright and a master of constructing the unanticipated situation, suggests is that the easiest thing for Moses to have done, the path of least resistance, would have been to rely on precedent: daughters don't inherit. That's the law. But the law was created to promote justice and mercy, and, inevitably, there will arise situations in which the application of the law would result in a miscarriage of justice and a denial of mercy. It takes a visionary to know when the existing laws are elastic enough to cover novel situations and when new legislation must be drafted to accommodate the spirit of the law. Moses under-stood the injustice of the law as it pertained to the daughters of Zelophehad. He was fortunate enough to have recourse to a court of higher authority.

17. Why didn't Moses judge them himself? Women cry easily, and Moses was afraid lest their tears influence him. Tears are also a form of bribery.

(Aharon Greenberg, 1900–1963, Poland and Israel)[32]

At first glance, this Hasidicly inclined commentator (and anthologist of *Torah Gems*) might be viewed as engaging in baseless sexist stereotyping. What reason do we have to think that these five exceptionally strong and brave women would weep? The Torah certainly gives no indication that the women would cry. But, given the emotional charge of the moment, isn't it entirely plausible that the women (some women/one woman) would express that intensity through tears? In Rabbi Hammer's depiction of the scene (com-ment nine), Mahlah does just that. Moses, struggling to maintain fidelity to God's Will in the face of such a heart-rending petition, recognizes that he cannot remain impartial. He does not trust himself to rise above the pathos of five orphans pleading for a holding in the Land as a memorial to their father. Moses, himself, had earlier exhorted: "You shall not ill-treat any widow or orphan" (Exod. 22:21). Since, as the Talmud says, tears unlock the gates of heaven (b. *Baba Metzia* 59a), it is all the more understandable that a man of flesh and blood could not remain closed to their influence.

Greenberg, however, implies that the women would cry in order to manipulate Moses. Bribes are intentional. This uncharitable reading of the daughters stands in contrast to the generally positive Rabbinic evaluation of them. Ironically, the origin of such a reading goes back to a medieval commentator on precisely that section of the Talmud that seems to be singing the women's praises. Comment ten explains that the women were wise because they spoke at the appropriate moment when Moses was dealing with issues of inheritance. On the page of Talmud where that comment appears (b. *Baba Batra* 119b), Rashbam explains that the women had been opportunistically awaiting a pretext to bring forward their claim.[33] Rashbam reads the women as wily rather than wise. A younger contemporary of Rashbam, Rambam, would later contend that wisdom includes the fine art of craftiness.[34] As for Greenberg's comment, although in modernity crying is sometimes associated with weakness, the biblical figure who cries most is David, Israel's wise and wily King. Indeed, according to Jeremiah, the messianic days will be characterized by all of Israel "weeping as they go to seek the LORD their God" (Jer. 50:4).

The Heavenly Torah

18. Just as Onkelos translated it: properly [Onkelos]. "That's how this section is written before Me in the heavens" [Sifre]. This tells us that the women's eyes perceived what Moses' eyes did not [Tanhuma].

(Rashi; incorporating Onkelos, *Sifre*, and *Tanhuma*)

Although Rashi is technically a medieval commentator, he's thoroughly Rabbinic. In fact, Rashi rarely has an original comment; more than three quarters of his commentary is from Rabbinic sources. Here he cites three sources from the Rabbinic period. His genius as a Torah commentator stems not from his originality, but from his ability to discern which of the multitude of Rabbinic sources best captures the problematics of the text and by his arrangement of those sources.

In our case, Rashi is explaining the Hebrew word *ken* from verse 7. Rashi cites the third-century translator of the Torah into Aramaic, Onkelos, who translated *ken* as *properly*. "The daughters of Zelophehad spoke properly." The NJPS offers the less literal translation in which the plea of Zelophehad's daughters is just. *Ken*, in this sense of true or correct, appears relatively infrequently in the Torah and, therefore, invites comment.

On the surface, our story seems to be a case of an amendment to the Torah. In other words, the legislation up until this point in the story was incomplete because it didn't take into account the contingency of a father's death when there are daughters but no sons. But the idea of an incomplete Torah goes against the Rabbis' assumption that the Torah is perfect. Eventually, the belief that the Oral Torah was given at Sinai simultaneous to the giving of the written Torah would serve as an explanation why certain laws were not included in the written Torah. But here the written Torah seems to be adding on to itself.

The Rabbis believed that the Torah was created even before the world. They imagined that God has a Torah in the heavens, a Torah pre-existent to the one Moses received at Sinai.[35] In this provocative midrash from the *Sifre*, God listens to the plea of Zelophehad's daughters, as proffered by Moses, and rather than rendering judgment, God looks into his own unabridged edition of the Torah. The Rabbis then claim to cite God's full response to Moses that our own Bible had abbreviated. "That's how this section is written before Me in the heavens." The daughters did not innovate law; they discovered it.

And that's where the comment from *Tanhuma* comes in. The daughters perceived what Moses, the greatest of all prophets, did not. Undoubtedly, the *Tanhuma* would not overturn Moses' status as the greatest prophet of all time. Nevertheless, not even the greatest prophet can always see most clearly. The comment from *Tanhuma*, by itself, is only about the daughters' perspicacity. They understood something about how society should function that Moses did not. But when Rashi places that comment immediately following the *Sifre*, the daughters become prophetesses, seeing the Torah which is before God in the heavens. And, at least regarding this section, they had a better view than did Moses. The authoritative tradition views the Torah one way. Rashi, who himself had only daughters, reminds us that our different perspectives might allow us, as individuals, to view God's Torah with even greater insight than has the tradition.

> 19. *It is known that in those sections in which a specific event occurs, like the Golden Calf (Exod. 32) or the Spies (Num. 13) or something similar, the letters are jumbled. But after the event, the correct sequence of letters arrives and from them we make the section that is in front of us. Thus the law of inheritance by daughters came to be revealed through the daughters of Zelophehad. "The daughters of Zelophehad merited and it was written on account of them" (b. Sann. 8a) and then the holy One, blessed be He, said to Moshe, "That's how this section is written before Me in the heavens."*
>
> (Moses Sofer, 1762–1839, Hungary)

Moses Sofer, known as the *Chatam Sofer*, gives us the prequel to Rashi's comment. The *Chatam Sofer*, the ideological father of the Ultra-Orthodox, begins by citing a Kabbalistic notion that letters are jumbled in certain sections of the Torah until human beings, through their actions, unjumble them.[36] This mystical notion, developed by the sixteenth-century Kabbalists, Moses Cordevero and Isaac Luria, penetrated into the writings of both eighteenth-century Hasidim and Mitnagdim (their opponents). What the *Chatam Sofer* adds to this tradition is that the daughters of Zelophehad's actions are on par with the act of disobedience in the Garden of Eden, the sin of the Golden Calf, and the evil report of the spies. As significant as those acts were for the development of Torah, the acts of the daughters were equally so, though for positive reasons rather than negative. The beginning of gender equality under the law precipitates a paradigm shift in the meaning of the Torah.

The Talmudic passage which Sofer cites, in its simple sense, has nothing to do with this Kabbalistic tradition. The Talmud, in its context, is bothered by what seems to be an amendment to the Torah. The Talmud suggests that the merit of the daughters was so great that this section of the Torah was written on their account. It's not that Moses was unworthy or that the original legislation was incomplete or that Moses did not know the law; God simply wanted to reward the women by having them associated with the laws of inheritance. But for the Talmud, these laws are written in *our* Torah.

The *Chatam Sofer,* by interpreting Rashi in light of the Kabbalah, audaciously imagines that God's Torah in the heavens is rewritten on the daughters' account. We human beings can rewrite God's Torah! For the *Chatam Sofer,* the Torah may be eternal but it's not immutable. Through our righteous deeds (or wicked acts), we can reconfigure the letters in the Torah of God. Then we can amend our own Torah to be consonant with God's new version. The father of Ultra Orthodoxy, who is famous for his saying, "All innovation is prohibited by the Torah!" opens the door to innovations *within* the Torah. The non-Orthodox would, of course, concur that new times demand new readings of Torah. One wonders which laws and stories next await our actions to unjumble God's Torah and our own.

Gained in Translation

20. It is significant that the suffixes used in verse seven referring to the daughters are in the masculine, lahem, avihem *(to them, their father). That says: You are to give them masculine rights of inheritance as if they were sons.*

(Rabbi Samson Raphael Hirsch, 1808–1888, Germany)

Friedrich Nietzsche once wrote: "It was subtle that God learned Greek when he wanted to become an author—and that he did not learn it better."[37] What Nietzsche wrote about the Greek of the New Testament also applies, though less noticeably, to the Hebrew of the TANAKH. Since one of the Rabbinic assumptions about the Torah is that it is perfect, at a minimum one would expect there to be no grammatical mistakes. After all, shouldn't God be an inerrant grammarian?

But every so often the Torah makes a mistake, or so it seems. A grammatical irregularity is found earlier in the Torah in the Cain and Abel story. In the very difficult verse that has sin "couching" or "crouching" at some undesignated entrance, the noun *sin (chatat)* is feminine, but the predicate is masculine. The Rabbis of *Genesis Rabbah* suggest that the temptation to commit a sin is first weak like a woman, but after indulging in the vice, the strength of the temptation grows until it is strong like a man.[38]

In verse 7 of our story, we find four suffixes, two of which are masculine and two of which are feminine. The problem is that since the verse is referring to the daughters, all the suffixes should be in the feminine. Since English doesn't specify the gender of nouns, this inconsistency is lost in translation.

Hirsch was writing in a time and place when and where the academic study of the Bible was beginning to seep into the understanding of Sacred Scripture by some religious denominations. For instance, in the Reform Movement's Pittsburgh Platform of 1885, the conclave of mostly German or German-trained Rabbis endorsed the academic notion that there were multiple, human authors of the Torah. Anyone concurring with such a theory could ascribe the grammatical irregularities in our verse to sloppy writing or poor editing. However, Rabbi Hirsch, the founding figure of Modern Orthodoxy, could not resort to such an explanation. Although he admitted the irregularity, he insisted that it was intentional. For Hirsch, it was impossible that there should be a mistake in the Torah. Hence, the masculine suffixes are grammatical hints that in those cases when women inherit, they are to be treated just like sons.[39]

To Heir Is Human

21. The law occasioned by the daughters of Zelophehad, that daughters inherit only when there are no sons, was restricted to the allocation of real estate upon entrance to the Land of Israel. Subsequently, daughters and sons inherit equally, both real estate and moveable property.

(from the Karaites, a medieval Jewish sect)[40]

The Karaites are a medieval Jewish sect who represent the road not taken. They emerged in the eighth century by rejecting certain Rabbinic assumptions about the Torah. The Hebrew word for scripture is Mikra, and the Karaites were scripturalists who rejected the midrashic readings of the Rabbis in favor (usually) of more plain-sense readings. Rabbanites, like Abraham ibn Ezra and Sa'adia Gaon, championed the classical Rabbinic readings of Torah and *halakhah* against Karaite exegesis, and their writings often contain polemics against the Karaites.[41]

The Rabbis could have adopted the Karaite's time-bound interpretation of our story. Indeed in the Second Temple period, before the rise of the Rabbis, this was the prevailing interpretation, and a reasonable one at that.[42] But since the Torah is not a historical artifact for the Rabbis, but a revelation of the living God, they were uncomfortable relegating the episode of Zelophehad to a mere historical footnote, an archaic law. They understood that this story was still relevant for them as well as for their heirs. So they found other ways of providing for their daughters while preserving this story as a precedent for future inheritance laws.[43]

The Karaites were not always more literal, nor more liberal, than the Rabbis. For instance, the Karaites extrapolate from the Torah's prohibition against plowing on the Sabbath (Exod. 34:21) a prohibition against sexual intercourse on this day. In this case, the Karaites regard plowing as metaphorical. (The Rabbis understand the Sabbath to be the perfect time for physical intimacy.)[44] The Karaites, however, did interpret literally the biblical law of an "eye for an eye," *lex talionis*, whereas Rabbinic *halakhah* understands it to mean that bodily injury requires monetary compensation.[45] Yet the tendency exhibited by the Karaites, to favor the literal meaning of the Torah, is also in evidence in the medieval Rabbanite community with the rise of the *peshat* commentators who, like the Karaites, often reject the traditional Rabbinic assumptions that the Torah is cryptic, contains no repetitions, and is relevant to contemporary life.

Marital Anomalies

22. The daughters of Zelophehad were wise, exegetes, and righteous. . . . They were righteous in that they only married those who were worthy of them. Rabbi Eliezer, son of Jacob taught: Even the youngest of them didn't marry until she was at least forty.[46]

(Gemara, Baba Batra 119b)

23. Not only are the daughters of Zelophehad named, but we find in the account of their marriage [Num. 36:11–12] a complete reversal of the normal biblical formula. Instead of having the husband named and the wife anonymous, here the wives are named but not the husbands. . . . The daughters by taking on the male role of inheritor, were also given the male status in terms of the marriage narrative. This is the only case in the Torah where we are told specifically that a named woman got married and yet the husband remains anonymous.

(Zvi Ron, contemporary, United States)[47]

24. The text presumes that the sisters chose their husbands, and not the other way around. . . . What is more, by all marrying cousins, there is a greater chance that they will stay close to one another.

(Hara E. Person, contemporary, United States)[48]

The record of the daughters' marriages occurs in the final chapter of the *Book of Numbers*. As all of the above commentators point out, there are some very unusual aspects about the description of their marriages. What is most interesting is that the Talmud deems their discrimination in selecting a marriage partner as an indication of their righteousness, even though the delay cost them precious child-bearing years. Since righteousness does not usually go unrewarded in the world of the Rabbis, the ensuing Talmudic passage records a miracle on the women's behalf which granted them children in their middle age.

"Every person shall cleave to his portion" (Num. 36:9).

The epilogue to our story rolls back some of the gains made by the daughters of Zelophehad by imposing marital restrictions on daughters who inherit. If those daughters were to marry men from outside the tribe, the land which they inherited would become part of another tribe's holdings. In order to avoid such a situation and to preserve the territorial integrity of each tribe's initial allocation, daughters who inherit land must marry within the tribe.[49] Of course, whether propertied women marry within their tribe or not, either their husbands or their male children inherit their real estate. Thus what the daughters of Zelophehad retain is not so much their own portion in the Land, but their portion in the Torah and Jewish tradition.[50]

25. The Israelites will cleave to their portion in life and peace.

(Joseph Bechor Shor, 1140–1190, France)

By the twelfth century, the Israelites had been dispossessed of their portion in the Land for well over a millennium. In this comment, Bechor Shor seeks to distract his audience from the fact that Christian Crusaders were occupying the Land, having recently routed the Muslims. Bechor Shor implores his readers to cleave not to the Land, but more importantly, to cleave to life and to peace. That should be their true portion.

26. The Israelites were commanded to see beyond the territorial and to cleave to God, as the LORD said earlier, "I am your portion" (Num. 18:20).

(Meshi)

There was a popular and controversial figure within the early Zionist movement named Vladimir Jabotinsky (1880–1940). He and his followers offered a vision of Zionism, called Revisionism, which forcefully promoted a Jewish state in the entire Land of Israel. (The Balfour Declaration of 1917 originally called for the establishment of a national home for the Jewish people in Palestine, which then included what is today the Kingdom of Jordan.) Meshi, a contemporary commentator from the diaspora, offers a qualification to the single-mindedness of Revisionist Zionism and their contemporary adherents on the right of Israel's political spectrum.[51]

By innovating a *g'zerah shavah* which links two passages through the word they share in common—*portion (nachalah)*—and reading "his portion" of real estate (Num. 36:9) as "his portion" in the Divine (Num. 18:20), Meshi argues that even more important than nationalism and real estate is striving to unite with and embody the Divine will.[52] The TANAKH provides ample evidence of how difficult it is to cleave to God in the Land. Indeed, Israel's eponymous founder, Jacob, was crippled in his struggle to return to and live in the Land (Gen. 32:25–33). The legacy of Mahlah, Noah, Hoglah, Milcah, and Tirzah is the hope that with wisdom, righteousness, and exegetical acumen, their heirs may be able to cleave both to God and to live on their portion of the Land in peace.

Ending with a Bang, Not a Whimper

In the final chapter of the *Book of Numbers* (Num. 36), the elders of the Manassite clan appeal to Moses to prevent the daughters from marrying outside the tribe, since that would ultimately result in a loss of land for the tribe as a whole. In a virtual replay of *Numbers 27*, Moses takes the query to God who agrees with the elders. The daughters of Zelophehad must marry within the tribe. They do—and that's the end of the book.

Genesis ends with the death of Jacob, the father of the twelve tribes. Exodus culminates with God's presence filling the newly constructed Tabernacle. But *Numbers* just fizzles out with another law pertaining to inheritance. The Hasidic Master, Mordechai Joseph Leiner of Isbitza (1802–1854), also known as the *Mei HaShiloach*, offers a rehabilitating interpretation.

> 27. The whole point is to understand, at every moment, the Will of God in the words of the Torah, knowing His will at all times, within the context of that particular time. Thus light emanates from the words of Torah to the hearts of Israel in order for them to understand the depth of the will of God, according to the time. Therefore this section was written after the completion of the entire Torah, in order to let Israel understand that details emerge from the Torah at all times, at each moment. The words of the Torah are words of advice to let human beings understand what the blessed God wants of us now, and to do it. Therefore this section was written (at the end), for it too is active only for a specific time.
>
> (Mei HaShiloach, Masei)

The Isbitzer Rebbe, sounding strikingly unorthodox, sharpens our question: Why does *Numbers* conclude with this seemingly prosaic and provisional law about tribal intermarriage? After all, this law applies only to the generation entering the Land of Israel from the desert.[53] Moreover, since Deuteronomy contains a repetition of the laws, Numbers basically ends the laws of the Torah.

The *Mei HaShiloach* argues that there could be no better climax to the Torah than this appendix to the laws of inheritance. This story safeguards us against "bibliolatry," the idolizing of the Bible.[54] The Torah may contain eternal truths, but these truths are concretized in language and contexts that are specific to that historical moment. It is a betrayal of our covenant with God to apply these laws to historical contexts in which God's light no longer emanates from the words of Torah. As the Isbitzer says, the whole point of the Torah is to understand God's will within the context of our particular moment in history. The change of law brought about by the petition of the daughters of Zelophehad, as well as the later clarifications of these laws, are perfect examples of that phenomenon of recontextualizing the Torah to respond to new circumstances. (The *Chatam Sofer* might say unjumbling the letters.)

Conservative Judaism, originally known as the Positive-Historical School, emerged from Germany at about the same time as the *Mei HaShiloach* was writing.

It is based on precisely this principle of recontextualization. The Positive-Historical School understands that Judaism is a *historical* religion whose laws evolve over time rather than remaining fixed at the moment of revelation at Sinai. This unfolding of the principles of Sinai and their application in concrete laws is regarded as *positive* for the continued flourishing of Jewish life. Early Reform Judaism, by contrast, used the fact that the Torah was a human, historical document to undermine the Divine authority of traditional *halakhah*. The Isbitzer Rebbe argues that the Torah charges us with understanding "the depth of the will of God, according to the time." Thus, understanding the Torah in our own particular time is not only positive, it's the whole point, and, therefore, the best possible ending.[55]

Summary of Comments

Comment	Problem	Resolution	Textual Mechanism	Historical Circumstance
1.	Why does the genealogy go back to Joseph? Why the repetition?	Similarity between Joseph and his descendants	Joseph is the end of the line	None
2.	What's the difference between the women coming near in verse 1 and standing before Moses in verse 2?	They came near to each other to take counsel. They did not come near to Moses until verse 2	Two different verbs	Patriarchal discrimination
3.	What was Zelophehad's sin?	He violated the Sabbath by collecting wood	G'*zerah shavah*/"In the wilderness" used in both scenes	None
4.	What was Zelophehad's sin?	Improper speech	Shape of cantillation sign	Mystical attention to both visual stimulation and ethics
5.	Why mention that Zelophehad sinned?	He was already punished by dying without sons	Reading the end of verse 3 as a consequence of his sin/ambiguity of *ki*	Patriarchal culture where sons are preferred to daughters
6.	Why mention that Zelophehad sinned?	He was already punished by dying for his sin	None	None
7.	Why mention that Zelophehad sinned without mentioning the sin?	Daughters demonstrate understanding of *teshuvah*/sin was self-righteousness	Plasticity of preposition *bet*	Hasidic emphasis on religious psychology

continued

Comment	Problem	Resolution	Textual Mechanism	Historical Circumstance
8.	Why repeat that he had no sons?	Daughters demonstrate wisdom and exegetical skill	None	None
9.	Who is speaking? Why repeat that he had no sons?	More than one daughter spoke, one after the other	Verb in verse 2 is in plural	None
10.	It's unusual for commoners (especially women?) to speak to Moses	They were wise	Census from previous chapter (biblical context)	None
11.	Why do the women want an inheritance?	Part of the grieving process	None	None
12.	Men are weak	In that generation, women were stronger	None	None
13.	Men are weak	Women are stronger	None[56]	None
14.	Why did Moses refer the case to God?	To demonstrate humility	Large *nun*	None
15.	Why did Moses refer the case to God?	Too controversial a case to decide himself	None	Modern concern with women's rights, openness to proselytes and other religious practices
16.	Why did Moses refer the case to God?	He didn't want to rely on an inappropriate precedent	None	None
17.	Why did Moses refer the case to God?	He was afraid he would lose objectivity if the women cried	Contextual. It's an emotionally charged scene	Modern association with women, crying and weakness
18.	What does *ken* mean?	Properly	None	Rabbinic notion of pre-existent Torah
19.	How is it that God's Torah and our Torah sometimes differ?	Both change, but God's changes first depending on human deeds	None	Kabbalistic notion of Torah with jumbled letters
20.	Grammatical inconsistencies	Male pronouns point to daughters being treated equally to men	Equal number of male and female suffixes	Rise of biblical criticism and Reform Judaism

continued

Comment	Problem	Resolution	Textual Mechanism	Historical Circumstance
21.	Is the law universal? Does the law apply to moveable property?	The law concerns only real estate for the generation going into the Land	Context	Karaite preference for plain sense
22.	How did the daughters bear children if they waited so long to marry?	They were righteous, waited for fitting partners, and were the recipients of miracles	None	Universal
23.	Why the naming of the daughters repeatedly and not the husbands?	They take the status of men in the marriage	Repetition and anonymity of men	Modern feminist sensibilities
24.	Why are the women described as marrying rather than being married?	They chose their husbands	Reversal of normal biblical marriage language	Modern feminist sensibilities
25.	How can Jews continue to bind themselves to their portion even when living outside the Land?	Bind themselves to their portion of life and peace, not Land	None	Living in diaspora outside the Land (but relevant for living in the Land, as well)
26.	Is cleaving to the Land an ultimate value?	No. Cleaving to God is the ultimate value.	G'zerah shavah with nachalah/portion	Israeli-Palestinian conflict
27.	Why does the book end on such a prosaic note?	To demonstrate the unfolding of Torah over time	None	Widespread concern with how Torah can be both eternal and responsive to particular historical moments

NOTES

1. Jerusalem and Israel are absolutely central for Jews wherever they may live. Yoel Bin-Nun offers a halakhic analysis of the relationship. A warmer account including a brief history of the events leading up to the modern State of Israel can be found in Abraham Joshua Heschel's *Israel: An Echo of Eternity.*

2. An excellent academic treatment of women in early halakhic literature is Judith Romney Wegner's *Chattel or Person: The Status of Women in the Mishnah.*

There is an extensive literature on women in the Bible and the Jewish tradition. In addition to the sources mentioned in this chapter, there are several recent books that deal with the depiction of women, usually in an aggadic context, from the Torah through the Kabbalah.

Tikva Frymer-Kensy's *Reading the Women of the Bible* is a wonderful treatment of this theme from a contemporary academic. *Midrashic Women: Formations of the Feminine in Rabbinic Literature* by Judith Baskin focuses on the women of the Rabbinic world rather than the biblical world. From a more traditional perspective, *The Women of the Torah* by Barbara Ronson presents Rabbinic and kabbalistic commentary. Athalya Brenner has done extensive work on women in the Bible. Her most recent book combines her scholarship and midrashic sensibilities, *I Am—: Biblical Women Tell Their Own Stories.*

3. y. *P'sachim* 6:1.

4. Perhaps the most difficult of all commandments to keep are those related to speech. Joseph Telushkin's *Words that Hurt, Words that Heal: How to Choose Words Wisely and Well* is a wonderful entrée into this area of Jewish thought.

5. *Moshav Z'kenim* on b. *Baba Batra* 119b.

6. b. *Shabbat* 97a. Shlomo Wexler develops this connection in his novel, *The Daughters Victorious* (New York: Gefen Books, 2002).

7. b. *Nedarim* 37b. Rabbi Yehudah He-Hasid (c. 1150–1217) writes that Moses transmitted the Torah to the Israelites in the same tune that God sang it to him! (*Sefer Hasidim*, 241.) For accessible reading on biblical grammar and cantillation, see Joshua R. Jacobson, *Chanting the Hebrew Bible.*

8. b. *Sanhedrin* 4a.

9. An alternative, and more pious interpretation, is that Joseph repeatedly refused her invitations (*Numbers Rabbah* 14). In that case, the *shalshelet* would represent the back and forth between the two of them, rather than Joseph's internal vacillations.

10. Ramban, commenting on Lev. 19:2, wrote that one can be fully observant of Jewish law and still be a despicable person.

11. *Honor thy Father and Mother: Filial Responsibility in Jewish Law and Ethics* by Gerald Blidstein covers the halakhic requirements as well as the psychological aspects of this commandment.

12. *Itturei Torah*, 5:173.

13. b. *Nazir* 23b.

14. b. *Baba Batra* 115b. This inheritance scheme is unique to that generation entering the Land for the first time.

15. *Sisters at Sinai: New Tales of Biblical Women* (Philadelphia: The Jewish Publication Society, 2001), 142.

16. The most elaborate dramatization of our story is Shlomo Wexler's *The Daughters Victorious.* Wexler writes as an Orthodox Rabbi convinced of the historicity of the biblical account and prone to accepting many Rabbinic midrashim as historically accurate, as well. Although I cannot endorse his approach, he does bring the story to life.

17. b. *Baba Batra* 109a.

18. *The Women's Torah Commentary*, ed. Elyse Goldstein (Woodstock: Jewish Lights Publishing, 2000), 313.

19. The *Kli Yekar* suggests that Moses should have sent women to reconnoiter the land!

20. m. *Avot* 4:1.

21. b. *Yoma* 69b.

22. For an introduction into the textual nuances of the Hebrew Bible, including large letters, see Emanuel Tov's *Textual Criticism of the Hebrew Bible*.

23. Rabbi David Abudarham, fourteenth-century Spain.

24. In addition to our verse, Lev. 24:10–22, Num. 9:6–14, and Num. 15:32–36.

25. *ReVisions*, 84ff.

26. *JPS Torah Commentary: Numbers* (Philadelphia: The Jewish Publication Society, 1990), 482.

27. Ibid.

28. *Numbers Rabbah* 9:49 and Zohar 2:195a, et. al.

29. Michael Silber, "The Invention of Ultra-Orthodoxy," in *In The Uses of Tradition: Jewish Continuity in the Modern Era*, ed. Jack Wertheimer (New York: Jewish Theological Seminary of America, 1992), 23–84.

30. *Exodus Rabbah* 18:10 establishes the precedent of considering the *'erev rav* as virtuous.

31. *Five Cities of Refuge: Weekly Reflections on* Genesis, Exodus, Leviticus, *Numbers, and* Deuteronomy (New York: Schocken Books, 2003), 125ff.

32. *Torah Gems.*

33. Rashi wrote a running commentary on almost the entire Talmud. For those sections that Rashi was unable to finish, his grandson, Rashbam, completed the task.

Rashbam's commentary on the Torah is not fully extant. In particular, his commentary on this section of *Numbers* is missing. Although it is reasonable to assume that Rashbam believed that the daughters of Zelophechad were wily, it is important to point out that Rashbam is commenting on the Talmud, not *Numbers*. Rashbam is known to sometimes distinguish his own understanding of the Torah from the traditional Rabbinic understanding of the text.

34. The *Guide for the Perplexed*, 3:54.

35. Rabbinic comments assuming a pre-existent Torah include the opening of *Genesis Rabbah* where God looks into his Torah and creates the world. Of the nine lists of things that pre-existed the world, Torah heads seven of them. See Ephraim Urbach, *The Sages*, 287, 685.

36. Gershom Scholem, the father of the academic study of Jewish mysticism, discusses the history of the idea of jumbled letters in the Torah in *On the Kabbalah and Its Symbolism*, 66–77. Moshe Idel has continued the discussion of Kabbalah and interpretation in his *Absorbing Perfections*.

37. *Beyond Good and Evil: Prelude to a Philosophy of the Future*, pt. 4, aphorism 121.

38. *Genesis Rabbah* 22:6.

39. Two essays in *The Jewish Study Bible* are helpful in understanding biblical criticism and its relationship to the Jewish study of Scripture: "Modern Jewish Interpretation" by S. David Sperling and "Textual Criticism of the Bible" by Adele Berlin and Marc Zvi Brettler. From more traditional perspectives, see Carmy, *Modern Scholarship in the Study of Torah*.

40. Cited by Jacob Milgrom, *JPS Bible Commentary: Numbers*, 484.

41. The essay in *The Jewish Study Bible* by Barry D. Walfish covers the broad swath of medieval Jewish biblical interpretation and deals briefly with the Karaites. For a sustained treatment, see Frank's *Search Scripture Well: Karaite Exegetes and the Origins of the Jewish Bible Commentary in the Islamic East.*

42. *Megilat Ta'anit* 33. Cited by Milgrom, 484.

43. Judith Hauptman, *Rereading the Rabbis: A Woman's Voice* (Boulder: Westview Press, 1998), 177–195. In the State of Israel, due to rabbinic legislation during the British Mandate, daughters inherit on an equal basis with sons.

44. b. *Ketubot* 62b and *Zohar* 2:89a/b, et. al.

45. Exod. 21:24, m. *Baba Kamma* 8:1 and related gemara.

46. The Tosafot, an early school of Talmudic commentators in the generation of Rashi's grandsons, suggest that Rabbi Eliezer assumes that Zelophehad was the wood gatherer. Since forty years elapsed since his execution and the marriage of Zelophehad's daughters, all the daughters must have been at least 40.

47. "The Daughters of Zelophehad," *Jewish Bible Quarterly* 26, no. 4 (1998): 261.

48. *Women's Torah Commentary*, ed. Goldstein, 326ff.

49. Tal Ilan has an insightful essay on this issue. "The Daughters of Zelophehad and Women's Inheritance: The Biblical Injunction and Its Outcome," in *Exodus to Deuteronomy: A Feminist Companion to the Bible*, ed. Athalya Brenner (Sheffield: Sheffield Academic Press, 2000), 176–186.

50. I thank my student, Joanna Caravita, for this observation. Cf. *Genesis Rabbah* 98:18.

51. For different views of classical Zionism, see *The Zionist Idea*, ed. Hertzberg. For a more recent collection of Zionist views, see Carol Diament, *Zionism: The Sequel.*

52. Although, as we have seen, the Talmud prohibits the innovation of a *g'zerah shavah*, Meshi relies on the modern precedent of R. Meir Simcha of Dvinsk for doing just that. See his comment on Exod. 20:22 in *Meshech Chochmah.*

53. b. *Baba Batra* 120a.

54. Yeshayahu Leibowitz coined this term. See his "Religious Praxis: The Meaning of Halakhah," in his *Judaism, Human Values and the Jewish State*, 11.

55. An appendix in Idel's *Absorbing Perfections* is entitled, "On Oral Torah and Multiple Interpretations in Hasidism." There is a rich collection of excerpts and analyses by Elliot N. Dorff on theories of *halakhah* within Conservative Judaism in *The Unfolding Tradition: Jewish Law after Sinai.*

56. There is actually a *g'zerah shavah* between the two verses in this comment that does not translate into English well.

EPILOGUE

In chapter two, the angels debated creating humanity. It was two against two. Loving-kindness and Justice were in favor. Peace was opposed, as was Truth who warned that we would be a lying lot. Rather than futilely arguing with Truth, God cast him to the earth, and the tie was broken.

The coda of this midrash from *Genesis Rabbah* is that the angels rebuke God for hurling Truth, the Divine seal, from the heavens. Citing the psalm from which our *darshan* had manufactured the image of the contentious angels, he has them say to God, "Grow Truth from the ground!"[1] In other words, bring Truth back up here where it won't become soiled and sullied.

This midrash is blatantly anti-Platonic. Truth, the Rabbis insist, is not in heaven. It's not a static, never-changing idea. One hundred years ago, William James promoted the notion that truth is dynamic. It grows from the ground, from our experience with lived reality. The Rabbis scooped him. The truth, and therefore our understanding of God's Will as expressed in the Torah, grows over time. As Abraham Joshua Heschel wrote, "The Bible is a seed, God is the sun, but we are the soil. Every generation is expected to bring forth new understanding and new realization."[2] Why? Because, as every good vintner knows, soil changes according to time and place, and we never know prospectively which combination will yield a quality vintage.

Heschel's analogy goes further than the botanical model with which we began. For Heschel, the Torah is a seed, not a tree. A fig tree produces figs, whether now or later. But the grape produced from the seed has been affected by the changing soil so that the next generation of seed is unlike its immediate predecessor. The soil affects the seed. This botanical metaphor is radically evolutionary. The context changes the meaning, which changes the subsequent context, which changes the subsequent meaning, and so on. In Heschel's analogy, we are the soil. And *we* are a combination of history and hermeneutics, of historical context and textual interpretation.

The creation of humanity recounted in Genesis 1, initially, meant something very different than how Jews have come to read that story in the wake of its placement as the "introduction" to the creation of humanity of Genesis 2. Similarly, the three different law codes related to the Hebrew slave likely possessed different legislative intent until the biblical redactor placed them in the same text. Moreover, as we read these texts in later historical

189

contexts wherein there is discomfort with patriarchy and slavery, a different soil from which they may have been originally written, the yield is affected. The midrashic readings of the early Rabbis represent the next soil of interpretive context for Rabbinic Jews and produced the seeds for generations of gardens.

The roughly 130 comments in this book represent a sampling of the harvest of 2000 years of Jewish understanding of the Torah. As with wine, some comments mature over time, while others sour. My primary goal in *Torah Through Time* has been to educate tasters about the seeds and the soils, that is, the peculiarities of the Hebrew Bible and the idiosyncrasies of its commentators. One desired byproduct has been to illustrate how a religious tradition justifies its claim that its Scripture is a tree of life (Prov. 3:18) and not petrified wood.[3]

Medieval *pashtanim* and contemporary bible scholars, to return to Heschel's image, are akin to paleobotanists churning through layers of soil to find petrified seeds. They often want to know what the Bible meant in its earliest, most narrow context. Already in the 15th century, Isaac Arama voiced this complaint against his contemporary *pashtanim*: "Their purpose is only to explain the grammatical forms of words and the simple meaning of the stories and commandments. They have not attempted to fill our need or to exalt the image of our Torah to our own people by regaling them with gems from its narratives and laws."[4] My second purpose in *Torah Through Time* has been to exhibit some of the gems of Torah commentary and to provide a map for those who seek to return.

The botanical model of Rabbinic literary theory posits that new meanings emerge over time. The Rabbinic tradition, while being cautious to preserve Moses' unique status as the foremost prophet, was willing to accede that the daughters of Zelophehad saw what Moses did not. They said the same thing about Ezra and Rabbi Akiva.[5] Continuous revelation allows God's light to shine on the descendants of Moses at an angle that allows us glimpses of God's Torah that Moses himself could not perceive. "Had God revealed to the Israelites all of His goodness at once, they'd have died. . . . So God reveals to them bit by bit."[6] And as Aviva Zornberg reminds us through the words of the Sefat Emet, only the slave abdicates responsibility to listen for those intimations of revelation.

Finally, though more of a hope than a goal, *Torah Through Time* seeks to rouse its readers to join the tradition of Torah commentary. The generation of Rashi's grandsons produced many commentaries, among them was one called *Da'at Z'kenim*. They asked why the commandment to build an ark for the

Torah was given in the plural (Exod. 25:10), while in the surrounding verses dealing with the other furniture in the Tabernacle, the instructions are in the singular. Their answer is that everyone had to contribute to the ark because that's what holds the Torah.[7] The Torah is too valuable to be left in the hands of any small group; it needs broad participation.

The Rabbis of *Exodus Rabbah* suggest that everyone, alive and not-yet-alive, experienced revelation at Sinai—and the Rabbis of the Talmud go so far as to suggest that revelation was simultaneously broadcast in all languages.[8] In less mythical terms, revelation, like the sun, is universally accessible. If we are to heed the angels' demand to grow Truth from the ground, to bring forth new understandings and new realizations of God's will, to hear and respond to those intimations of revelation, it will require a collective effort.

NOTES

1. *Genesis Rabbah* 8:5 citing Ps. 85:12.

2. *God in Search of Man*, 274.

3. *Genesis Rabbah* 12:6.

4. Cited and translated by Marc Saperstein, *Jewish Preaching, 1200–1800: An Anthology* (New Haven: Yale University Press, 1989), 393.

5. *Numbers Rabbah* 19:6.

6. *Tanhuma* (Buber), Deuteronomy, 2.

7. Cited in Louis Jacobs, *Jewish Biblical Exegesis*, 62.

8. *Exodus Rabbah* 28:6 and b. *Shabbat* 88b. S. Y. Agnon has collected a wonderful treasury of midrashim on revelation in *Present at Sinai: The Giving of the Law*, trans. Michael Swirsky; intro. by Judah Goldin (Philadelphia: The Jewish Publication Society, 1994).

GLOSSARY OF TERMS

'Aggadah   Hebrew for *telling*, related to the word *Haggadah* which is used at the Passover meal. *Aggadah* is any non-legal text.

'Amidah   Central prayer in the Jewish prayer service, lit. standing.

Anthropocentric   Human beings at the center. In the Kabbalah, worthy human deeds empower the good side of the Godhead while bad deeds fuel the *sitra achra*.

'Apikorus   In Mishnaic Hebrew (m. San 10:1), someone who denies Divine intervention, or, more generally, is at odds with the Rabbis. Throughout Jewish history, the term has been used to designate someone who holds heretical ideas. The name probably derives from the Greek philosopher, Epicurus (341–270 BCE).

Aristotle   Ancient Greek philosopher (384–322 BCE) who argued that the world is eternal and unchanging. In the Middle Ages, many Muslims, Jews, and Christians attempted to synthesize elements of Aristotelian philosophy with their own theology.

'Avodah   Hebrew for *service*. In the Torah, it generally refers to sacrificial service, while in Rabbinic Hebrew, it generally refers to prayer service.

Bat Torah   Hebrew for daughter of the Torah.

Beit Midrash   Hebrew for *study house* where one engages in Talmud Torah.

B'rit   Hebrew for *covenant*. The idea of a covenant, going back to Avram (even before his name change to Abraham), is a symbiotic relationship between God and the Jewish people, each benefiting somehow from the relationship. Jewish boys undergo a *b'rit milah*, a covenant of circumcision, on the eighth day following their birth.

Conservative Judaism   Founded as the Positive-Historical School of Judaism in Germany in the mid 19th century. Its founders accepted Reform Judaism's assertion that the Torah and Jewish tradition were products of human beings, but they insisted that the *halakhah*, though constantly evolving, was still binding on the individual Jew.

Darshan   Writer of a midrash.

Derash   As a noun, it is a reading of a verse which is not obvious from the context. As a verb, it is the activity of weaving together a biblical verse with one's own worldview.

Dead Sea Sect   Separatists/Refugees from the Jerusalem Temple in the second century BCE who maintained a highly disciplined lifestyle and had more stringent ritual purity laws than other groups of Second Temple Jews. This community was destroyed by the Romans during the Great Revolt of 66–70. Some of the scrolls from their library were preserved in clay jugs in the caves above the Dead Sea and discovered in 1947.

'Erev Rav The mixed multitude who left Egypt with the Israelites (Ex. 12:38). Often used by traditionalists as scapegoats for Jewish transgressions.

'Eved Hebrew for servant, serf, or slave.

Gnosticism A complex of religious ideologies maintaining a dualism between a good god and an evil god. The evil god is responsible for physical creation. Humans are linked to the good god only through the soul. It is through the knowledge (*gnosis*) of this dualistic scheme that one attains salvation.

G'zerah Shavah The transitive property of Rabbinic logic. The Rabbis use this principle to learn about one context from a different context through the connection of an identical word or phrase. The Talmud prohibits students from innovating these independently.

Haftarah A passage, usually from the prophetic books, appended to the reading of the Torah portion. The Rabbis, or their predecessors, selected a *haftarah* with a linguistic or thematic connection, often both, to the Torah portion.

Halakhah Hebrew for *path* or *way*. The word signifies traditional Jewish law and practice.

Hammurabi's Code A legal code, c. 18 century BCE, from the ancient Near East that predates the Torah by many centuries.

Hasidism A religious renewal movement which swept through Eastern Europe in the 18th and 19th centuries. Focus is on religious psychology. The leader of any particular school is called the *tzaddik* and the disciples are called *hasidim*.

Havruta Aramaic for *companion* or *study buddy*. One can be a member of a *havruta* (the pair) or one can be Ploni Almoni's havruta (the individual).

Hellenism From the 4th century BCE much of Europe and Asia came under the influence of the Greek culture that Alexander the Great brought with him in his conquests. Greek philosophy, bath houses, circuses, and theatre all fall under this broad cultural umbrella of Hellenism.

Impassible Having no passions or emotions and thus not subject to needs.

Indeterminacy The impossibility of deciding on a single meaning among multiple interpretations of a text.

Jubilee Every 50 years, slaves would be released, debts forgiven, and real estate returned to its original owners within the biblical system.

Kabbalah Jewish mysticism, emerging in the 12th and 13th centuries, which uses a fluid system of symbolic clusters, the *s'firot*, to represent flows of energy within the Godhead. The Zohar becomes the principal text of Kabbalah.

Karaites Hebrew for *Scripturalists* or *Biblicists*. Karaites rejected Rabbinic Judaism's midrashic interpretations of the Torah. Emerged in the middle of the 8th century under the leadership of Anan ben David. Centered in Babylonia and offered a challenge to Rabbinic hegemony for several hundred years.

Kavanah   Hebrew for *direction, intention, inwardness,* or *awareness.* Although extolled by Rabbinic Judaism, *kavanah* was not required to fulfill most commandments. (Prayer is an exception.) In the Judaism practiced by medieval mystics, *kavanah* becomes an essential component to unite the fragmented elements of the Divine. *Kavanah* is also central to the development of devotional posture that characterizes Hasidism.

Lex Talionis   Latin for *the law of retaliation.* The biblical principle of an "eye for an eye" was understood by Rabbinic Judaism to mean that bodily injury required monetary compensation.

Manumission   The act of liberating a slave.

Mezuzah   In the Torah, a mezuzah is the lintel, or side post, of the door. In Rabbinic Hebrew, it became the term used for the scroll that is commanded to be affixed to the side post (Deut. 6:9). Today, many people use the term not for the scroll, but for the decorative casing of the scroll.

Midrash   An idea weaved to a biblical verse. Also a collection of individual midrashim (plural of midrash).

Mitzvah/Mitzvot   Commandment/s. Although in Yiddish the term has the sense of a *good deed,* in Hebrew, a mitzvah has greater force because it is commanded by the Commander.

Olam Ha-ba   Not Olam Ha-zeh. Olam Ha-ba can either indicate what this world will be like in the messianic future, or the world that awaits us after death. In the latter sense, Olam Ha-ba already exists for those who have made the transition from Olam Ha-zeh.

Olam Ha-zeh   This present world that we all inhabit, as opposed to Olam Ha-ba.

Omnisignificance   Term coined by scholar James Kugel to refer to the interpretability of every word, or even calligraphic flourish, in the Torah.

Ontology   A study of the very being or essence.

Pashtan   A commentator who seeks the *peshat.*

Peshat   Contextual, plain-sense meaning.

Pharisees   Intellectual ancestors of the Rabbis. Active in the period before the destruction of the Second Temple (70 CE). They had an oral tradition in addition to the *peshat* of the Torah and were concerned about purity issues outside the Temple for non-priests.

Ploni Almoni   Hebrew for *Joe Shmoe.* Makes his biblical debut in *Ruth* 4:1.

Pluripotence   The capacity of a Divinely charged, biblical word to generate multiple meanings.

Polysemy   The capacity of any word, sentence or text to inherently possess multiple interpretations.

Reform Judaism   Religious renewal movement starting in Germany in the 1820s, but later flourishing in the United States. Traditional *halakhah* is not obligatory in Reform Judaism.

Sadducees   In the period before the destruction of the Second Temple (70 CE), this group may have been connected to the priesthood and the urban middle class. They only considered the Pentateuch authoritative, avoided the midrashic reading style of the Pharisees, and thus denied the resurrection of the dead.

Sheol   The biblical underworld where all, both the good and the evil, descend upon death.

Shmittah   Hebrew for release. Every 7 years, the land will lay fallow and debts will be forgiven.

Shoah   The systematic extermination of six million European Jews in Nazi Europe during World War II. *Shoah* is Hebrew for *catastrophe*. "Holocaust," a term coined by Christian theologians, means a wholly-burnt sin offering.

Sitra Achra   In the Kabbalah, the Aramaic term for the "other side," dominated by evil.

Syncretism   The absorption by one religion of aspects from other religions.

Talmud Torah   Studying Torah, a paramount mitzvah in Judaism.

Teshuvah   Hebrew for *return* or *respond*. A preeminent value of Rabbinic Judaism. Frequently translated as repentance.

Theography   Divine geography. After the Temple was destroyed, Rabbinic Jews seek God in the Torah.

Theosophy   Describes the inner life of God. The *s'firot* are a Kabbalistic map of theosophic speculation.

Torah   Hebrew for *teaching*. Its range of meanings includes a particular teaching, the Pentateuch, the TANAKH, and all subsequent Jewish teaching.

Tzaddik   Hebrew for *righteous*. Also used in Hasidism as the leader of a particular school of Hasidim.

Tzorech Gavoah   Hebrew for *supernal need*. The central Kabbalistic concept that God has needs which can be filled by Jews performing the *mitzvot* with the proper *kavanah*.

Yetzer Ha-ra   The tendency to do evil, see Gen. 6:5.

Yetzer Ha-tov   The tendency to do good. The Rabbis coined this term, if not the psychological trait, to complement and compensate for the biblical Yetzer Ha-ra.

Zoroastrianism   A dualistic theological system influential in Persia. Second Isaiah responds to Zoroastrian theology after the destruction of the First Temple in 586 BCE. Zoroastrianism again became a theological foil for the Jews living in Babylonia after the destruction of the second Temple in 70 CE.

GLOSSARY OF TEXTS AND COMMENTATORS

Abraham ibn Ezra (1089–1164, Spain) Wrote two commentaries on the Torah, a long and short one. A frequent polemicist against Karaites and believer in astrology.

Albo, Joseph (1380–1435, Spain) Author of *Sefer Ha'ikkarim (Book of Principles)*, a philosophical work which posits three principles of Judaism: Divine existence, providence, and revelation.

Alphabet of Ben Sira (c. 9th century, Arab world) This text, likely to have been originally written as a farce, contains an early legend of Lilith.

Avot (3rd century) *Aggadic* tractate appended to the Mishnah.

Avot d'Rabbi Natan (c. 500, Land of Israel) Commentary on the opening sections of *Avot*.

Bahya ben Asher, Rabbeinu (1263–1340, Spain) Kabbalist who frequently interpreted Torah according to the traditional Pardes system: *Peshat, Remez* (philosophical allegory), *Derash* (Rabbinic), and *Sod* (secret/kabbalistic.)

Bahir (late 12th century, Spain) First text to incorporate mystical language of the *s'firot*.

Bechor Shor, Joseph (1130–1200, France) One of the earliest Torah commentators to focus on the plain-sense meaning. Involved in Christian polemics.

Beit Yakov see Leiner, Yakov.

Book of Education (Sefer Hachinuch) (13th century, Spain) Enumeration of 613 commandments, according to Rambam's count, in the order in which they appear in the Torah. Also provides reasons for many of the commandments.

Book of Principles (Sefer Ha'ikkarim) see Joseph Albo.

Bunim of Przysucha, Rabbi (1765–1827, Poland) Hasidic Master.

Eliyahu ben Shlomo Zalman, Vilna Gaon (1720–1797, Lithuania) The leading Talmudist in the 18th century who also wrote a Torah commentary.

Gemara Aramaic for learning. The Gemara forms the bulk of the Talmud. The Gemara begins by commenting on the Mishnah and then spins off through associative reasoning. There were two *gemarot*, one in the Land of Israel, called the Jerusalem Talmud, completed in the fourth-fifth century, and the Babylonian Talmud, edited about a hundred years later.

Genesis Rabbah   Midrashic compilation on Genesis. Statements attributed to Rabbis of 1ˢᵗ–4ᵗʰ centuries, edited by 5ᵗʰ century, Land of Israel.

Goldstein, Elyse   Contemporary Rabbi, director of Kolel: The Adult Centre for Liberal Jewish Learning in Toronto, and author of *ReVisions: Seeing Torah Through a Feminist Lens*.

Greenberg, Aharon   (1900–1963) Born in Poland and raised in a Hasidic home, Greenberg immigrated to Palestine and later served in the Knesset. He collected traditional interpretations of the Torah, primarily from the Hasidic masters, and included those of his own in '*Itturei Torah*, abridged and translated as *Torah Gems*.

The Guide for the Perplexed   (1190). Rambam's great philosophical work attempting to synthesize Aristotelianism and Judaism.

Gur Aryeh   see Judah Loew ben Bezalel.

Haktav v'hakabbalah   see Mecklenburg, Jacob Zvi.

Hammer, Jill   Contemporary Conservative Rabbi and author of *Sisters at Sinai* and *The Jewish Book of Days*.

Hayim ben Attar   (1696–1742) was born in Morocco, lived in Italy and the Land of Israel. Wrote Torah commentary, *Or Hahayim*, from within the mystical tradition.

Hirsch, Samson Raphael   (1808–1888, Germany) The father of Modern Orthodoxy, Rabbi Hirsch pioneered the model for the contemporary Jewish day school, defended traditional Judaism from Reform, and wrote a commentary on the Torah in German.

Hizkuni ben Manoah   (13ᵗʰ century, France) A disciple of Rashi and a *pashtan*.

Itturei Torah   see *Torah Gems*.

Jacob, Benno   (1862–1955, Germany) Used academic methods to support more traditional understandings of Hebrew Bible.

Judah Loew ben Bezalel, Maharal   (c. 1525–1609, Prague) Wrote super-commentary on Rashi, *Gur Aryeh*, as well as other important works.

Kagan, Yisrael Meir   (1838–1933, Poland) Authored a legal code and wrote a popular book on the laws of speech, *Chofetz Chayim*.

Karaites   A medieval sect concentrated in the Land of Israel and farther east which denied the authority of the Rabbinic Oral Torah. Their name means Scripturalists, and they had a tendency toward plain-sense interpretation.

Kimchi, David   see Radak.

Kli Yekar   see Shlomo Ephraim of Lunschitz.

Leibowitz, Nechama   (1905–1997, Israel) One of the great Torah teachers of the 20ᵗʰ century.

Leibowitz, Yeshayahu   (1903–1994, Israel) Controversial Israeli gadfly. A sampling of his thought can be found in *Judaism, Human Values, and the Jewish State*.

Leiner, Mordechai Joseph   (1802–1854, Isbitza, Poland) A radical Hasidic master who wrote the Torah commentary, *Mei HaShiloach*.

Leiner, Yakov   (1828–1878, Isbitza-Radzin, Poland) Successor and son of Mordecai Joseph Leiner. Wrote Torah commentary, *Beit Yakov*.

Lewin, Aharon   (1879–1941, Poland) Communal leader and author of *Haderash Ve'ha'iyun*. Murdered by the Nazis.

Maimonides, Moses   see Rambam.

Malbim   Meir Loeb ben Yechiel Michael (1809–1879). Torah commentator and Reform adversary in Germany and Central Europe.

Mamet, David   Contemporary playwright, director, and writer who joined Rabbi Lawrence Kushner to pen a commentary on the Torah: *Five Cities of Refuge*.

Masoretes   The vowels and cantillation marks in the TANAKH are the products of the Masoretes (tradition bearers). They lived in Tiberias on the Sea of Galilee for several centuries beginning around 600. The version of the TANAKH that they endorsed has become the authoritative Jewish Bible. Scholars often refer to this version as the Masoretic Text (MT).

Mecklenburg, Jacob Zvi   (1785–1865, Germany) He wrote a biblical commentary, *Haktav v'hakabbalah*, showing the compatibility of the Rabbinic tradition to the plain sense of Scripture.

Mei HaShiloach   Torah commentary by the Hasidic master Mordechai Joseph Leiner (1802–1854).

Meir Simcha HaKohen of Dvinsk   (1843–1926, Russia) He wrote a Bible Commentary, *Meshech Chochmah* and attempted to show the merit of Rabbinic interpretations of Torah.

Mekhilta   An early halakhic midrash on Exodus compiled in 3rd century, Land of Israel.

Mendelssohn, Moses   (1729–1786, Germany) A pioneer of the Jewish Enlightenment, Mendelssohn translated the Bible into German and provided a commentary defending traditional Rabbinic exegesis.

Meshech Chochmah   see Meir Simcha HaKohen of Dvinsk.

Meshi   Michael Shai Cherry, your author, b. 1966.

Milgrom, Jacob   Contemporary Bible scholar, b. 1923.

Mishnah   The foundation document of Rabbinic Judaism, largely the result of Rabbi Akiva and his students, compiled by Yehuda HaNasi around 220. The Mishnah is almost exclusively legal, but it is not a law code since it preserves minority opinions, dissenting opinions, and relates relevant anecdotes. The justification for its claim as the authoritative interpretation of Torah law was appended to the Mishnah several decades later, around 250, as the *aggadic* tractate of *Pirkei Avot*. *Mishnah* can either refer to a single section or the entire work. An *m.* precedes a mishnaic citation.

Mishneh Torah   Comprehensive law code by Rambam, late 12th century, Egypt.

Moshav Zekenim   A collection of Torah commentaries by the Tosafot (12th century).

Nachmanides, Moses   see Ramban.

Numbers Rabbah   *Aggadic* midrash compiled in the Land of Israel by the 9th century.

Onkelos   see *Targum* Onkelos.

Person, Hara E.   Contemporary Rabbi and contributor to *The Women's Torah Commentary*.

Pesikta d'Rav Kahana   Homiletic collection from the Land of Israel, perhaps from the 5th century.

Philo, Judaeus   (20 BCE–50 CE, Egypt) A Hellenistic Jew who anticipated the synthesizing work of Rambam in his effort to bring Judaism into line with current philosophical thinking. He is known for his allegorical interpretations of Torah.

Pirkei d'Rabbi Eliezer   A midrashic work written in the late Rabbinic period, perhaps 8th century.

Rabbeinu Bahya   see Bahya.

Radak   Rabbi David Kimchi (c.1160–c.1235, France) Grammarian and Torah commentator. *Pashtan.*

Rambam   Rabbi Moshe ben Maimon (1138–1204, Egypt) Rambam, aka Moses Maimonides, is the towering figure in medieval Jewry. His works include the halachic code, *Mishneh Torah* (1180), and his synthesis of Aristotelian philosophy and Judaism, *The Guide for the Perplexed* (1190).

Ramban   Rabbi Moshe ben Nachman (1194–1270, Spain) Ramban, aka Moses Nachmanides, wrote the first Torah commentary to incorporate Kabbalah. He was a Talmudist as well as a Kabbalist and represented the Jewish community in the Disputation of 1263 in Barcelona against the apostate Pablo Christiani. (*Pronunciation tip:* It is easy to confuse Rambam and Ramban. They were both rabbis and doctors whose first names were Moshe. By convention, Rambam is pronounced with the accent on the first syllable, RAMbam. Ramban, who was born later, has the accent on the second syllable, ramBAN.)

Rashbam   Rabbi Shmuel ben Meir (c. 1080–c. 1160, France) Rashi's grandson. Wrote a *peshat* commentary that sometimes veered from Rabbinic interpretation. He also wrote a commentary on the Talmud for those sections that Rashi did not.

Rashi   Rabbi Shlomo Itzchaki (1040–1105, France) Commentator extraordinaire on TANAKH and Talmud. About three quarters of his Torah commentary is gleaned from Rabbinic sources. More than 150 commentaries have been written on Rashi's commentary!

Ron, Zvi   Contemporary Orthodox Rabbi.

Sa'adia Gaon   (882–942, Babylonia) Leader of the Jewish community in Sura, foe of the Karaites, author of Torah commentary, and an early major work of Jewish philosophy, *Opinions and Beliefs.*

Sasso, Sandy Eisenberg   Contemporary American rabbi (ordained from the Reconstructionist Rabbinical College) and author of children's books.

Scolnic, Benjamin Edenic   Contemporary American rabbi (ordained from the Conservative movement).

Sefat Emet   see Yehudah Leib Alter of Ger.

Sefer Hachinuch   see *Book of Education.*

Shaviv, Yehudah   Contemporary Israeli Rabbi

S'forno, Ovadia   (1475–1550, Italy) A Torah commentator emphasizing *peshat.*

Shiur Komah   Early centuries of the Common Era, Land of Israel. A mystical text describing gigantic Divine dimensions.

Shlomo Ephraim of Lunschitz   (1550–1619, Prague and Poland) Author of Torah commentary *Kli Yekar.*

Sifra   Halachic midrashic collection on Leviticus compiled around 300, Land of Israel.

Sifre **Deuteronomy**   Halachic midrashic collection on Deuteronomy compiled around 300, Land of Israel.

Sifre **Numbers**   Halachic midrashic collection on Numbers compiled around 300, Land of Israel.

Sofer, Moses   (1763–1839, Hungary) Defended traditional Judaism against reforms and is viewed as the ideological father of Ultra Orthodoxy. He is often referred to by the name of his book, *Chatam Sofer* (in Ashkenazi pronunciation, *Chasam Sofer.*)

Soloveitchik, Joseph B.   (1903–1993 born in Lithuania) Lived in Boston and New York. The leading figure of Modern Orthodoxy in the 20th century. His book, *The Lonely Man of Faith,* offers a contemporary reading of the two creation stories in Genesis.

Talmud   A combination of the Mishnah, a predominantly legal text redacted in the early third century by Yehuda HaNasi, and the Gemara, a literature formally based around the Mishnah. The Talmud Yerushalmi was redacted by 450 in the Land of Israel (not in Jerusalem, but so named because of the centrality of the holy city in the Jewish imagination). The Talmud Bavli was redacted by 550 in Babylonia, is a more well-crafted document, and has tended to be more authoritative than the Yerushalmi for purposes of *halakhah.* Citations that are preceded by a *y.* are from the Yerushalmi, while those preceded by a *b.* are from the Bavli.

TANAKH   Acronym for Torah, Nevi'im (Prophets), Ketuvim (Writings), the three sections of the Hebrew Bible.

Tanhuma   Homiletic collection redacted in early Middle Ages but containing older material, Land of Israel. Subsequently edited in Babylonia and Europe.

Targum   Any number of Aramaic renditions of the TANAKH. Some, like *Targum Onkelos,* translate fairly closely to the Masoretic Text. Others, like *Targum Neophyti* and *Targum Pseudo-Jonathan,* contain much midrashic material.

Targum Onkelos A frequently literal translation of the Torah into Aramaic, dating from late first or early second century. Used by many later commentators in their attempt to understand the *peshat* of the Torah.

Targum Neophyti A midrashic *Targum*, going back perhaps to the second century, Land of Israel.

Targum Pseudo-Jonathan Although it contains earlier material, this *Targum* did not attain its final form until the Middle Ages.

Tikkunei HaZohar Written in Spain in the period immediately after the Zohar, c. 1300, this text offers 70 interpretations of the first chapters of Genesis.

Tosafot Commentators on the Talmud who tend to reconcile seemingly conflicting passages in different parts of the Talmud. They are Rashi's grandsons and their contemporaries (12th century France).

Tosefta The Tosefta includes much material from the Mishnah but also incorporates later material. It is structured like the Mishnah and was likely to have been redacted c. 300 CE in the Land of Israel. A text from the *Tosefta* is preceded by *t*.

Trunk, Yisrael Yehoshua (1820–1893, Poland) Halakhist and Hasidic colleague of Rabbi Yitzchak Meir of Ger.

Torah Gems Compilation of insights, mostly from the Hasidic Masters, arranged according to biblical verse. The Hebrew original, *'Itturei Torah*, has a fuller selection of comments. Compiled by Aharon Greenberg.

Wax, Pamela Contemporary Rabbi, Director of Religious Living for Union of Reform Judaism, and contributor to *The Women's Torah Commentary*.

Wexler, Shlomo A contemporary Orthodox Rabbi living in Jerusalem and author of *The Daughters Victorious*.

Wiesel, Elie Contemporary scholar, Nobel Laureate for Peace, and Shoah survivor.

Yalkut Shimoni A midrashic collection covering the entire TANAKH compiled around the 13th century.

Yehudah Hehasid (c. 1150–1217, Germany) *Sefer Hasidim* provides an interesting account of pious living in medieval Germany.

Yehudah Halevi (1080–1145, Spain) Wrote poetry and *The Kuzari*. Left for the Land of Israel in his old age.

Yehudah Leib Alter of Ger (1847–1905, Poland) A Hasidic master who wrote Sefat Emet.

Yitzchak Meir of Ger also known as Rim (1799–1866, Poland) Talmudist and founder of Ger Hasidism.

Zornberg, Aviva Contemporary Torah commentator living in Jerusalem.

Zohar Kabbalistic text from Northern Spain, late 13th century. Attributed to 2nd century sage, Shimon bar Yochai.

BIBLIOGRAPHY

Adams, Maurianne and John Bracey, eds. *Strangers & Neighbors: Relations between Blacks and Jews in the United States*. Amherst: University of Massachusetts Press, 1999.

Agnon, S. Y. *Present at Sinai: The Giving of the Law*. Translated by Michael Swirsky. Introduction by Judah Goldin. Philadelphia: The Jewish Publication Society, 1994.

Alter, Robert. *The Art of Biblical Narrative*. New York: Basic Books, 1981.

———. *The Five Books of Moses*. New York: W. W. Norton & Co., 2004.

Altmann, Alexander. "The Gnostic Background of the Rabbinic Adam Legends." In *Studies in Religious Philosophy and Mysticism*. Ithaca: Cornell University Press, 1969.

Appleman, Philip, ed. *Darwin: A Norton Critical Edition*, Third Edition. New York: W. W. Norton & Co., 2001.

Aschkenasy, Nehama. *Woman at the Window: Biblical Tales of Oppression and Escape*. Detroit: Wayne State University Press, 1998.

Bach, Alice, ed. *Women in the Hebrew Bible: A Reader*. New York: Routledge, 1999.

Barr, James. "Adam: Single Man, or All Humanity?" In *Hesed ve-Emet: Studies in Honor of Ernest Frerichs*, edited by Jodi Magness and Seymour Gitin, 3–12. Atlanta: Scholars Press, 1998.

Baskin, Judith R. *Midrashic Women: Formations of the Feminine in Rabbinic Literature*. Hanover, NH.: Brandeis University Press, 2002.

Becker, Hans-Jurgen. "The Magic of the Name and Palestinian Rabbinic Literature." In *The Talmud Yerushalmi and Graeco-Roman Culture*, edited by Peter Schafer, 3:391–407. Tübingen: Mohr Siebeck, 2002.

Beckwith, Roger T. "The Vegetarianism of the Theraputae, and the Motives for Vegetarianism in Early Jewish and Christian Circles." *Revue de Qumran* 13, 1–4 (1988): 407–410.

Berger, David. *The Jewish-Christian Debate in the High Middle Ages*. Philadelphia: The Jewish Publication Society, 1979.

Bergman, Samuel Hugo. *The Quality of Faith: Essays on Judaism and Morality*. Translated by Yehuda Hanegbi. Jerusalem: World Zionist Organization, 1970.

Berkovitz, Eliezer. *Faith after the Holocaust*. New York: Ktav Publishing, 1973.

Berlin, Adele, Marc Brettler, and Michael Fishbane, eds. *The Jewish Study Bible*. New York: Oxford University Press, 2004.

Bin-Nun, Yoel. "The Obligation of *Aliyah* and the Prohibition of Leaving Israel in the Contemporary Era, According to the Opinion of Rambam (Maimonides)." In *Israel as a Religious Reality,* edited by Chaim I. Waxman, 75–104. Northvale, N.J.: Jason Aronson, 1994.

Birnbaum, David. *God and Evil. A Unified Theodicy/Theology/Philosophy.* Hoboken, NJ: Ktav Publishing House, 1989.

Bleich, Judith. "Rabbinic Responses to Nonobservance in the Modern Era." In *Jewish Tradition and the Nontraditional Jew,* edited by Jacob J. Schachter. Northvale, N.J.: Jason Aronson, 1992.

Blidstein, Gerald. *Honor thy Father and Mother: Filial Responsibility in Jewish Law and Ethics.* Jersey City: Ktav Publishing House, 2005 Augmented edition.

Boyarin, Daniel. *Carnal Israel: Reading Sex in Talmudic Culture.* Berkeley: University of California Press, 1993.

———. *Intertextuality and the Reading of Midrash.* Bloomington: Indiana University Press, 1994.

Brenner, Athalya. *I Am—: Biblical Women Tell Their Own Stories.* Minneapolis: Fortress Press, 2005.

Brettler, Marc Zvi. *Biblical Hebrew for Students of Modern Israeli Hebrew.* New Haven: Yale University Press, 2002.

———. *How to Read the Bible.* Philadelphia: The Jewish Publication Society, 2005.

Breuer, Edward. *The Limits of Enlightenment: Jews, Germans, and the Eighteenth-Century Study of Scripture.* Cambridge: Harvard University Press, 1996.

———. "Naphtali Herz Wessely and the Cultural Dislocations of an Eighteenth-Century Maskil." In *New Perspectives on the Haskalah,* edited by Shmuel Finer and David Sorkin, 27–47. London: Littman Library of Jewish Civilization, 2001.

Brown, William P. "Divine Act and the Art of Persuasion in Genesis 1." In *History and Interpretation: Essays in Honour of John H. Hayes,* edited by M. Patrick Graham, et. al., 19–32. Sheffield: JSOT Press, 1993.

Buber, Martin. *Hasidism and Modern Man.* Translated by Maurice Friedman. New York: Horizon Press, 1958.

———. *Moses.* Oxford: East and West Library, 1946.

———. *On Judaism.* Edited by Nahum N. Glatzer and with a new Foreword by Roger Kamenetz. New York: Schocken Books, 1995.

———. *Tales of the Hasidim.* New York: Schocken Books, 1991.

Carmy, Shalom, ed. *Modern Scholarship in the Study of Torah: Contributions and Limitations.* Northvale, N.J.: Jason Aronson, 1996.

Cassuto, Umberto. *A Commentary on the Book of Genesis.* Translated by Israel Abrahams. Jerusalem: Magnes Press, 1961–1964.

Cherry, Shai. "Crisis Management via Biblical Interpretation: Fundamentalism, Modern Orthodoxy and Genesis." In *Jewish Tradition and the Challenge of Darwinism,* edited by Geoffrey Cantor and Marc Swetlitz. Chicago: University of Chicago Press, 2006: 166–187.

———. "Three Twentieth-Century Jewish Responses to Evolutionary Theory." *Aleph: Historical Studies in Science and Judaism* 3 (2003): 247–290.

Chill, Abraham. *The Mitzvot: The Commandments and their Rationale.* New York: Bloch Publishing Company, 1974.

Cohen, Jeremy. *"Be Fertile and Increase, Fill the Earth and Master It:" The Ancient and Medieval Career of a Biblical Text.* Ithaca: Cornell University Press, 1989.

Cohen, Shaye J.D. "Does Rashi's Commentary Respond to Christianity? A Comparison of Rashi with Rashbam and Bekhor Shor." In *The Idea of Biblical Interpretation: Essays in Honor of James L. Kugel,* edited by Hindy Najman and Judith H. Newman, 449–472. Leiden: Brill, 2004.

———. *From the Maccabees to the Mishnah.* Philadelphia: Westminster Press, 1987.

Dame, Enid, Lilly Rivlin, and Henny Wenkart, eds. *Which Lilith? Feminist Writers Recreate the World's First Woman.* Northvale, N.J.: Jason Aronson, 1998.

Dan, Joseph. *The Ancient Jewish Mysticism.* Tel Aviv: MOD Books, 1993.

———. *Jewish Mysticism and Jewish Ethics.* Northvale, N.J.: Jason Aronson, 1996.

Derrett, J. Duncan M. "The Case of Korah Versus Moses Reviewed." *Journal for the Study of Judaism* (34:1): 59–78.

Diament, Carol, ed. *Zionism: The Sequel.* New York: Hadassah, 1998.

Dorff, Elliot N. *The Unfolding Tradition: Jewish Law after Sinai.* New York: Aviv Press, 2005.

Draper, J. A. "'Korah' and the Second Temple." In *Templum Amicitiae: Essays on the Second Temple Presented to Ernst Bammel,* edited by William Horbury, 150–174. Sheffield: JSOT Press, 1991.

Eisen, Arnold. *Rethinking Modern Judaism: Ritual, Commandment, Community.* Chicago: Chicago University Press, 1998.

Eisen, Robert. *Gersonides on Providence, Covenant, and the Chosen People: A Study in Medieval Jewish Philosophy and Biblical Commentary.* Albany: State University of New York Press, 1995.

———. *The Book of Job in Medieval Jewish Philosophy.* New York: Oxford University Press, 2004.

Elior, Rachel. *The Three Temples: The Emergence of Jewish Mysticism.* Translated by David Louvish. Oxford: Littman Library of Jewish Civilization, 2004.

Elman, Yaakov. "The Rebirth of Omnisignificant Biblical Exegesis in the Nineteenth and Twentieth Centuries." *Jewish Studies, an Internet Journal* 2 (2003): 199–249.

Etz Hayim: Torah and Commentary. The Rabbinical Assembly. Philadelphia: The Jewish Publication Society, 2001.

Faur, Jose. "Basic Concepts in Rabbinic Hermeneutics." *Shofar* 16:1 (Fall, 1997): 1–12.

———. *Golden Doves with Silver Dots: Semiotics and Textuality in Rabbinic Tradition.* Bloomington: Indiana University Press, 1986.

Feldman, Louis H. "Josephus' Portrait of Korah." *Old Testament Essays* 6:3 (1993): 399–426.

Fishbane, Michael. "Hermeneutics." In *Contemporary Jewish Religious Thought: Original Essays on Critical Concepts, Movements, and Beliefs,* edited by Arthur A. Cohen and Paul Mendes-Flohr, 353–361. New York: The Free Press, 1982.

———. *The Garments of Torah: Essays on Biblical Hermeneutics.* Bloomington: Indiana University Press, 1989.

———. *The JPS Bible Commentary: Haftarot.* Philadelphia: The Jewish Publication Society, 2002.

Fossum, Jarl E. "Gen 1,26 and 2,7 in Judaism, Samaritanism, and Gnosticism." *Journal for the Study of Judaism* 16:2 (1985): 202–239.

Fox, Everett, trans. *The Five Books of Moses.* With introduction, commentary, and notes by Everett Fox. New York: Schocken Books, 1995.

Fox, Marvin. *Interpreting Maimonides: Studies in Methodology, Metaphysics, and Moral Philosophy.* Chicago: University of Chicago Press, 1990.

Fraade, Steven D. *From Tradition to Commentary: Torah and its Interpretation in the Midrash Sifre to* Deuteronomy. Albany: State University of New York Press, 1991.

———. "Moses and the Commandments: Can Hermeneutics, History, and Rhetoric be Disentangled?" In *The Idea of Biblical Interpretation: Essays in Honor of James L. Kugel,* edited by Hindy Najman and Judith H. Newman, 399–422. Leiden: Brill, 2004.

Frank, Daniel H. *Search Scripture Well: Karaite Exegetes and the Origins of the Jewish Bible Commentary in the Islamic East.* Boston: Brill, 2004.

Frank, Daniel H. and Oliver Leaman. *The Cambridge Companion to Medieval Jewish Philosophy.* New York: Cambridge University Press, 2003.

Friedman, Richard Elliott. *Who Wrote the Bible?* New York: Harper & Row Publishers, 1987.

———. *Commentary on the Torah With a New English Translation.* New York: Harper-Collins, 2001.

Frisch, Amos. "R. Jacob Zvi Mecklenburg's Method in the Issue of the Patriarchs' Sins." *Journal of Jewish Studies* 8:1 (Spring, 2002): 107–119.

Frymer-Kensky, Tikva. *Reading the Women of the Bible.* New York: Schocken Books, 2002.

Garbini, Giovanni. In *Myth and History in the Bible,* translated by Chiara Peri. Sheffield: Sheffield Academic Press, 2003.

Geller, Yakov. "The Malbim: Leadership and Challenge." In *Studia et Acta Historiae Iudaerom Romaniae,* 176–182. Bucharest: Editura Hasefer, 2002.

Gillingham, Susan E. *The Image, the Depths and the Surface: Multivalent Approaches to Biblical Study.* London: Sheffield Academic Press, 2000.

Gillman, Neil. *The Death of Death: Resurrection and Immortality in Jewish Thought.* Woodstock: Jewish Lights Publishing, 1997.

Goldstein, Elyse. *ReVisions: Seeing Torah Through a Feminist Lens.* Toronto: Key Porter Books, 1998.

———, ed. *The Women's Torah Commentary.* Woodstock: Jewish Lights Publishing, 2000.

Goodman, Lenn Evan. *God of Abraham.* New York: Oxford University Press, 1996.

———. *RAMBAM: Readings in the Philosophy of Moses Maimonides.* New York: Viking Press, 1976.

Gordis, Robert. "'Be Fruitful and Multiply'—Biography of a Mitzvah." *Midstream* 28:7 (1982): 21–29.

Goshen-Gottstein, Alon. "The Body as Image of God in Rabbinic Literature." *Harvard Theological Review* 87:2 (1994): 171–195.

Gould, Steven Jay. *Wonderful Life: Burgess Shale and the Nature of History.* New York: W. W. Norton & Co., 1989.

Green, Arthur. *Ehyeh: A Kabbalah for Tomorrow.* Woodstock: Jewish Lights Publishing, 2003.

———. *A Guide to the* Zohar. Stanford: Stanford University Press, 2004.

———. *The Language of Truth: The Torah Commentary of the* Sefat Emet *Rabbi Yehudah Leib Alter of Ger.* Philadelphia: The Jewish Publication Society, 1998.

———. *Menahem Nahum of Chernobyl: Upright Practices, The Light of the Eyes.* New York: Paulist Press, 1982.

———. "Typologies of Leadership and the Hasidic Zaddiq." In *Jewish Spirituality,* edited by Arthur Green, 2:127–56. New York: Crossroad, 1994.

Green, Arthur and Barry W. Holtz, eds. and trans. *Your Word is Fire: The Hasidic Masters on Contemplative Prayer.* New York, Paulist Press, 1977.

Green, William Scott. "Romancing the Tome: Rabbinic Hermeneutics and the Theory of Literature." *Semeia* 40 (1987): 147–168.

Greenberg, Aharon Yakov, ed. *Torah Gems.* Translated by Shmuel Himelstein. New York: Chemed Books & Co, 1998.

———, ed. *'Itturei Torah* [Hebrew]. Tel Aviv: Yavne Publishing House Ltd., 1996

Greenberg, Moshe. *Studies in the Bible and Jewish Thought.* Philadelphia: The Jewish Publication Society, 1995.

Greenstein, Edward L. "Deconstruction and Biblical Narrative." In *Interpreting Judaism in a Postmodern Age,* edited by Steven Kepnes, 21–54. New York: New York University Press, 1996.

Grenholme, Christina and Daniel Patte. *Reading Israel in Romans: Legitimacy and Plausibility of Divergent Interpretations.* Harrisburg: Trinity Press International, 2000.

Grossman, Avraham. "The School of Literal Jewish Exegesis in Northern France." In *Hebrew Bible/Old Testament: The History of Its Interpretation* I:2 ed. Magne Saebo, Göttingen: Vandenhoeck & Ruprecht, 2000.

Halbertal, Moshe. *People of the Book: Canon, Meaning, and Authority.* Cambridge, Harvard, 1997.

Halbertal, Moshe and Avishai Margalit. *Idolatry.* Translated by Naomi Goldblum. Cambridge: Harvard University Press, 1992.

Halivni, David Weiss. *Peshat and Derash: Plain and Applied Meaning in Rabbinic Exegesis.* New York: Oxford University Press, 1991.

Hammer, Jill. *Sisters at Sinai: New Tales of Biblical Women.* Philadelphia: The Jewish Publication Society, 2001.

Handelman, Susan A. *The Slayers of Moses: The Emergence of Rabbinic Interpretation in Modern Literary Theory.* Albany: State University of New York Press, 1982.

Harris, Jay M. *How Do We Know This? Midrash and the Fragmentation of Modern Judaism.* Albany: State University of New York Press, 1995.

Hauptman, Judith. *Rereading the Rabbis: A Woman's Voice.* Boulder: Westview Press, 1998.

Hertzberg, Arthur, ed. *The Zionist Idea: A Historical Analysis and Reader.* Philadelphia: The Jewish Publication Society, 1997.

Heschel, Abraham Joshua. "The Concept of Man in Jewish Thought." In *To Grow in Wisdom: An Anthology of Abraham Joshua Heschel,* edited by Jacob Neusner with Noam M. M. Neusner, 97–145. New York: Madison Books, 1990.

———. *Heavenly Torah: As Refracted Through the Generations.* Translated and edited by Gordon Tucker with Leonard Levin. New York: Continuum, 2005.

———. *God In Search of Man: A Philosophy of Judaism.* New York: Farrar, Straus and Cudahy, 1955.

———. *Israel: An Echo of Eternity.* New York: Farrar, Straus and Giroux, Inc., 1967.

———. *Man's Quest for God: Studies in Prayer and Symbolism.* New York: Crossroad Publishing, 1954.

———. *A Passion for Truth.* New York: Farrar, Straus and Giroux, Inc., 1973.

———. *The Prophets: An Introduction.* 2 vols. New York: Harper Torchbooks, 1962.

Hezser, Catherine. *Jewish Slavery in Antiquity.* Oxford: Oxford University Press, 2005.

Higger, Michael. "Intention in Talmudic Law." In *Studies in Jewish Jurisprudence,* edited by Edward M. Gershfield, 1:235–292. New York: Hermon Press, 1971.

Hirsch, Samson Raphael. *The Pentateuch.* Translated by Isaac Levy. Gateshead, England: Judaica Press, 1976.

Hoffman, Lawrence A. ed. *My People's Prayer Book.* Vol. 5. *Birkhot Hashachar.* Woodstock, Jewish Lights Publishing, 2001.

Holtz, Barry W., ed. *Back to the Sources: Reading the Classic Jewish Texts*. New York: Summit Books, 1984.

Horwitz, Rivka. "Revelation and the Bible According to Twentieth-Century Jewish Philosophy." In *Jewish Spirituality: From the Seventeenth-Century Revival to the Present*, edited by Arthur Green, 346–370. New York: Crossroad, 1987.

Hurowitz, Victor (Avigdor). "'His Master Shall Pierce His Ear with an Awl' (Exodus 21:6)–Marking Slaves in the Bible in Light of Akkadian Sources." *Proceedings— American Academy for Jewish Research* 58 (1992): 47–77.

Idel, Moshe. *Absorbing Perfections: Kabbalah and Interpretation*. New Haven: Yale University Press, 2002.

Ilan, Tal. "The Daughters of Zelophehad and Women's Inheritance: The Biblical Injunction and Its Outcome." In *Exodus to Deuteronomy: A Feminist Companion to the Bible*. Edited by Athalya Brenner, 176–186. Sheffield: Sheffield Academic Press, 2000.

Jacob, Benno. *The First Book of the Bible: Genesis*. Translated and edited by Ernest I. Jacob and Walter Jacob. New York: Ktav Publishing House, 1974.

Jacobs, Louis. *Jewish Biblical Exegesis*. New York: Behrman House, Inc., 1973.

Jacobson, Joshua R. *Chanting the Hebrew Bible*. Philadelphia: The Jewish Publication Society, 2005.

Jacobson, Yoram. *Hasidic Thought*. Translated by Jonathan Chipman. Tel Aviv: MOD Press, 1998.

Japhet, Sara. "The Tension between Rabbinic Legal Midrash and the 'Plain Meaning' (*Peshat*) of the Biblical Text—An Unresolved Problem?: In the Wake of Rashbam's Commentary on the Pentateuch." In *Sefer Moshe-The Moshe Weinfeld Jubilee Volume: Studies in the Bible and the Ancient Near East, Quram, and Post-Biblical Judaism*, edited by Chaim Cohen, Avi Hurvitz, and Shalom M. Paul. Eisenbrauns: Winona Lake, IN, 2004: 403–425.

Jenkins, Jr. Everett. *The Creation: Secular, Jewish, Catholic, Protestant and Muslim Perspectives Analyzed*. Jefferson, N.C.: McFarland & Co., 2003.

Jonas, Hans. *Mortality and Morality: The Search for the Good After Auschwitz*. Edited by Lawrence Vogel. Evanston: Northwestern University Press, 1996.

Kadushin, Max. *Worship and Ethics: A Study in Rabbinic Judaism*. New York: Bloch Publishing Company, 1963.

Kalechofsky, Roberta. *Judaism and Animal Rights: Classical and Contemporary Responses*. Marblehead, MA: Micah Publications, 1992.

Kant, Immanuel. *Critique of Practical Reason*. Translated by Lewis White Beck. 3rd ed. New York: Macmillan Publishing Company, 1993.

Kaplan, Mordecai M. *The Future of the American Jew*. New York: Macmillan Company, 1948.

Kass, Leon. "Farmers, Founders, and Fratricide: The Story of Cain and Abel." *First Things* 62 (April 1996): 19–26.

Kearney, Peter J. "Creation and Liturgy: The P Redaction of Ex 25–40." *Zeitschrift für die Alttestamentlische* Wissenschaft 89:3 (1977): 375–387.

Kellner, Menachem M. *Must a Jew Believe Anything?* Oxford: Littman Library of Jewish Civilization, 2006, 2nd edition, expanded.

Kook, Abraham Isaac. *The Lights of Penitence, The Moral Principles, Lights of Holiness, Essays, Letters, and Poems.* Translated and introduced by Ben Zion Bokser. New York: Paulist Press, 1978

Knohl, Israel. *The Divine Symphony: The Bible's Many Voices.* Philadelphia: The Jewish Publication Society, 2003.

Kugel, James L. *The Bible as it Was.* Cambridge: Harvard University Press, 1997.

———. "Cain and Abel in Fact and Fable: Genesis 4:1–16." In *Hebrew Bible or Old Testament? Studying the Bible in Judaism and Christianity,* edited by Roger Brooks and John J. Collins, 167–190. Notre Dame: University of Notre Dame Press, 1990.

Kushner, Lawrence S. and David Mamet. *Five Cities of Refuge: Weekly Reflections on Genesis, Exodus, Leviticus, Numbers, and Deuteronomy.* New York: Schocken Books, 2003.

Kushner, Lawrence S. and Kerry M. Olitzky, eds. *Sparks beneath the Surface: A Spiritual Commentary on the Torah.* Northvale, N.J: Jason Aronson, 1993.

Lamm, Norman. *The Shema: Spirituality and Law in Judaism.* Philadelphia: The Jewish Publication Society, 2000.

Lawee, Eric. "The 'Ways of Midrash' in the Biblical Commentaries of Isaac Abarbanel." *Hebrew Union College Annual* 67 (1996): 107–142.

Leibowitz, Nehama. *Studies in* Exodus, trans. Aryeh Newman. Jerusalem: World Zionist Organization, 1981.

Leibowitz, Yeshayahu. *Judaism, Human Values and the Jewish State,* edited by Eliezer Goldman, translated by Eliezer Goldman, et. al. Cambridge: Harvard University Press, 1992.

Levenson, Jon D. *The Hebrew Bible, the Old Testament, and Historical Criticism.* Louisville: Westminster/John Knox Press, 1993.

Lieberman, Saul. "Rabbinic Interpretations of Scripture." In *Essential Papers on the Talmud,* edited by Michael Chernick, 429–460. New York: New York University Press, 1994.

Loewe, Raphael. "The 'Plain' Meaning of Scripture in Early Jewish Exegesis." In *Papers of the Institute of Jewish Studies London,* edited by J. G. Weiss, 1:140–185. 1964.

Maimonides, Moses. *The Guide for the Perplexed.* 2 vols. Translated by Shlomo Pines. Chicago: University of Chicago Press, 1963.

Matt, Daniel C. "The Mystic and the Mizwot." In *Jewish Spirituality,* edited by Arthur Green, 1:367–404. New York: Crossroad Publishing House, 1994.

Matthews, Honor. *The Primal Curse: The Myth of Cain and Abel in the Theatre*. New York: Schocken Books, 1967.

Meyer, Michael A. *The Origins of the Modern Jew: Jewish Identity and European Culture in Germany, 1749–1824*. Detroit: Wayne State University Press, 1967.

Milgrom, Jacob. *JPS Torah Commentary: Numbers*. Philadelphia: The Jewish Publication Society, 1990.

Nabokov, Vladimir Vladimirovich. *Pale Fire*. New York: Putnam, 1962.

Nachmanides, Moses. *The Disputation at Barcelona*. Translated and annotated by Charles B. Chavel. New York: Shilo Publishing House, 1983.

———. *Writings and Discourses*, 2 vols. Translated by Charles B. Chavel. New York: Shilo Publishing House, 1978.

Neusner, Jacob. "*Genesis Rabbah* as Polemic." *Hebrew Annual Review* 9 (1985): 253–265.

Neusner, Jacob and Tamara Sonn. *Comparing Religions through Law: Judaism and Islam*. New York: Routledge, 1999.

Nietzsche, Friedrich. *Beyond Good and Evil: Prelude to a Philosophy of the Future*. Translated by Walter Kaufmann. New York: Vintage Books, 1989.

Noonan Jr., John T. *A Church that Can and Cannot Change: The Development of Catholic Moral Teaching*. Notre Dame: University of Notre Dame Press, 2005.

Oz, Amos. "Strange Fire." In *Where the Jackals Howl and Other Stories*, translated by Nicholas de Lange and Philip Simpson. New York: Harcourt Brace Jovanovich, 1981.

Pagels, Elaine. "Exegesis and Exposition of the Genesis Creation Account in Selected Texts from Nag Hammadi." In *Nag Hammadi, Gnosticism, and Early Christianity*, edited by Charles W. Hedrick and Robert Hodgson, Jr., 257–285. Peabody, MA: Hendrickson Publishers, 1986.

Person, Hara E. *The Women's Torah Commentary*. Edited by Elyse Goldstein. Woodstock: Jewish Lights Publishing, 2000.

Peters, Simi. "'Na'aseh Adam': Should We Make *Adam?* A Midrashic Reading of Genesis 1:26." In *Torah of the Mothers: Contemporary Jewish Women Read Classical Jewish Texts*, edited by Ora Wiskind and Susan Handelman, 291–306. New York: Urim Publications, 2000.

Quinones, Ricardo J. *The Changes of Cain: Violence and the Lost Brother in Cain and Abel Literature*. Princeton: Princeton University Press, 1991.

Rawidowicz, Simon. "On Interpretation." In *Studies in Jewish Thought*, ed. Nahum N. Glatzer, 83–126. Philadelphia: The Jewish Publication Society, 1974.

Reif, Stefan C. "Aspects of the Jewish Contribution to Biblical Interpretation." In *The Cambridge Companion to Biblical Interpretation*, edited by John Barton, 143–159. New York: Cambridge University Press, 1998.

Ron, Zvi. "The Daughters of Zelophehad." *Jewish Bible Quarterly* 26:4 (1998): 260–262.

Ronson, Barbara L. *The Women of the Torah: Commentaries from the Talmud, Midrash, and Kabbalah*. Northvale, N.J.: Jason Aronson, 1999.

Rosenberg, Shalom. "Emunat Hakhamim." In *Jewish Thought in the Seventeenth Century*, edited by Isadore Twersky and Bernard Septimus, 285–341. Cambridge: Harvard University Press, 1987.

Sagi, Avi. "Contending with Modernity: Scripture in the Thought of Yeshayahu Leibowitz and Joseph Soloveitchik." *Journal of Religion* 77, no. 3 (1997): 421–441.

Salzman, Jack and Cornel West, eds. *Struggles in the Promised Land: Toward a History of Black-Jewish Relations in the United States*. New York: Oxford University Press, 1997.

Saperstein, Marc. *Jewish Preaching, 1200–1800: An Anthology*. New Haven: Yale University Press, 1989.

Sarna, Nahum. *Studies in Biblical Interpretation*. Philadelphia: The Jewish Publication Society, 2000.

———. "Zedekiah's Emancipation of Slaves and the Sabbatical Year." *Orient and Occident* (1973): 143–149.

Sasso, Sandy Eisenberg. *Cain & Abel: Finding the Fruits of Peace*. Woodstock: Jewish Lights Publishing, 2001.

Schimmel, Solomon. *The Seven Deadly Sins: Jewish, Christian and Classical Reflections on Human Nature*. New York: Free Press, 1992.

Scholem, Gershom. *The Messianic Idea in Judaism and Other Essays on Jewish Spirituality*. New York: Schocken Books, 1971.

———. *On the Kabbalah and its Symbolism*. New York: Schocken Books, 1960.

———. *On the Mystical Shape of the Godhead*. Translated by Joachim Neugroschel. New York: Schocken Books, 1991.

Schwartz, Eilon. "Judaism and Nature: Theological and Moral Issues to Consider While Renegotiating a Jewish Relationship to the Natural World." In *Judaism and Environmental Ethics: A Reader*, edited by Martin D. Yaffee, 297–308. New York: Lanham Books, 2001.

Schwartz, Richard H. *Judaism and Vegetarianism*. New York: Lantern Books, 2001.

Scolnic, Benjamin Edidin. "How to Read the Torah's Laws of Slavery." *Conservative Judaism* 47:3 (1995): 37–41.

Scott, James M. "Korah and Qumran." *The Bible at Qumran*, ed. Peter W. Flint, 182–202. Grand Rapids: William B. Eerdmans Publishing Company, 2001.

———, ed. *New International Biblical Commentary: 2 Corinthians*. Peabody, MA: Hendrickson Publishers, 1998.

Shapiro, David S. "Be Fruitful and Multiply." *Tradition* 13:4 (1973): 42–67.

Shaviv, Yehudah. *Between the Haftarah and the Torah Portion* [Hebrew]. Jerusalem: Reuven Mas, 2000.

Signer, Michael A. "How the Bible Has Been Interpreted in Jewish Tradition." In *The New Interpreter's Bible*, 65–82. Nashville: Abingdon Press, 1994–2002.

Silber, Michael. "The Invention of ultra-Orthodoxy." In *The Uses of Tradition: Jewish Continuity in the Modern Era*, edited by Jack Wertheimer, 23–84. New York: Jewish Theological Seminary of America, 1992.

Soloveitchik, Joseph B. "The 'Common-Sense' Rebellion against Torah Authority." In *Reflections of the Rav, 139–149*. Jerusalem: Department for Torah Education, 1979.

———. *The Lonely Man of Faith*. New York: Doubleday, 1965.

Somers, H. H. "The Riddle of a Plural (Gen 1:21 [sic]): Its History in Tradition." *Folia: Studies in the Christian Perpetuation of the Classics* 9 (1955): 63–101.

Sommer, Benjamin D. "The Source Critic and the Religious Interpreter." *Interpretation* 60, no. 1 (January 2006): 9–20.

Sperling, S. David, "Modern Jewish Interpretation." In *The Jewish Study Bible*, edited by Adele Berlin, Marc Zvi Brettler, and Michael Fishbane, 1908–1919. New York: Oxford University Press, 2004.

———, ed. *Students of the Covenant: A History of Jewish Biblical Scholarship in North America*. Atlanta: Scholars Press, 1992.

Steinsaltz, Adin. *The Talmud: A Reference Guide*. New York: Random House, 1989.

Stern, David. "The *Alphabet of Ben Sira* and the Early History of Parody in Jewish Literature." In *The Idea of Biblical Interpretation: Essays in Honor of James L. Kugel*, ed. Hindy Najman and Judith H. Newman, 423–448. Leiden: Brill, 2004.

———. *Midrash and Theory: Ancient Jewish Exegesis and Contemporary Literary Studies*. Evanston: Northwestern University Press, 1996.

Stern, Josef. "Language." In *Contemporary Jewish Religious Thought: Original Essays on Critical Concepts, Movements, and Beliefs*, edited by Arthur A. Cohen and Paul Mendes-Flohr, 543–551. New York: The Free Press, 1982.

———. *Problems and Parables of Law: Maimonides and Nachmanides on Reasons for the Commandments*. Albany: State University of New York, 1998.

Talmage, Frank. "Apples of Gold: The Inner Meaning of Sacred Texts in Medieval Judaism." In *Jewish Spirituality: From the Bible Through the Middle Ages*, ed. Arthur Green, 313–55. New York: Crossroad, 1986.

Talmage, F. E., ed. *Disputation and Dialogue: Readings in the Jewish-Christian Encounter*. New York: Ktav Publishing House, 1975.

Telushkin, Joseph. *Words That Hurt, Words That Heal: How to Choose Words Wisely and Well*. New York: W. Morrow and Co., 1996.

Tov, Emanuel. *Textual Criticism of the Hebrew Bible*. Minneapolis: Fortress Press, 2001.

Twersky, Isadore. "Joseph ibn Kaspi: Portrait of a Medieval Intellectual." In *Studies in Medieval Jewish History and Literature*, edited by Isadore Twersky, 231–257. Cambridge: Harvard University Press, 1979.

Urbach, Ephraim. *The Sages*. Cambridge: Harvard University Press, 1975.

Vermes, Geza, trans. *The Complete Dead Sea Scrolls in English*. New York: Penguin Classics, 2004.

Walfish, Barry D. "Medieval Jewish Interpretation." In *The Jewish Study Bible*. Edited by Adele Berlin, Marc Zvi Brettler, and Michael Fishbane, 1876–1900. New York: Oxford University Press, 2004.

Waskow, Arthur. "Brothers Reconciled." *Sojourners* (July/Aug. 1999): 42–46.

———. *Down to Earth Judaism: Food, Money, Sex, and the Rest of Life*. New York: William Morrow & Co., 1995.

Waskow, Arthur, ed. *Torah of the Earth: Exploring 4,000 Years of Ecology in Jewish Thought*. Woodstock: Jewish Lights Publishing, 2000.

Wegner, Judith Romney. *Chattel or Person: The Status of Women in the Mishnah*. New York: Oxford University Press, 1988.

Weinfeld, Moshe. "Sabbatical Year and Jubilee in the Pentateuchal Laws and their Ancient Near-Eastern Background." In *The Law in the Bible and its Environment*. 39–62. Finnish Exegetical Society. Göttingen: Vandenhoeck & Ruprecht, 1990.

Wexler, Shlomo. *The Daughters Victorious*. New York: Gefen Books, 2002.

Wiesel, Elie. *Messengers of God: Biblical Portraits and Legends*. Translated by Marion Wiesel. New York: Simon & Schuster, 1976.

Wiley, Tatha. *Original Sin: Origins, Developments, Contemporary Meanings*. New York: Paulist Press, 2002.

Wolfson, Eliot R. "The Hermeneutics of Visionary Experience: Revelation and Interpretation in the Zohar." *Religion* 18 (1988): 311–345.

———. "On Becoming Female: Crossing the Gender Boundaries in Kabbalistic Ritual and Myth." In *Gender and Judaism: The Transformation of Tradition*, edited by Tamar R. Rudavsky. New York: New York University Press, 1995.

Yaffe, Martin D., ed. *Judaism and Environmental Ethics: A Reader*. Lanham, MD: Lexington Books, 2001.

Yehoshua, Abraham B. *The Terrible Power of a Minor Guilt*. Translated by Ora Cummings. Syracuse: Syracuse University Press, 2000.

Zevit, Ziony. "Invisible and Unheard in Translation: How New Discoveries in Hebrew Grammar Affect Our Understanding of Tanakh." *Conservative Judaism* 55, no. 2 (Winter 2003): 38–48.

Zornberg, Aviva Gottleib. *The Particulars of Rapture: Reflections on Exodus*. New York: Doubleday, 2001.

Subject Index

Abel: avarice of, 88; Cain's appeal to, 91–92; God, 75, 79; Moses as reincarnation of, 138, 139; silence of, 91, 97

Abudarham, David, Rabbi, 171, 187n23

adam: creation of, 43–44; *dimyon*, 47, 48, 64; Eve, 49, 53; gender of, 50, 51, 53, 64; Lilith, 53; opposition to creation of, 43, 44

adon, 115, 116, 128

Akiva, Rabbi, 33–34, 61, 141, 164, 190, 198

Albo, Joseph, 60, 70, 82, 99n15, 196

alien slave (*'eved canani*), 104

The Alphabet of Ben Sira, 53, 196

angels, 43, 44, 63, 64, 189

animals, 58, 59–60, 65, 66

Arabic language, 18, 96

Arama, Isaac, 190

Aramaic language, 19

Aristotelians, 192; God in, 22, 23, 46, 76, 77; image understood by, 46, 64; on origin of the world, 106; Rambam and, 22, 76, 77, 83; on sin, 83, 96

arrogance, 108, 109, 145, 146

Aryeh Leib, Rabbi (Shpoler Zeide), 111

assimilation, 29, 56, 136, 145, 155, 157

Avot d'Rabbi Natan, 11, 90, 196

Babylonia, 8, 16, 121, 128, 145

Bahir, 46, 196

Bahya, Rabbeinu, 23, 83, 84, 102, 171, 172, 196

bal taschit, 70n42

Bar Kokhva Revolt, 61

Bechor Shor, Joseph, 106–7, 180, 181, 196

Ben Bag Bag, 1, 13–14

Berlin, Naftali Zvi Yehuda, Rabbi, 29

biblical exegesis: botanical model, 32, 33, 39n69, 189, 190; braided narratives, 132–33, 140–41, 154; in Christianity, 16; *g'zerah shavah*, 139, 140, 156, 164, 181, 183, 188n52, 193; haftarah in, 120–22, 193; Islamic scholarship, 18–19, 96, 106; limits on, 14, 36n22; omnisignificance in, 10, 11, 14, 15, 25, 26, 194; pluripotence in, 14, 24–25, 27, 194; in post-Temple era, 15–16; rationalism, 18, 19, 20; silences in, 87, 89, 92, 93, 97. *See also derash* commentary; historical contexts; peshat commentary; individual rabbis (e.g. Rashi)

Bin-Nun, Yoel, 185n1

botanical model of Creation, 32, 33, 39n69, 189, 190

Boyarin, Daniel, 3, 46

braided narratives, 132–33, 140–41, 154

Breuer, Edward, 38n57

b'rit, 76, 77, 192

The Brothers Karamozov (Dostoevsky), 90, 99n33

Buber, Martin, 144, 150–51

Bunam of Przysucha, Rabbi, 48, 79, 196

Cain: and Abel's silence, 91–92; *The Brothers Karamozov* (Dostoevsky), 90, 99n33; character of, 75, 79–81, 85–86, 90–92, 94, 100n38, 139; God and, 75, 81, 86, 96; puns on name (*koneh, kinah*), 88, 139; reincarnations of, 138, 139, 140, 156; sister as wife of, 88, 89, 99n26; teshuvah (repentance) of, 94–95, 97

Cain and Abel narrative: breakdown in communication between brothers, 91–92; Cain not understanding the concept of sin (Malbim), 85; divine justice v. human injustice, 81–82; missing dialogue in, 87, 91, 97; murder as misunderstanding of divine mandate, 85; Philo on, 94; preferential treatment by God, 77–79, 80, 81; sacrifices in, 76, 78, 81, 86; sisters in, 87, 88–89, 99n26

214

Classical Source Index